A Common Journey

**The Bishop Henry McNeal Turner Studies
in North American Black Religion**

Editor:

James H. Cone,
Union Theological Seminary, New York

The purpose of this series is to encourage the development of biblical, historical, theological, and pastoral works that analyze the role of the churches and other religious movements in the liberation struggles of blacks in the United States and the Third World. What is the relationship between black religion and black peoples' fight for justice in the U. S.? What is the relationship between the black struggle for justice in the U. S. and the liberation struggles of the poor in Asia, Africa, Latin America, and the Caribbean? A critical investigation of these and related questions will define the focus of this series.

This series is named after Bishop Henry McNeal Turner (1834–1915), whose life and work symbolize the black struggle for liberation in the U. S. and the Third World. Bishop Turner was a churchman, a political figure, a missionary, a pan-Africanist—a champion of black freedom and the cultural creativity of black peoples under God.

**The Bishop Henry McNeal Turner Studies
in North American Black Religion
Volume VI**

George C. L. Cummings

A Common Journey

Black Theology (USA) and
Latin American Liberation Theology

ORBIS BOOKS

Maryknoll, New York 10545

The Catholic Foreign Mission Society of America (Maryknoll) recruits and trains people for overseas missionary service. Through Orbis Books, Maryknoll aims to foster the international dialogue that is essential to mission. The books published, however, reflect the opinions of their authors and are not meant to represent the official position of the society.

Library of Congress Cataloging-in-Publication Data

Cummings, George C. L.
  A common journey : Black theology (USA) and Latin American
liberation theology / George C. L. Cummings.
    p. cm. — (The Bishop Henry McNeal Turner studies in North
American Black religion ; v. 6)
  Includes bibliographical references and index.
  ISBN 0-88344-825-4
  1. Black theology. 2. Liberation theology. 3. Theology,
Doctrinal — United States — History — 20th century. 4. Theology,
Doctrinal — Latin America — History — 20th century. I. Title.
II. Series: Bishop Henry McNeal Turner studies in North American
Black religion ; vol. 6.
BT82.7.C85 1993
230'.046 — dc20
                                                    93-16995
                                                       CIP

Contents

v

Acknowledgments

Without the contributions of the following people, this book would never have been completed. James Cone, my mentor and teacher, provided a persistent and critical challenge to sharpen the arguments being articulated in this project. My teachers at Union Theological Seminary, Cornel West and Christopher Morse, provided me with a stimulating environment for the development of my critical skills. My colleagues in the BT Forum, Dwight N. Hopkins, Will E. Coleman and James Noel, contributed by providing me with an ongoing dialogue that was the context for many provocative conversations and penetrating criticisms. The staff and faculty of the American Baptist Seminary of the West provided me with some visible models of scholarship and a location in which to pursue my work. Robert Ellsberg, the editor-in-chief of Orbis Books, gave me guidance in bringing this project to its fruition. My wife, Althea Grannum-Cummings, and our daughters Chantal and Charisse, provided me with a warm home and family, without which this project would not have been finished. Finally, without the encouragement of my grandmothers, who taught me to believe, and my connection to my ancestral community, my understanding of the vocation I have been given, this task would have no meaning.

G. C. L. C.

Introduction

The development of formative elements of liberation theology during the last three decades affords contemporary theologians the opportunity to scrutinize their development, both independently of one another and in relationship to one another. In the late 1960s, Black Theology in the United States (BTUSA) and Latin American Liberation Theology (LALT) emerged simultaneously, yet independently, as some Christian theologians sought to explicate the meaning of the Christian faith in the context of social upheaval in the United States and in Latin America.[1]

These two liberation theologies emerged in order to respond to the question: What does the Gospel of Jesus Christ have to do with the concrete struggles of exploited, suffering and oppressed people?[2] BTUSA sought to explicate the meaning of the Christian faith in the context of the struggle for racial and cultural justice in the United States, and LALT sought to do the same in the context of the socio-economic struggle against oppression on the Latin American continent. In this regard, particularly, both BTUSA and LALT are theologies which acknowledge the historical ground and subjective character of the theological enterprise. They are theologies which acknowledge that the theological enterprise in which they are engaged is "contextual language — that is, defined by the human situation that gives birth to them."[3] It was, they claimed, the suffering of the oppressed, the exploited and the disenfranchised, and their ongoing struggle for justice and freedom, which defined the context and content of this new theological development.

While black Christians reflected on the relevance of white images of Christ in the black struggle for freedom and social justice, Christians in Latin America were reflecting on the relationship among the ecclesiastical structures, political power and the struggle for socio-economic and political independence. Theological concerns about the significance of Jesus Christ (Christology), the role of the church (ecclesiology) and the ultimate hope and goals of the Christian movement (eschatology) were at the core of these liberation theology traditions.

Black Christians challenged the images of a white Jesus, and Latin American Christians sought to define their Christian identity amid suffering and oppression. In a sense, the question of theodicy — that is, the relationship between the existence of evil and Christian claims concerning a benevolent and just God — was being reticulated in the light of the material conditions of those who were experiencing evil in the world. What does the Gospel of Jesus Christ mean from the perspective of the suffering victims of racial oppression and economic exploitation? What is the witness of the liberating Gospel? What is the vision of the Kingdom of God discussed in the Scripture? These questions, liberation theologians believed, defined the context and content of their discourse.

BTUSA and LALT, in contrast to the dominant Euro-North American theological traditions of the twentieth century, aimed to clear the ground for a theological discourse that emerged from the perspective of the victims, the oppressed, the poor and the wretched of the earth.[4] In the process of clearing the theological terrain, a new paradigm of theology was created: liberation theology.[5]

We will examine BTUSA and LALT as two distinct, yet similar, voices within the tapestry of liberation theologies which have developed in recent years. The primary purpose of this effort is to critically interpret BTUSA and LALT in relationship to each other. This will necessarily entail studying each theology in its own context and on its own terms, with explicit attention to the particular voice of each tradition, and then evaluating them in relationship to each other. Underlying this enterprise is the fundamental premise that liberation theology is a theology committed to an integral vision of liberation and that each liberation tradition, with its distinct emphasis and nuance, can contribute to the evolution of a more comprehensive vision of liberated creation.[6]

By *integral* I am referring here to the fact that the biblical concept of liberation is the unifying principle of the Gospel and has significance for the breadth and depth of human existence.[7] The liberation theologians remind us that the biblical concept of liberation extends to all dimensions of human existence: politics, culture, economics, religion and theology.

The development of such an integral vision is the stated commitment of liberation theologians who participate in the dialogical encounter of liberation theology traditions in the Ecumenical Association of Third World Theologians (EATWOT).[8] The final statement of the fifth EATWOT Conference (India, 1981) clearly affirms this when it defines one of its priorities as "developing a synthesis between the two major trends in third world theologies: The socio-economic and the religio-cultural, both of which are essential for integral liberation."[9]

The dialogical encounter between BTUSA and LALT, in EATWOT and in other contexts, while not the major focus of this book, provides us with the historical grounds for evaluating them in relation to each other, as well as one of the means for doing such an examination. This project will answer the following questions: What are the commonalities and differences between BTUSA and LALT, and what can they contribute to the formation of a higher synthesis?

Both Black Theology in the United States and Latin American Liberation Theology understand religio-cultural, socio-economic and political liberation as essential to the Gospel message and can contribute to each other in the evolution of a more comprehensive theology of socio-economic, religio-cultural and political liberation.

Thus, the overreaching interests that shape this study are:

1. To examine each theological tradition, in its own context and development, in order to identify its major emphases
2. To evaluate BTUSA and LALT in relationship to each other in order to see what they can contribute to each other
3. To demonstrate that they can assist each other in developing a theology of religio-cultural, socio-economic and political liberation for Latin America and the United States.

Accordingly, then, chapter 1 sets the historical context for the development of BTUSA and LALT. This exploration of their respective contexts is vital to my argument, since the commonalities and different nuances of these theological traditions are connected to the peculiar circumstances out of which each emerged. An examination of the historical, political, cultural religious and economic context of these two theologies will provide us with the clues to both common ground and differences.

Chapter 2 will be a critical examination of three theologians who represent BTUSA, in order to discover their unique contributions to Black Theology. These three theologians, James Cone, Gayraud Wilmore and Deotis Roberts, have been significant in the early development of black theological thought and show an appreciation of dialogue with the Latin American theologian tradition.[10]

Chapter 3 will assess three representative theologians of liberation from the Latin American continent. Gustavo Gutiérrez, José Míguez Bonino and Hugo Assmann were chosen because of their formative contributions to the development of a Latin American theology of liberation and because they have been a part of the dialogical process with black theologians from the USA.[11]

Chapter 4 will explore the methodological and contextual differences and similarities between these two theologies in order to discern their mutual contributions to each other. Here, the aim will be to answer the question, "What can they say to each other?"

Chapter 5, the last chapter, will elaborate four areas in which BTUSA and LALT can further work toward developing a theology of religio-cultural, socio-economic and political theology of liberation. The primary aim of this last chapter is to establish the contours of the development and growth of these respective liberation theology traditions and to answer the question, "Where do we go from here?"

The project is being undertaken in the hope of contributing to the theological enterprise in four ways. First, no one has undertaken a major comparative study of Black Theology in the United States and Latin American Liberation Theology. There is a need to compare, evaluate and examine these two traditions and to interpret them, theologically, in relation to each other. Thus this book will pursue, secondarily, answers to the following questions:

1. What gave rise to contemporary BTUSA and LALT?
2. What is the relationship between their distinct emphasis on religio-cultural liberation (by BTUSA) and on socio-economic liberation (by LALT)?
3. What are the theological themes in BTUSA and LALT?
4. What are their commonalities and differences?
5. What can they learn from each other?
6. What can I learn from both traditions as I attempt to develop a theologically holistic understanding of liberation?

Second, a comparative study can address the need for a more comprehensive understanding of liberation and liberation struggles in each context. Both black theologians in the USA and Latin American liberation theologians, in their work in EATWOT, have acknowledged the need for a more integral synthesis.

Third, I hope to contribute to the concrete struggles of the oppressed in the United States and Latin America as they attempt to achieve a measure of socio-economic, religio-cultural and political liberation. A comprehensive understanding of oppression and of the notion of liberation can shape the strategy and commitment of the oppressed as they struggle amid the conditions of oppression.

Fourth, it is my hope to contribute to the Euro-American theological enterprise with a reminder that the Gospel message is holistic in its implications. The Gospel of liberation is a Gospel of religio-cultural, socio-economic and political liberation.

The scope of this enterprise will be limited to the period from 1968 to 1986. Since this book will primarily be scrutinizing the origins and early development of BTUSA and LALT in order to analyze the differences and similarities between the two, the emphasis will be placed upon the earlier period of their respective development and dialogue with each other. It is during the initial section of this period, from 1968 to 1980, that their development and dialogue with each other focused upon the fundamental difference between LALT's stress on class analysis and BTUSA's emphasis on race.

Later (after 1980), both theological traditions began to incorporate, if only tentatively, the insights that they had introduced to each other. The period of our study will begin with 1968, the year in which the ideas of James Cone were published in his essay, "Christianity and Black Power," where the seminal views of his first published book on Black Theology and Black Power (1969) were articulated.[12] It was also in 1968 that Gustavo Gutiérrez presented a theological paper in Chimbote, Peru, which constituted the essentials of his book, *Hacia Una Teología de la Liberación,* published in 1971 (*A Theology of Liberation,* Eng. edition, 1973).[13] The year 1968, then, constituted the initial publishing of BTUSA and LALT, with their challenges to the dominant theological traditions.

The scope of my study will be limited to the period ending in 1986. In 1986 EATWOT held its second international assembly — its seventh international conference. The reports of that meeting reflect the growth that has characterized their encounter with each other and manifests the fact that BTUSA and LALT can learn from each other.[14] Despite the fact that this book will primarily focus on tensions which characterized their dialogue, there is a need to acknowledge the growth of the two traditions; hence my choice of the period from 1968 to 1986.

To ensure the comprehension of this study, some definitions are included here:

The Americas. A term that in the time of colonization was used to refer to North, Central and South America, as well as the islands of the Caribbean. Thus the "African-American" reality could be viewed as extending beyond the confines of the United States to the other parts of the Americas, and the "Latin American" reality can be viewed as extending beyond South and Central America into North America and the Caribbean.[15]

Black. A term often used interchangeably with Afro-American or African or African-American. It refers to the identity of persons who are of African descent but who currently inhabit the Americas.

Black Theology USA. The theological school associated with theologians such as James Cone, Gayraud Wilmore, Deotis Roberts, Major Jones, Albert Cleage, and others, who emerged in the 1960s in order to explicate the meaning of the Gospel from the perspective and through the experiences of black oppressed people in the United States of America.[16]

Latin American Liberation Theology. The theological school associated with theologians such as Gustavo Gutiérrez, Juan Luis Segundo, Sergio Torres, Rubem Alves, Hugo Assmann, José Míguez Bonino, and others, which emerged in the late 1960s in order to explicate the meaning of the Gospel from the perspective and through the experiences of the oppressed.[17]

Political. This term will be used to refer to those theologies of liberation that view the struggle as primarily one that must transform political systems, governments and the power relationships in an oppressive society.

Religio-Cultural. This term will be used in this project to refer to those theological traditions which emphasize culture and religion as the dominant sources in developing a theology of liberation, and who view the spheres of religion and culture as a critical aspect of oppression and exploitation.

Socio-economic. This term will be used to refer to those liberation theologies which emphasize the role of economic structures as the dominant factor in oppression. In this context, the battle is waged against economically determined social structures that must be transformed in order to achieve liberation.

The definition of these categories in this way is not intended to suggest that they are discreet categories, but to clarify the manner in which they will be used in this paper. My own perspective is that the spheres of politics, culture, religion and economics are mutually interpenetrating factors in shaping human societies. However, for the sake of establishing the distinct nuances of BTUSA and LALT, these definitions are provided.

CHAPTER ONE

Black Theology (USA) and Latin American Liberation Theology

The Historical Context

Black Theology (USA): Its Historical Roots

The gift of black faith was wrought out of the distinctive way God was revealed to pre-colonial Africa and it was shaped for five hundred years, by the experience of suffering and struggle related to oppression. Its lasting contribution will be its demonstration of what it takes for a people to survive and achieve inner and external liberation under the strange circumstances of being downtrodden under the heel of white Christian racists.

> Gayraud S. Wilmore
> *Black Religion and Black Radicalism*

Black Theology (USA) emerged during the 1960s in order to challenge the Christian assumptions of white theologians and preachers in North America. It stands against the background of a long history of communal struggle grounded in a commitment to the Gospel and the Church; a struggle that consistently joined spirituality and activism in the struggle for wholeness and liberation. BTUSA can only be understood within the context of the African slave trade, the middle passage, 244 years of slavery and 100 years of segregation as African-American people struggled to affirm their God-given humanity and to attain liberation. It is, therefore, necessary to evaluate the development of Black Theology in the sixties against this historical background, and to recognize that one cannot comprehend it apart from that history.

The origins of BTUSA lie in events and movements on the North American continent in the 1960s that brought to the fore the sentiments of a

1

community that had a long history of correlating black faith with political struggle for justice and equality.[1] In this sense Black Theology, like other theological movements, emerged in relationship to specific political, cultural and social realities which characterized their contexts. Herbert O. Edwards aptly describes this process of theological development:

> The history of Christian theologies reveals that they almost always have been "theologies of response." The responses have generally been to "winds of change." Sometimes hopeful and full of promise, the changes were usually characterized by socio-economic and political upheavals or pregnant with those possibilities . . . Consequently the fact that black theology as a modern phenomenon was in part a response to the Civil Rights Movement and black power simply suggests that new theological movements continue to follow in the wake of, or in the midst of, the "winds of change."[2]

BTUSA was the product of the black revolt of the sixties, but was grounded in a struggle for freedom that went back to the beginning of the black experience of enslavement. BTUSA emerged within the context of Martin Luther King and civil rights, Malcolm X and Black Power and the insurrections in the streets of black ghettos in the United States. It was in this context that black Christians were forced to face difficult questions concerning the Christian faith and its relationship to the "love ethic," power and justice. Indeed, what did the Gospel of Jesus Christ mean in the midst of "the black revolution?"

BTUSA, then, is deeply rooted in the historical American conflict regarding the exploitation of black people on the basis of the color of their skins, and can only be understood against the broad framework of six realities:

1. The African slave trade and American slavery
2. Segregation in post-emancipation America
3. Martin Luther King, Jr., and the civil rights movement associated with him
4. Malcolm X and the Black Muslim movement
5. Black power and the black rebellions in the 1960s
6. The struggle of black Christians to define their identity and mission within the context of African-American life.

The Black Story in the New World: Its Historical Roots

Black radicalism emerged as an expression of the rejection of white racist attitudes and values, and as an affirmation of the unique social, religious, cultural and historical consciousness of African peoples in the New World. Cedric Robinson, in his text *Black Marxism*, and Gayraud Wilmore in *Black Religion and Black Radicalism*, both affirm that from the beginning, black resistance in the New World was directly opposed to white racism and to its ideological partner, white supremacy, and that the preservation of black humanity's capacity to affirm its right to be was grounded in the Africans' ability to maintain their own peculiar culture, religion, values and life-styles, despite the impositions of the white world.[3]

From the very beginning of their enslavement in white Christian America, blacks began to reflect on the meaning of their faith in the light of their religious experience, and to assert that slavery was not Christian. Indeed, black religion, understood as all those religio-cultural sensibilities and values — African, European, and American — that converged to form the core of the black religious experience in America, functioned as the fulcrum of protest against black oppression. Black religious thought came out of this historical situation of oppression, and black slaves sought to understand their faith and to find the resources for survival. Blacks reflected on the meaning of their faith but did not necessarily have the tools that are associated with the discipline of theology. Thus, it is better to refer to these earlier reflections not as Black Theology, in the technical sense, but as the development of a radical tradition of black religious thought.[4] It would be inappropriate to define these early religious affections as Black Theology, for as James Cone has aptly pointed out:

> Theology as "rational reflection" about God was foreign to the intellectual and religious sensibilities of African slaves. Most could not read or write, and the few who could were almost forced to apply what they believed about God to the survival and liberation of their people rather than to consider it systematically.[5]

Black religion emerged as a resource in the struggle against the dehumanizing conditions of racist exploitation in America, and black religious thought developed its distinctive character in that context. Black religious thought began when African slaves, laboring in sweltering heat on white-owned plantations, tried to make sense of their experiences of servitude in the light of the Bible, hymns and Christian testimonies.[6] Some documents have been preserved that point to various events that witness to both the existence of black religious reflection and its critical function early in the sojourn of Africans on the American continent.

In 1779 black slaves wrote:

> We perceive by our own reflection, that we are endowed with the same faculties with our masters, and there is nothing that leads us to a belief, or suspicion, that we are any more obliged to serve them, than they us, and the more we consider this matter, the more we are convinced of our right (by the laws of nature and by the whole tenor of the Christian Religion, so far as we have been taught) to be free.[7]

From the time of their earliest experiences, black people declared their views that the legitimation of slavery was incompatible with the Christian faith and with an egalitarian approach to human society.[8]

The encounter of African slaves with the Gospel of Euro-American civilization became the context for the evolution of a peculiarly African expression of faith which empowered black slaves to believe that their struggle for freedom was a right and just cause.

Gayraud Wilmore, while acknowledging the existence of a more conservative religious tradition in the black community, has indicated that prophetic black radical religion was also present and was a critical dynamic in the struggles of blacks against oppression.[9] Robert Bruce Simpson has called this " 'enabling religion,' a religion of protest about this world," in distinction to " 'coping religion' [which] was concerned with surviving this world in preparation for the next."[10] Black religion enabled black slaves to develop a perspective on Christian faith which was characterized by the notion of "freedom—untrammelled, unconditional freedom to be, to exist, and to express the power of being fully and creatively for the sheer joy and profound meaning of Muntu, Man [sic]."[11]

This black Christian viewpoint not only understood the Gospel to be unequivocally opposed to slavery, but played a role in initiating many of the slave revolts. The religion of the slaves provided the resources for daily resistance to slavery, in the revolts and development of institutions whose primary vocation was the struggle of black people.[12]

On August 30, 1800, a young slave named Gabriel Prosser led an unsuccessful revolt in Virginia. It has been noted that religion played a significant role in Prosser's revolt.[13] The organization for revolt occurred in the context of religious meetings where Prosser's brother, Martin, was reputed to have utilized biblical texts to affirm the success of their plot. Prosser was captured, tried and executed on October 7, 1800.

Denmark Vesey, a rebellion leader in South Carolina in 1822, was a leader in the local African church and used scriptural texts to win supporters for the insurrection. A deposition against Vesey accuses him precisely of linking religion and antislavery:

> His general conversation was about religion which he would apply to slavery, as for instance, he would speak of the creation of the world in which he would say all men had equal rights, black as well as whites—all his religious remarks were mingled with slavery.[14]

In 1831 the bloodiest revolt in the history of the United States took place under the leadership of Nat Turner, whose reputation as a prophet and preacher was well known. Questioned concerning his motives, Turner replied that God had directed him, through the Scriptures and visions, to lead the slaves to revolt.

Among several documents expressive of early black religious thought is the Ethiopian Manifesto. Its author is explicit concerning the fate of the slaveholder:

> Ah. Doth your expanding judgement, base slaveholder, not from here descry that the shackles which have been by you so undeservingly forged upon a wretched Ethiopians's frame, are about to be forever from him unlinked. Say ye, this can never be accomplished? If so, must indeed the power and decrees of infinity become subservient to the will of depraved man. But learn, slaveholder, thine will rests in thine hand; God decrees to thy slave his rights as a man.[15]

Perhaps the most important written critique of slavery was David Walker's "Appeal to the Colored Citizens of the World." Wilmore calls Walker's excoriation of the Christian religion "the most devastating since Voltaire's 'Catéchisme de l'honnête homme,'" and writes: "Walker's appeal is steeped in biblical language and prophecy. It is certainly one of the most remarkable religious documents of the Protestant era."[16] Throughout the appeal, David Walker questioned the patent hypocrisy of white Christianity and challenged blacks to stand up for the freedom inherent in the message of the Gospel. It was a stinging indictment.[17]

In such words and deeds of protest, the black Christian faith that evolved in the context of the initial encounter between American slaves and the Gospel was manifested against the dehumanizing racism of America. An additional, very direct response of that faith, in protest to the racist structures of America, was embodied in the development of the independent black church. This is the church with which such varied figures as Henry M. Turner, Henry Highland Garnett, Richard Allen, Absalom Jones, Adam Clayton Powell, and Martin Luther King are associated. Wilmore asserts that the independent black church movement "must be considered ipso facto, an expression of black resistance to white oppression — the first black freedom movement."[18]

The black church emerged in the context of the development of the "invisible institution" and independent black church traditions. The "invisible institution" was the experience of community worship and organizing which occurred away from the eyes and ears of the slave master. Often at night, the slaves would steal away to worship in their own way. In the secrecy of their lives from sundown to sunup, slaves forged an extensive religious and cultural worldview that made Christianity their own and enabled their struggle.

There in those meetings, the African High God met Yahweh, the God of the Hebrews, and African-American Christianity was nurtured. At the same time, independent Christian denominations emerged as blacks rejected the racism of white Christian institutions and organized their own churches.

In the broad context of American society, black life was one of intense disenfranchisement characterized by economic dependency and exploitation, political powerlessness, social degradation, and segregation. In the black church—understood here to mean all the diverse African-American Christian communities—persons who lived with daily exploitation and dehumanization could find comfort and affirmation:

> As the one institution which freed blacks were allowed to control, the church was the center of social, economic, educational and political activity. It was also the source of continuity and identity for the black community. In their churches, black worshippers continued for decades to pray, sing, preach and shout as they or their parents had during slavery.[19]

It is clear that resistance and struggle were also cornerstones of the black church, characterized as it was by leaders whose spiritual commitment impelled them into the battle for freedom. The eloquent preacher Henry Highland Garnett, for example, challenged blacks to resist dehumanization. He encouraged them in a speech before the National Negro Convention in Buffalo, New York, in 1843, to rise up and seize their liberty.[20] In Wilmore's words:

> Born in protest, tested in adversity, led by eloquent and crusading black preachers, the black church was, during most of the nineteenth century, the cutting edge of the freedom movement among both slaves and freedmen, and thereby a living witness against the ambivalence and faithlessness of lost white Christianity during that period.[21]

Inevitably the magnitude of American racism led some among these black leaders to conclude that hopes for the future lay, not in America, but in the rise of black nationalism and Pan-Africanism. Their commitment to returning to the African continent was based on their theological critique of the institutional racism in the United States. This view is supported by Wilmore's studies of Martin Delaney, Alexander Crummel, and Edward Blyden; men who, perhaps more than all others, articulated a black religious thought which contributed to the development of a black prophetic tradition. Delaney's stance was characteristic, according to Wilmore:

> God, said Delaney, did not provide mystical solutions for the hard problems of power and self-realization, nor did He expect blacks to accept white definitions of reality when those definitions presumed white jurisdiction over black progress.[22]

Thus Delany rejected explicitly the interpretation of the faith given by the white oppressors and challenged black Christians to determine their own destiny.

Episcopalian priest Alexander Crummel, another prominent figure in the nineteenth century, also espoused black self-determination and supported nationalism and colonization.

Crummel was one of the earliest black religious leaders to identify self-love as an important aspect of the Christian principle of love. He argued that oppressed blacks must affirm their selfhood in the process of being viewed as equals in the broader society.[23]

Thus, the black church as an agency and institution independent of white structures made a considerable contribution to the development of racial pride, the independence and the organizational skills requisite for the development of nationalist movements in the black community. In the twentieth century, black nationalist movements, from Garvey to Malcolm X, owed a great debt to the black church for its preparatory work on behalf of black freedom.

It is, however, important to note that the radical tradition of black Christianity was in time subsumed under a more accommodationist spirituality that led to a more complacent black church at the turn of the twentieth century. This development can be accounted for by reference to several factors.

First, the postreconstructionist era was characterized by a commitment to integration into "American society." Thus followed the tendency to downplay the black militant antiracist Christian tradition and turn to white Christianity for identity and association.[24]

Second, some black scholars have argued that rapid urbanization and the persistence of racism have also contributed to the process whereby the black church lost sight of its specific vocation as an instrument in the struggle for black liberation.[25]

James Cone has persuasively argued that the "deradicalization of the black church" resulted from several factors: the persistence of black suffering after the civil war; the institutionalization of the black church; the movement of blacks from the rural South to Northern urban areas; and the influence of the accommodationist philosophy of Booker T. Washington.[26] Cone goes on to argue that the rise of a conservative posture among the religious leadership and the abandonment of the political struggle by most ministers "created the conditions that gave rise to the civil rights movement."[27] The black church, whose historic vocation had been a commitment to the struggle for black freedom, now shared the leadership of the freedom movement with "secular" organizations which had taken up the cause of justice and equality for blacks in America.

Despite the debate on the retention of Africanisms, the evolution of a distinctly black Christian faith, thought and practice in the United States, shaped by the cultural and religious traditions of Africa, as well as the Gospel as it had been encountered in the New World, provided blacks with the resources for the liberation struggle into the twentieth century.[28] At this point, however, the black church focused on a conservative spirituality which severed it from its radical roots.

The civil rights movement, Martin Luther King, Jr., Malcolm X and the Black Muslim movement were heirs of the deeper, older tradition of black religious activism. Behind them stood the historical background of black prophetic radical leadership, apart from which they and Black Theology cannot be understood.

The Emergence of Black Theology in the 1960s

The Civil Rights Movement was led by Martin Luther King, Jr., a preacher, theologian and activist who utilized the Christian faith as a motivating force in the freedom struggle. The white criticism that the Civil Rights Movement was unchristian led black thinkers such as Martin Luther King, Jr., to reflect critically upon the role of white Christianity as an instrument of the status quo.[29] In 1955, Martin Luther King, Jr., a new preacher in Montgomery, Alabama, was swept up in events not of his own making, and by 1956 found himself the head of a movement which would change American society.

On December 1, 1955, when Rosa Parks refused to give up her bus seat to a white male, her cause became the occasion for the beginning of one of the significant mass movements in American history. In Montgomery, Martin Luther King, Jr., was a Baptist pastor carrying on a legacy of ministry inherited from both his parents. He was to become the leader of the Civil Rights Movement, first in Montgomery, then in the South, and finally throughout the United States. King had studied Gandhi, Rauschenbusch, Niebuhr, and Brightman during his educational career and was prepared to provide the intellectual foundations for a nonviolent activist protest movement.[30] He was committed to institutionalized social processes of change as the means of solving the problem of racial discrimination. On this matter, he wrote:

> Through education, we seek to change attitudes; through legislation and court order, we seek to regulate behavior. Through education, we seek to change internal feelings (prejudice, hate, etc.); through legislation and the court orders, we seek to control the external effect of these feelings; through education, we seek to break down the spiritual barriers to integration; through legislation and court orders, we seek to break down the physical barriers of integration.[31]

From the first year (1955), when King was thrust into the leadership of the movement, to the tragic day of his assassination (April 4, 1968), he worked to gain access to the resources of American life and society for blacks. Out of his cultural, social and educational background he created a framework for mobilizing the black masses to act on their own behalf for freedom.

According to King, religion was a force that had to have practical relevance for human lives:

> Any religion that professes to be concerned with the souls of men and is not concerned with the slums that damn them, the economic conditions that strangle them, and the social conditions that cripple them is a dry-as-dust religion — the kind the Marxists like to see — an opiate of the people.[32]

The nonviolence he advocated was never conceived of as a passive acquiescence, but as a positive, organized, resisting force to the violence of white racism. It allowed the dominated to remain true to the moral and religious fabric of the universe, while saying the radical "No!" to their oppression. King believed this approach was the most effective means for blacks to ensure their freedom, and he articulated the vision in a manner that resonated with the sentiments of major constituencies within the black community. In an attempt to explain this vision theologically, he wrote:

> The cross is the eternal expression of the length to which God will go in order to restore broken community. The resurrection is a symbol of God's triumph over all the forces that seek to block community. The Holy Spirit is the continuing community reality that moves through history. He who works against community is working against the whole of creation. ... I can only close the gap in broken community by meeting hate with love. If I meet hate with hate, I become depersonalized, because creation is so designed that my personality can only be fulfilled in the context of community.[33]

Christologically, King explained, the basis of the black community's struggle for justice and liberation, as well as its hope for the future, was God's suffering presence on the cross: an eternal witness to God's identification with those who suffer.[34] Pneumatologically, King indicated that God's presence, the Holy Spirit, was the ongoing basis for humanity's will and struggle for wholeness and shalom.[35]

When eight white Alabama pastors published a statement entitled, "An Appeal for Law and Order and Common Sense," challenging his active participation in the Civil Rights Movement, King responded with his classic "letter from a Birmingham Jail."[36] He said: "Injustice anywhere is a threat to justice everywhere."[37] He chastised the institutional church for its focus on a completely other-worldly religion that makes a strange, unbiblical distinction between body and soul, between sacred and secular. For King, the paradigm offered by the New Testament church was clearly opposed to injustices perpetrated within society:

In those days, the church was not merely a thermometer that recorded the ideas and principles of popular opinion; it was a thermostat that transformed the mores of the society.[38]

By the year 1963, the movement for freedom had spread contagiously throughout black America. It raged through America at a fever pitch, and by the time it had peaked, many blacks had gained access to the schools, hotels, parks, restaurants and jobs. However, the year 1963 also brought to fruition the slowly rising frustration among blacks in an explosion of marches and riots. Token changes did not erase the pervasive unemployment and ghetto realities that marked most black lives. King identified racism as the "chief moral dilemma" in the twentieth century. Concerning racism, he wrote:

This long-standing racist ideology has corrupted and diminished our democratic ideal. It is this mangled web of prejudice from which many Americans now seek to liberate themselves realizing how deeply it has been woven into their consciousness.[39]

The ever-growing militancy of the advocates of black revolution and Black Power was expressed in the advocacy of counterviolence, in race riots, bombings, marches and demonstrations. Ministers, especially, found themselves searching for theological and ethical guidelines for their actions. What did the Gospel have to say about the intransigence of white racists? What did the love ethic of Jesus Christ mean for black advocates who called the church into the struggle? Was it appropriate to utilize the church sanctuary as a haven and meeting place for those who advocated violence? These were some of the questions which issued forth in black theological reflection.

While it is important to view Martin Luther King, Jr., and the Civil Rights Movement as an important factor in the development of BTUSA, BTUSA owes an even greater debt to Malcolm X and the Black Power Movement. BTUSA owes its origin to the struggle for black empowerment amid a world of suffering and powerlessness, and behind the Black Power Movement stood the presence of El Haj Malik El Shabazz (Malcolm X). Malcolm X had emerged on the American scene preaching the teachings of the Nation of Islam: black self-love, the human right of self-defense, black unity, black nationalism and Christianity as the religion of the white man. He was murdered at the age of thirty-nine, on February 21, 1965, but left the legacy of black nationalism which reemerged among the black power advocates of the late sixties. Albert Cleage, speaking about Malcolm X's influence on Stokely Carmichael, an early Black Power advocate, wrote in 1967:

Malcolm X laid the entire foundation for everything Stokely Carmichael says. Stokely hasn't said one word that was not completely implicit in everything that Malcolm X taught. He is just a voice carrying on upon the basic foundation that Malcolm X put down.[40]

Malcolm X's significance must be evaluated in relationship to that of Martin Luther King and the Civil Rights Movement.[41] While King, a Baptist preacher, believed that Christian religion could inform the black struggle for liberation, Malcolm X, a Muslim minister, believed that Christianity was an instrument for supporting the white oppression of black people. While King preached integration and affirmed the quest for the beloved community, Malcolm spoke of the need for separate development and black unity. As James Cone wrote:

> While Martin King spoke from the perspective of faith and the hope that black people of good will would create a just and humane society, Malcolm spoke from the perspective of history, seeing no hope that an appeal to conscience would lead white people to treat blacks and others as human beings.[42]

In comparing King and Malcolm X, Cone has advanced the claim that both perspectives informed the development of BTUSA. While Martin called the black church back to its unique historical vocation in the black liberation struggle, it was Malcolm who raised difficult questions about the role of Christianity in defining black struggle and hope.[43] Malcolm articulated a difficult theological problem for the black Christian community when he said:

> Christianity is the white man's religion. The Holy Bible is in the white man's hands and his interpretations of it have been the greatest single ideological weapon for enslaving millions of non-white human beings.[44]

Despite their differences at the level of ideology and practical strategy, Malcolm X and Martin Luther King, Jr., were both a part of the same tapestry of black prophetic leadership that viewed its historical vocation as black liberation, and they must be understood in relationship to each other. Malcolm, for example, was a product of the black ghetto, and emphasized the need for utilizing black culture as a basis for black self-affirmation while rejecting Christianity as the religion of the whites. Martin Luther King, Jr., a product of the black middle class, emphasized the importance of integrating into the American mainstream and sought to affirm the Christian faith as relevant to the black struggle for civil rights.

James Cone has indicated that a rapprochement of their views on America was emerging later in their careers.[45] This would support the growing conviction among some black scholars that this growing affinity contained the promise of a synthesis for the future. Cornel West, for example, supports this idea by expressing the belief that integration had proven as hopeless a strategy as had separatism.[46] Thus, the need to utilize both tendencies in the developing of a creative strategy for black struggle in the USA. The precondition for a synthesis of this kind must be the appropriation of an analytical framework that is absent in either Martin or in Malcolm, but which must do justice to the comprehensive problem of diverse oppressive forms, including racism, classism and sexism.

When the cry for black power emerged in 1966, white religious leaders were appalled at the nationalistic turn of the freedom movement. The Civil Rights Movement had achieved limited results and had been confronted by the more subtle oppression of the North. Black activists, particularly the young soldiers of the movement who had been on the battle lines in the Southern states, had become frustrated with the slow process of change in American society. Some were becoming convinced that the movement for racial justice in American society had to be redefined in such a manner as to address the issue of power for the powerless in a racist and unjust world. In this context, the Black Power theme became a forceful new ideology. According to Wilmore:

> Black Power meant that only by black people solidifying their ranks through a new consciousness of history and culture, building political and economic power, and being willing to legitimize ethnocentrism, group self-interest and even defensive violence if necessary, could they hope to survive the onslaught of repression following the wake of disillusioned white liberalism, and take control of their own future.[47]

Stokely Carmichael, Rap Brown, John Lewis, Julian Bond, James Forman and others in that activist group were members of the Student Nonviolent Coordinating Committee. This organization and its members had served as a major organizing force in the South during the Civil Rights Movement. They were seasoned veterans of the Civil Rights Movement who were beginning to experience and express genuine frustration regarding the slow process of integration. The influence of Malcolm X was spreading. His focus on nationalism pervaded their thinking, and they came to see him as someone who articulated the sentiments of the black masses. In addition, some of the SNCC activists had read and analyzed Fanon, Camus and Sartre, and had begun to have grave doubts about King's emphasis on nonviolence. Indeed, according to Robert Brisbane: "By the time of its elections in May 1966 . . . SNCC had moved a long way from the philosophy of love and nonviolence. It was adopting new creeds and new heroes."[48]

Prior to his winning the election and taking over the direction of SNCC on May 17, 1966, Stokely Carmichael had been organizing blacks in the deep South. It was there, in Mississippi, Alabama, and the rest of the South, that political power, economic power and self-determination began to emerge as cornerstones of contemporary black political thinking.[49]

Although Richard Wright had published, in 1954, a book entitled *Black Power,* analyzing the African political situation, the earliest use of the term "black power" in the United States is attributed (by many historians) to Adam Clayton Powell, Jr., who said in an address at Howard University on May 19, 1966: "Human rights are God-given. Civil rights are man-made . . . Our life must be purposed to implement human rights . . . to demand these God-given rights is to seek black power . . . the power to build black institutions of splendid achievement."[50] Many of the SNCC leadership had been present to hear these words and, according to Brisbane, the term "Black Power" was the major topic of conversation at dinner that night.[51] When the opportunity came, with the "Meridith Mississippi Freedom March," in June, 1966, Carmichael was newly equipped with a term that would soon be on the tongues of many Americans. On the march, which was being jointly sponsored by SCLC, SNCC and CORE, Carmichael had decided to seize the initiative and prepared his supporters by indicating to them that "Black Power" would be the slogan for the day.[52] In Greenwood, Mississippi, the new slogan was proclaimed and, thanks to the media, the words Black Power were sent streaming across the country, frightening some and intriguing others.[53]

Amid the confusion and rhetoric, the term Black Power did not seem to have a clear definition and meaning. The multiplicity of interpretations of its meanings suggests that the term was "a slogan in search of a meaning."[54] Carmichael and the leadership of SNCC soon attempted to clarify their understanding of the term by publishing a position paper in the New York *Times* that outlined their position.[55] To them, the term referred to the need for blacks to be proud of their black heritage and to utilize that proud past as a motivating force in the liberation struggle. Furthermore, it meant self-determination for blacks (i.e., control of the cultural, political, economic, and social institutions that affect black life). For Carmichael, there was a necessary connection between black self-esteem and the power blacks might exercise. In the words of Nathan Wright, Jr.: "The concept of black power directly involves a forthright claim to the inherent dignity and worth of black people. Life does have worth, and that worth is related when it has or appropriates the power to become what it should be."[56]

As might have been predicted, the white establishment was disapproving of this new slogan, and white liberals especially urged their black friends to try to limit the impact of this new direction. White churchmen sought out black churchmen to urge them to reject the Black Power Movement and to accept love as the greatest principle of faith. As Gayraud Wilmore remembers, it was in this context, in July 1966, that a number of black churchpersons convened a meeting at the Interchurch Center in New York City to discuss the hysteria that seemed to be evolving among white clergy, the inability of the SCLC to creatively respond to the new situation, and to develop strategies for mobilizing the increasing numbers of radical black clergy. Shortly after their meeting, this ad hoc group of black churchpersons issued a Black Power statement outlining their response to the events. These representatives of the black church rejected the notion that the black yearning for power was wrong. They asserted:

> The fundamental distortion facing us in the controversy about "black power" is rooted in a gross imbalance of power and conscience between Negroes and white Americans. It is this distortion, mainly, which is responsible for the widespread, though often inarticulate, assumption that white people are justified in getting what they want through the use of power, but that Negro Americans must, either by nature or by circumstance, make their appeal only through conscience.[57]

They affirmed that although they did not condone violence, they were nevertheless caught up in a freedom movement that expressed itself in Black Power and sought Black Power. Fellow clergymen were reminded that there was a necessary connection between power and human freedom, and that there could be no genuine expression of love on the part of blacks without the ability to participate as a people with political and economic power. Power exercised in a responsible manner, consistent with gospel intentions, was a power that included justice, freedom and equality for all. Liberation was a necessity, and Black Power was understood to be an important part of the process of achieving it.

It was power, not love, that was at issue. It was within this group of churchpersons, soon to become the National Conference of Black Churchmen (NCBC), and within various other black religious caucuses, that black theological reflection upon the meaning of the Christian faith for the struggle of black freedom was now taken up with a new spirit and focus. On May 4, 1969, NCBC accepted and affirmed James Forman's "Black Manifesto," which located the African-American struggle within the international context of the worldwide struggle of nonwhite peoples against white domination, and in June 1969, under the influence of James H. Cone, they issued a statement of black theology. According to the drafters of that statement:

> Black theology, based on the imaginative black experience, was the best hope for the survival of black people ... Black theology is a theology of black liberation ... it seeks to plumb the condition in the light of God's revelation in Jesus Christ, so that the black community can see that the Gospel is commensurate with the achievement of black humanity.[58]

From 1966 to 1970, documents, articles and books on Black Theology (USA) proliferated as black theologians sought to define their work within the context of this movement for black power. This was the period when the term Black Theology came into explicit use.[59] Much ambiguity, as yet, surrounds the explicit origin of the term Black Theology. Wilmore suggests that the term was probably in use by the theological commission of NCBC prior to the publication of Cone's *Black Theology and Black Power* in 1969.[60] Cone concurs that it was probably in the context of the NCBC theological commission, but also indicates that it was also used in print on several occasions in 1968.[61]

In the documents of the era, the shift from theological dependency to self-determination is evident.[62] First the necessity to define theological sources grounded primarily in black cultural, religious and political traditions was stressed:

It intended to speak to the black church and community about the ethnic pride, political realism, and religious radicalism hidden in the deepest recesses of the black experience, but almost forgotten by black people in their rush to embrace white standards and values.[63]

The newly developed general sense of independence was nowhere more clearly expressed than in the "Black Declaration of Independence" issued by the NCBC on July 1970:

We, therefore, the black people of the United States of America, in all parts of this nation, appealing to the Supreme Judge of the world of rectitude of our intentions, do, in the name of our good people and our black heroes—Richard Allen, James Varick, Absalom Jones, Nat Turner, Frederick Douglass, Marcus Garvey, Malcolm X, Martin Luther King, Jr. . . . solemnly publish and declare that we shall be and of right ought to be, free and independent from the injustice, exploitative control, institutionalized violence and racism of white America.[64]

Black faith also declared itself to be no longer dependent upon the confessional standards of white denominations and the writings of white theologians as the primary sources and standards for its theologizing. In the NCBC, in black caucuses, in white denominations, and in some of the historical black denominations, the debate concerning the need for black theological reflection began in earnest. It should also be noted that the development of black theology was characterized as a setback in race relations by the then-president of the National Baptist Convention, U.S.A., Inc., Dr. J. H. Jackson. This denomination constitutes the largest number of black Christian churches in America. Blacks would do for themselves what no one else could do—provide the theological framework for the interpretation and guidance of the struggle for black liberation.

BTUSA emerged in the context of the Civil Rights and Black Power movements, Malcolm and Martin, and the insurrections which wreaked havoc on America from 1964 to 1968, when black America rebelled in the wake of King's death.[65] The insurrections and the counterviolence of the black community, as a response to the violence of racist American and as an indication of the heightened frustration of the oppressed black community, provided a context for black pastors and religious leaders to reflect on the meaning of Christian faith. Black pastors had to struggle with the meaning of black suffering and to interpret the meaning of the Gospel in a community torn by racial animosity and violence.

Another significant factor in the development of BTUSA was the publication in 1964 of Joseph Washington's book on black religion.[66] The discussion of the role of black religion in the black community, and its sources and content, had been the object of continuing discussion in academic circles for several decades. Washington claimed, contrary to E. Franklin Frazier, that there was a distinctive black culture and religion to be placed alongside Judaism, Protestantism, Roman Catholicism, and secularism.

However, inasmuch as black religion existed only because of the exclusion of blacks from Christianity by white Christians, it had developed primarily as a folk religion that was not substantially Christian, but only had Christian trappings. According to Washington, the black church was an amusement center, an arena for politics, a context for leadership development and worship, but it was not a Christian institution and did not have a Christian theology:

> Without communication with the white community and their source of direction, the Negro has been without theology, except that of the severely limited eschatology of the spirituals . . . The real weakness in the mission of Negro religious groups is the lack of theology.[67]

Concomitantly, Washington argued that it was because of its separation from white Christianity that the black church had no theology and consequently had mistakenly connected faith with the elusive goal of racial freedom by means of protest and social action. Wilmore has stated that the publication of this book accelerated the development of Black Theology by way of negative reaction.[68] Black ministers and scholars responded to Washington's thesis with an outpouring of protest and reaction. Wilmore asserts that most of the black clergy found Washington's claim incredible and rejected his conclusion that "the Negro now must close his house of worship and enter the white congregation of his choice en masse."[69]

BTUSA developed, in part, as black ministers and scholars sought to respond to Washington's thesis.[70] According to Cone: "The black clergy wanted to correct two flagrant misconceptions: 1) that black religion is not Christian and thus has no Christian theology, and 2) that the Christian gospel has nothing to do with the struggle for justice in society."[71]

Black clergymen and scholars — James H. Cone, Albert Cleage, Jr., J. Deotis Roberts, C. Eric Lincoln, Gayraud Wilmore, and others — began to produce a wealth of written material that sought to reject Washington's interpretation and to articulate a perspective grounded in black faith. In 1969 James Cone published the first book to use the term Black Theology in its title — *Black Theology and Black Power* — in which he argued that Black Theology and Black Power were expressions of black rejection of white racist definitions and an affirmation of the unique contributions of the black Christian community.[72]

Cone's book issued a challenge to blacks and whites alike in asserting that Black Power was consistent with God's liberating movement in a world of oppression. The theological terrain was radically disrupted by the claims of Cone's work. Other scholars, such as Wilmore, sought to demonstrate that there was continuity between the Christian theological reflection of the black slaves through the nineteenth century to current times and that the peculiar contribution of the black Christian tradition was precisely its insistence that the Gospel had radical implications for justice in society.

Albert Raboteau's *Slave Religion* and Wilmore's *Black Religion and Black Radicalism* are but two books that emerged in the 1970s as products of the turn to the radical Christianity of eighteenth- and nineteenth-century black Christians. Although they were not always in complete agreement with one another, black scholars of religion — clergymen, historians, theologians, and ethicists — affirmed, in contrast to Washington, the distinctive character of the black Christian tradition, stressed the centrality of the struggle for justice and righteousness in the black Christian tradition, and rejected the necessity for the validation of white people in the religious life of the black community.

Indeed some of the black theologians, notably Albert Cleage, Jr., and James Cone, in the tradition of their forebears in the time of slavery, insisted that it was white religion that was apostate and unchristian and asserted that the only authentically Christian theology was the theology of the black church, which clearly articulated and enacted the liberation action of the Gospel in the world of a people dehumanized by racist oppression. The Gospel was the liberating good news that God, in Jesus Christ, was engaged in the struggle for black freedom. Cone, for example, asserted:

> By defining black religion as an instrument of social protest and excluding it as a genuine historical manifestation of Christianity, Washington undermined the connection between the Christian faith and political struggle as found in the history of the black church. The discipline of Black Theology was developed partly to correct this distortion. In view of the continuity of the secular and sacred in our African heritage and the biblical location of God's revelation in history, many of us believed that it would be a serious mistake to sever the connection between theology and politics.[73]

Since his first book, Washington has published several texts in which he drastically revised his original conclusion. While I acknowledge the importance of Washington's text in understanding the development of BTUSA, I would consider it to be of secondary significance when evaluated alongside the Black Power and Civil Rights Movements, and the suffering of the black community during the sixties, as they sought to respond to the violence of a racist social system. The black theological discourse that emerged in the late sixties was a response to the dynamic events that surrounded blacks' ongoing struggle for justice and freedom. It was a theology which emerged to respond to questions being raised in the streets of black communities all over the nation.

BTUSA emerged from an oppressed community that had reinterpreted the meaning of the Gospel in the context of the black freedom struggle. Although a systematized discourse was absent in the eighteenth- and nineteenth-century black churches, it is apparent that black Christians viewed the radical dimensions of the Gospel as explicitly supporting their claim that God did not wish blacks to be slaves in a society that claimed a Christian heritage. Thus, black radicalism, even in its incipient stages, is to be understood as an affirmation of the religio-cultural particularity of Africans in America, in the face of white racism, and as a declaration of independence from white society. Black Theology is a continuation of this radical tradition.

Having considered the origins and emergence of BTUSA, let me now turn to a similar consideration of that of LALT.

Latin American Liberation Theology: Its Historical Roots

Latin American Liberation Theology (LALT) emerged in the sixties as a response to the need for Christians on that continent to decolonize their theological traditions and develop an independent theology reflecting their situation. Like BTUSA, the emergence of LALT in the contemporary context can only be understood against the backdrop of the historical struggles of a colonized peoples to rid themselves of their colonial and neocolonial oppressors.

Camilo Torres, a Colombian priest, wrote in the 1960s, "I believe that the revolutionary struggle is a Christian struggle and a priestly one. Indeed, in the present specific conditions of Colombia, participation in that struggle is the only way men can show love for their neighbors as they should."[74] Torres and many other Latin Americans had come to view neocolonialism, imperialism and class domination as the central contradictions confronting their attempts to build a just and free society.

The words of Camilo Torres echoed the sentiments of many Latin American Christians as they confronted the realities of Latin American life. The questions that Torres's statement sought to answer are implicit in it and give us a hint of life in Latin America. LALT developed amid the ongoing attempts of Christians to explicate the meaning of the Gospel in the light of their socio-economic and political circumstances.

In recent decades, Latin America has been undergoing socio-economic and political upheaval, as the people have attempted to extricate themselves from a state of dependence upon the developed nations of the world.[75] In the midst of this situation, Christians have struggled to explicate the meaning of faith for the revolutionary struggle. The historical roots of LALT can be traced directly to the upheavals that were manifested in the peoples' desire to become independent, free from the neocolonial forces that dominated their homelands.

The challenge that issued from this struggle — the challenge to develop a liberation theology proper to Latin America — entailed the attempt to develop an anticolonial tradition self-consciously focused on the reality of Latin America. In light of its long colonial (1492–1808) and neocolonial (1808–1968) history, this challenge was to be of decisive importance to Latin American Christians.[76]

In a paper entitled "Theological Understanding in European and Latin American Theology," Jon Sobrino stated the motivating force of liberation theology when he raised the following questions: "What is the interest of the theologian? Why does one do theology in the first place? For who is one theologizing and from whose perspective?" As with BTUSA, his presupposition is that theology is never neutral; it always, implicitly or explicitly, has practical and ethical dimensions. Sobrino concludes that in Latin America the essential problem with which the liberation theologians were concerned was the recovery of meaning in a situation in which there was poverty and misery. LALT, he argues, was seeking to confront the concrete human situation of life in Latin America. Thus, the origins of LALT were to be found rooted in the historical context on that continent. Basic to the situation on that continent is the class struggle.

The Historical Roots of the Struggle for Liberation in Latin America

The development of a liberation theology indigenous to the region is to be understood within the broad framework of seven realities:
1. The role of Christianity in Latin America
2. Economic and political factors that shaped the social fabric of Latin American life
3. *La Violencia*
4. The radicalization of the popular masses into movements of liberation
5. The Cuban revolution of 1959
6. Vatican II and Medellín
7. The struggle to be Christian in Latin America.[77]

In his important text, *Doing Theology in a Revolutionary Situation*, José Míguez Bonino characterizes the situation of Latin American Christians as undergoing a crisis in identity and conscience. The situation entailed a crisis in identity because Christianity, both Protestant and Catholic, had become linked to the ideological superstructures of an oppressive social order. It entailed a crisis in conscience because Latin American Christians were becoming increasingly aware of the complicity of Christianity in the rampant oppression that characterized Latin America. Míguez Bonino points out:

> Christianity faces in Latin America the crisis unleashed by the collapse of the two historical projects to which it had become intimately related. Catholicism suffered the first crisis at the time of the emancipation. To the extent that it has clung to the old semi-feudal society, it still has this crisis in front of it.[78]

According to Míguez Bonino, Catholicism "and Protestantism share the crisis of modernistic-liberal ideology. Co-opted into the colonial and neocolonial systems as religious sanction and ideological justification, Christianity faces an agonizing experience of self-criticism."[79] Ninety percent of the 320 million Latin Americans were Catholics, with the rest broadly coming under the banner of Protestantism.[80] Thus it is not surprising that the predominant texture of the religion and theology that emerged out of that context should be Catholic. Both the Catholic and Protestant churches in Latin America had been guilty of allying themselves with the dominant interests in Latin America:

> Protestantism . . . is clearly linked with the whole North Atlantic ideological, cultural, economic and political thrust beginning with the nineteenth century and up to the present. Protestantism, in terms of its historical origin . . . came into our world as the religious accompaniment of free enterprise, liberal, capitalist democracy.[81]

And, on the other hand, "Roman Catholicism, clinging with all of its force to its conservative continuation, fought hard against the introduction of the modern world."[82]

Christianity thus entered Latin America under these two historical movements: Catholicism, with the conquest and colonization of the sixteenth century, and Protestantism, with the modernization and neocolonialism of the nineteenth and twentieth centuries. Latin American Christians found themselves, in recent years, attempting to evaluate the historical role of Christianity in Latin America, as well as developing new and more authentic Christian models for that situation.

The factors that resulted in this crisis for the Christians of Latin America were the appalling conditions of the Latin American masses. The crisis in conscience was precipitated by a Latin America characterized by the overwhelming poverty of rural and urban workers in a situation where starvation, suffering and disease were rampant. Further, the bulk of the land and wealth was controlled by a few families who exploited the labor of the lower classes.

According to one United Nations report, cited in Míguez Bonino's text, the Latin American continent was characterized by (1) massive undernourishment, (2) illiteracy among three-fourths of the population, (3) rampant infectious diseases among the poor, (4) landlessness among the majority of the people, (5) an economy dependent on overseas investments and foreign economic factors, (6) underdevelopment, (7) rampant unemployment, and (8) exploitation of the masses as sources of cheap labor.[83] This was the real situation with which Christians in Latin America were confronted. As the initial meeting of Latin American Christians for Socialism asserted in its final document:

The socio-economic, political, and cultural situation of the Latin American people challenges our Christian conscience. Unemployment, malnutrition, alcoholism, infant mortality, illiteracy, prostitution, and ever increasing inequality between the rich and the poor, racial and cultural discrimination, exploitation, and so forth, are facts that define a situation of institutional violence in Latin America.[84]

The Latin America to which they had turned their attention had been a victim of gross exploitation and was experiencing the effects of the economic, political and cultural domination by neocolonial forces. Latin American intellectuals — theologians, sociologists, economists, political scientists — began to understand that their continent was afflicted by dependence on its colonial and neocolonial oppressors, underdevelopment and violence, and they began to realize that these factors were natural consequences of the particular economic policies that had been applied to the region. As Míguez Bonino asserts:

For a growing number of Latin Americans ... the reason for the failure lies ... in the very nature of the economic system. The Christians meeting in Santiago expressed it this way: "This unjust society has its objective basis in the capitalist relations of production that necessarily generate a class society.[85]

According to Míguez Bonino, they began to realize that Latin America "has been incorporated into the modern world indeed, but not as a junior partner with increasing participation in the total enterprise but as a dependent, serving the further development of the owners' profit."[86]

The notion of development, Gustavo Gutiérrez points out and documents, is a term that "has synthesized the aspiration of poor peoples during the last decades."[87] Development is a total social process that includes economic, political, social, cultural and religious factors as they shape the progress of a society.

The "development" model had been proposed by the United Nations in 1950, when it declared the first decade of development, and had continued in the sixties with John F. Kennedy's launching of the Alliance for Progress in 1961. The expectation, based on a number of misguided assumptions, was that development would be the process for addressing the historic inequities between the developed and underdeveloped nations. Edward Cleary, in response to the question, "Why is Latin America underdeveloped?" immediately points in the direction of the development model.[88] He writes:

> The "development" model was proposed for Latin America and the third world because of the reconstruction of Europe and Japan through the Marshall Plan . . . because the Marshall Plan had worked so well with former enemies, why not apply essentially the same plan to friends to the South?[89]

By 1960, U Thant of the United Nations had declared the 1960s "the decade of development," and President John Kennedy and his advisors had established an instrument of implementation in the Alliance for Progress. Upon careful economic analysis, however, Latin American economists, social scientists, theologians and political leaders came to view the ideal of development as detrimental to Latin America. Míguez Bonino indicates that "soon after the launching of the Alliance for Progress, the failure [of this policy] was already visible."[90]

Míguez Bonino notes that the development model was a failure in Latin America: "The chasm between the developed and the underdeveloped world was growing wider instead of narrower."[91] Applications of the development mode to Latin America had been based on "a historical and mechanistic analysis which makes at least three fundamental mistakes":

> The first is to believe that history is unlinear and that a society can move to previous stages of other existing societies. . . . Secondly, the model did not take into account the political factors: There is an "Effect of Demonstration" which moves the masses to demand participation in wealth and welfare, and therefore the "slave labor" that was available in the early states of the developed societies cannot be obtained today—hence social unrest and repression. Thirdly, the theory took for granted that the developed countries were the "normal" model for the underdeveloped.[92]

Through a process of study, analysis and inquiry, Latin Americans recognized that underdevelopment was a consequence of domination and exploitation by Europe and North America.

Underdevelopment was a category used to describe the uneven social and economic development of one society by comparing it to another, as well as to describe a particular relationship of exploitation between one country and another. Walter Rodney states, "All of the countries named as 'underdeveloped' in the world are exploited by others; and the under-development with which the world is now preoccupied is a product of capitalist, imperialist and colonialist exploitation.'"[93] Thus any development program designed according to this perspective would perpetuate the underdevelopment of Latin America and cultivate what Latin Americans called *dependencia*.[94] In fact, Latin American emergence in the colonial period, it was concluded, was as an exploited and dependent continent. Development and underdevelopment had been two dimensions of colonial and imperialist activity by the developed nations as they sought to exploit that part of the world.

It had become increasingly evident that, from Mexico to Chile, Latin America was a dependent region of the world, and this fact profoundly affected its struggling societies. Latin American Christians were to realize that dependency was applicable not only to politics and economics but also to culture, religion and theology. It is therefore not surprising that Latin Americans rejected development as reformist and dependency as imperialist in favor of a more appropriate vision of liberation (i.e., self-determination). It is important to note here that the shift from development to liberation was through a long process of social analysis of Latin America.

Violence had become a hallmark of the Latin American situation. In addition to the well-documented atrocities of various military dictatorships, it was public knowledge that in Brazil, El Salvador, Guatemala, Nicaragua (under Somoza), and Argentina, right-wing death squads were regularly at work. Violence, one writer argues, had been an endemic part of modern Latin America from the time of the European conquest:

A spiral of violence . . . is one of the chief characteristics of Latin American life to this day. As Malcolm Lowry noted in *Under the Volcano,* the sickness that engulfs Latin America came to the New World with the conquistadors. The killings and torture—the total disregard for human rights in a majority of Latin American countries—can be understood only when seen through the prism of colonial Spain and Portugal.[95]

Violence as an instrument of repression was so prevalent in many parts of Latin America that in Colombia it was referred to as *La Violencia*. In a major address, Camilo Torres touched on the spiral of violence in Colombia:

The government's violence, financed by the oligarchy, taught the peasants many lessons. It taught them that their real enemy is the oligarchy. It also taught them to flee; then to defend themselves; and finally to take the offensive in order to get what the oligarchy had got by means of violence; namely, farms, harvests, cattle . . . and power.[96]

The violence of the oligarchy was not always replaced by victorious revolutionaries, but by new forms of political repression. The modern, liberal democratic state (Argentina, Brazil, Chile, Peru, etc.) was dying, and in successive military coups, a new kind of state had developed: the National Security State. The dominant ideology of liberalism was replaced by the ideology of national security. Democratic participation was being replaced by authoritarian integration. The state was identified with the nation, and all opposition was savagely repressed as a grave threat to national or continental security.

Even the institutional church was increasingly faced with a choice between becoming integrated into the state or of being repressed as an enemy of the state. This was the case with Archbishop Romero of El Salvador, who was to become a martyr of the Latin American church. Christians everywhere in Latin America were being forced to choose between state violence and the violence of revolutionary movement. Much like American black Christians in the turbulent 1960s, Latin American Christians found themselves looking for new ways of theologically interpreting their faith in the light of their circumstances.

During the period in which these events unfolded, an event of revolutionary significance occurred that stimulated the radicalization of popular movements in Latin America. The event to which I refer is the victorious Cuban revolution of 1959. This event, along with the repression of workers' and students' movements, the party's left, and the church in other contexts, served to radicalize the masses. The revitalization of popular movements among the poor played a preparatory role for the development of liberation theology, because it forced certain theological questions to the forefront for Latin American Christians. Gutiérrez writes:

The revolutionary ferment in Mexico (in its more popular aspects) as well as in Bolivia and Guatemala, in the 1950's, played a preparatory role. The socialist revolution in Cuba—whatever analysis some observers may make today—opened up new outlooks. The year 1965 marked a high point in armed struggle in Latin America and hastened a political radicalization even of persons who had hoped to find other avenues for their revolutionary activity. Camilo Torres and "Che" Guevara symbolized so many others—anonymous, committed, setting an indelible seal on the Latin American process, raising questions and exerting definitive influence in Christian circles.

Indeed, from these years onward, an increasing number of Christians—in Brazil especially, at first—have become active agents in this process, and consequently in the process of discovery of the world of the exploited of Latin America. In most instances this has simply meant becoming aware of their own world.[97]

Awareness of one's own world (Latin America) meant for Gutiérrez:

An increasing awareness of the world of the "other"—of the poor, the oppressed, the exploited class. For in a social order drawn up economically, politically, and ideologically by the few for the benefit of the few, the "others"—the exploited classes, oppressed cultures, and ethnic groups that suffer discrimination—have begun to make their own voice heard.[98]

The struggle of oppressed Catholic and Protestant Christians to define their own Latin American identity and theology must be viewed within this framework of circumstances. As Gutiérrez has written:

This is the context in which the theology of liberation was born and grew. It could not have come to be before the popular movement itself and its concrete, historical liberation praxis had achieved a certain degree of development and maturity. These struggles are the locus of a new way of being men and women in Latin America and thereby as well of a new manner of living the faith, a new mode of encounter with the Father and with one's sisters and brothers.[99]

Another dimension of the background of LALT is Medellín and the activities that led to that historic conference of Catholic bishops. Medellín, and the parallel developments of radical theology in Protestant Christian circles, constituted an important part of the struggle of Christians in Latin America.

According to Phillip Berryman in *The Religious Roots of Rebellion,* Medellín "gave the Catholic Church in Latin America its own identity, that is, its issues were no longer those emanating from the Vatican council and its aftermath but those arising out of native soil and articulated by Latin Americans."[100]

Cardinal Archbishop Juan Landazuri Ricketts, of Lima, Peru, the Co-President of the Latin American Episcopal Council (CELAM—*Consejo Episcopal Latino Americano*) speaking at the inaugural meeting of the Medellín Conference, indicated that the reason for their presence in Colombia for the conference could be deduced from the title of the conference, "The Church in the Present Day Transformation of Latin America in the Light of the Council." The conference could be traced to Bishop Manuel Larrain who, at the close of the Vatican II Council, had expressed the need for a major conference of Latin American Catholics.[101]

The second meeting of CELAM was held in Medellín, Colombia, in 1968. This meeting of bishops, unlike the first meeting in Rio de Janeiro in 1955, was to prove decisive for the Catholic Church in Latin America. Prior to Medellín, however, was the Second Vatican Council in Rome, from 1962 to 1965. In order to understand Medellín, it is necessary to view it in the light of Vatican II. Much debate has taken place concerning whether the meeting at Medellín was intended for the purpose of "applying" the conclusions of Vatican II to Latin America. Edward L. Cleary observed that "Oliveros and others argue that what took place at Medellín was an interpretation of Vatican II in the light of the Latin American situation—rather than simply an application."[102]

Vatican II was essentially a call for the renewal of the Catholic Church in light of the challenges of the modern world. Cleary speaks of Vatican II correctly when he writes, "Vatican Council II was a modern plan for renewal of the universal church to which the Latin American Church actively responded."[103]

Of greater significance, however, was the fact that by 1962 the non-European Catholic churches in Asia, Africa and Latin America had a markedly higher representation in the worldwide episcopacy. Enrique Dussel, a Latin American historian, compares the role and representation of Latin American bishops in Vatican I and Vatican II:

> There were sixty-five Latin American bishops at Vatican I, but they did not take an active role and merely approved what Rome proposed. ... At Vatican II, the Latin American presence was much more substantial, even though it might well have been even greater in proportionate terms. Over six hundred Latin American bishops were present at the Council: i.e., 22 percent of the total. But the Catholic population of Latin America is 38 percent of the world Catholic population—hence considerably more than was proportionately represented at the Council.[104]

Cleary indicates that the election of Pope John XXIII, who had "an openness to religions and cultures outside Europe," played a significant role in setting in motion the process of the updating of the Catholic church.

Despite the pope's "openness" and the Latin American Bishops' substantial participation in Vatican II, it was quite evident that the agenda had been organized and determined by the dominant European participants. As a result the council appeared to have been called to modernize the church in the light of the reality of Europe, rather than in the light of the diverse localities in which the church was to be found:

> Except for having a part to play in the preparation of one document and the occasional noteworthy intervention of a few Latin American bishops, the Latin American church did not go to the council as a pacesetter. It went rather as a learner.[105]

The Latin American church (the bishops and their advisors) became painfully aware of the absence of any reference to Latin America in the deliberations of the meeting, but they learned some important essentials that would facilitate the development of a theology of liberation indigenous to Latin America.

First, the Latin American bishops utilized the opportunity to strengthen their ties with one another and to build informal networks with various ecclesial groups. As much as time provided, the Latin Americans used this time to caucus in the halls and established networks for communications and collaboration. At Vatican II, Latin American bishops could interact with one another and also with other bishops from other parts of the Third World.[106] Their interaction with other non-European bishops helped them to become more aware of the common experiences that bonded them together as colonial churches.

Secondly, their awareness of the absence of the particular social context of modern Latin America led to the realization of the need to interpret Vatican II in the light of the modern realities of Latin America. Manuel Larrain was the Latin American bishop who exerted the most significant influence at the council. According to Cleary:

Larrain formed the idea of having a Latin American conference apply what was being expressed at Vatican II to the Latin American situation. At the psychologically appropriate moment, Larrain proposed this to other Latin American bishops at the last session of the Council (1965).[107]

Larrain was elected president of CELAM in 1963, the second year of the council.[108] Concerning the strengthening of ties within CELAM, Cleary notes that the "four-year experience of the council brought them together in a way that no other experience had."[109]

Thirdly, the bishops' use of advisors, who were mostly young Latin American graduates of European theological institutions, gave these young theologians an arena in which to apply their considerable intellectual skills.[110] It is out of this group that the most articulate Latin American theologians have come. It is, however, important to note that these young men were educated in European schools, far away from the reality of Latin America. Their education in European culture and values is one factor which contributed to their failure to integrate the perspectives of black and indigenous peoples in their early discourse on liberation theology. About these advisors Cleary remarks, "They acted as the intellectual bridges for the Latin American church, interpreting what was taking place in council discussions and eventually reinterpreting for Latin America the ideological thrust of the council."[111]

Fourthly, the Latin American church took seriously the call of Vatican II that the church's mission was to the world, a world that was outside the church and with which the church had to become involved. Gustavo Gutiérrez has written about the impact of Vatican II. He observes:

At the opening of the second session of Vatican II . . . Pope Paul VI spoke of the church's desire and duty of coming at last to a full understanding of its true nature. And a year later he spoke once again of the need for the church to deepen its awareness of the mission it must carry out in the world. The Council faced up to this task; and the church has continued to do this, often in unexpected ways, in the years following the end of the Council. Going beyond the strict letter of its documents, the Council opened up perspectives that have not ceased to provoke wondrous surprise, fear, alarm—depending on one's point of view.[112]

The call to clarify their mission in the world led the Latin American bishops on a journey to new awareness of their world—the world of Latin America. All these factors contributed to the organization of the Medellín Conference of August 1968, which would provide a significant impetus to the theology of liberation in Latin America.

In the years between 1965 and 1968, the Latin American bishops committed themselves to a process of continued study and reflection on their reality, and at their annual meeting in 1966, a critical decision was made:

To set a new direction for the forthcoming extraordinary conference at Medellín. In contrast to canonical representation (delegates from ecclesiastical regions), Medellín would have pastoral representation (delegates from functional or apostolic sectors). The decision was crucial: it meant that the church would be analyzed and defined from the bottom up.

The same CELAM meeting brought about another structural change of note: the conference would use a now-famous methodology that would follow the trinomial of the Vatican II *Gaudium at Spes (The Church in the Modern World)*: It represented a shift from a perspective that was dogmatic, deductive and top-to-bottom to one that was exploratory, inductive and bottom-to-top.[113]

These two decisive and fundamental shifts were to be of great significance in the development of LALT. It also suggests that the Latin Americans had deeper intentions than those mentioned by Cleary: assimilation and Latin Americanization. Assimilation was bringing the Latin American church into conformity with the teachings of Vatican II, and Latin Americanization was interpreting Latin America in the light of Vatican II.[114] The intention of the bishops and their advisors was really to analyze Latin America and to reinterpret Vatican II teaching in light of the Latin American social context, thus creating a theology for Latin America and accomplishing what Noel Erskine has called the "decolonizing" of Latin American theology.[115]

The need for facts and analysis of causes and effects in various social situations in Latin America was taken up with new zeal by the young religious intellectuals in a network of development institutes that had sprung up in Latin America. The three major sources of inspiration for these institutes were François Houtart of Louvain University, French Dominican Louis Joseph Lebret, and the Jesuits. Centers were established in all the major regional cities of Latin America, eventually leading Houtart to form a coordinated network called the Federation of Religious and Social Studies.[116]

Louis Joseph Lebret and his followers established several centers in Uruguay, Argentina and Bolivia. The Jesuits, often in collaboration with other existing organizations, began to establish centers for social investigation and action. Cleary writes that the establishment of these centers, focusing on various dimensions of Latin American life, was important for many reasons. Most importantly:

> A number of the more talented, younger, Latin American Jesuits went off to major universities, usually outside Latin America, to obtain advanced degrees in social leadership within the social science enterprise, government circles, (as in Nicaragua), the theology of liberation, or church administration . . .
>
> The CIAS (Centers for Social Investigation and Action) model led the Jesuits away from merely academic concerns to emphasis on social problems. This major shift has had important consequences for the Jesuits and for Latin American society. Nowhere is this more evident than in Paraguay or in Central America where Jesuit social commentators and activists helped the church confront manifestly unjust social structures.[117]

It was in these centers, staffed by young priests, that research was performed in order to establish a clear, precise picture of the facts of Latin American life. In the process of preparing for Medellín, commissions and consultations were organized and a comprehensive view of the human and religious situation in Latin America was discussed. The view that emerged was that of a world characterized by dependency, underdevelopment, and violence, suffering from two evils: external dominance and internal colonialism. Gutiérrez's words capture the emerging picture well:

> The true face of Latin America is emerging in all its naked ugliness. It is not simply or primarily a question of low educational standards, a limited economy, an unsatisfactory legal system, or inadequate legal institutions. What we are faced with is a situation that takes no account of the dignity for human beings or their most elemental needs, that does not provide for their biological survival or their basic right to be free and autonomous. Poverty, injustice, alienation, and the exploitation of human beings by other human beings combine to form a situation that the Medellín Conference did not hesitate to condemn as "institutional violence."[118]

It is important to note that attention to social investigation as an important dimension of theology developed as Latin American Christians tried to understand their role in contemporary Latin America. It is also significant that some of the theologians of the Latin American church began to see the investigation of the social sciences as an indispensable aspect of the theological task. Another aspect of this important development was that:

> Theologians had to focus their thoughts on practical affairs such as education, missions and social action. It was theology at the side of those immersed in practical activities—a considerable change from the theology that had typically been taught in Latin American schools of theology.[119]

Medellín stands as a conference of decisive significance to the churches of Latin America. The conclusions of Medellín, Dussel writes, "gave a voice to a new tone and a new idiom in the language of the Latin American church."[120] The final document spells out a new vision for the church in the world of Latin America:

> It is the same God who, in the fullness of time, sends his Son in the flesh so that he might come to liberate all men from the slavery to which sin has subjected them: hunger, misery, oppression, and ignorance, in a word, that injustice and hatred have their origin in human selfishness.[121]

"Therefore," the writers of the document continue:

> The Christian . . . recognizes that in many instances Latin America finds itself faced with a situation of injustice that can be called institutional violence. This situation demands all-embracing, courageous, urgent and profoundly renovating transformations.[122]

The Medellín conclusions reflected the shift from the theology of development or revolution to a theology of liberation. Confronting the Latin American situation, the participants called for liberation:

> Because all liberation is an anticipation of the complete redemption of Christ, the church in Latin America is particularly in favor of all educational efforts which tend to free our people . . . A deafening cry pours from the throats of millions of men, asking their pastors for a liberation that reaches them from nowhere else.[123]

This realization of the new call to liberation meant an acknowledgment that the church's structures are inadequate for the world in which it lives.

It showed up as outdated and lacking in vitality when confronted with new questions. Thus the church had to ask anew what it means to be a church in these circumstances in Latin America. The Latin American Christian community was forced to confront these essential questions: "What does being Christian mean?" "How can the church truly be the church in the new circumstances that surround it?"[124] At Medellín the bishops agreed that the Church had to choose the side of the poor and the oppressed and that new models had to be developed that would provide answers to the questions. In summing up his analysis of the meeting, Cleary writes:

> In sum, a new ideology for the Latin American church had been born. Progressive thinkers had assumed intellectual leadership of the church and set it on a new course of change. The highest church membership in Latin America endorsed an ideology that would become increasingly clarified and elaborated as the theology of liberation . . . The shift from development to liberation, with spiritual as well as material overtones, had been made. The most important event in the modern era of the Latin American Church had taken place.[125]

The evolution of the Catholic Church in Latin America from Vatican II to Medellín was the context for the growth of the young theologians of liberation in Latin America. These new thinkers understood theology as a partner to pastoral action, and they understood social analysis as one dimension of the theological task. It was within this framework that Gutiér-rez, Juan Luis Segundo, José Comblin, Eduardo Pironio, and others emerged as articulators of this new Latin American theological tradition. These same intellectuals had participated in a series of informal consultations on Latin American theology organized by Monsignor Ivan Illich in 1960.[126] Gustavo Gutiérrez and Juan Luis Segundo presented influential papers that led to a series of meetings throughout Latin America (1964–1968) and "opened the way toward a Latin American theology and expressed concerns that were to become richer, more systematic statements of liberation thought."[127]

The Protestant dimension, which paralleled and sometimes overlapped the developments in the Catholic Church, is of great importance to the development of LALT, because it emphasizes the ecumenical aspect of LALT. During the 1960s and 1970s, many Protestants were experiencing a similar development in international meetings, often sponsored by such organizations as the World Council of Churches (WCC), the National Council of Churches in the U.S.A. (NCC), and Church and Society in Latin America (ISAL). Liberal Protestantism's openness to modernity and its willingness to adapt itself to the modern world also created massive pressures on the Catholic Church, which for the most part had resisted such changes since the time of the Reformation.

The WCC Second World Assembly discussed the notion of development in 1954, and the WCC promoted it through the 1950s, but its members began to recognize its inadequacy as they participated in discussions with Christians from the Third World. For example, at the World Conference on Church and Society in Geneva in 1966, Christians from "underdeveloped countries" began to challenge openly the reformist positions that up to then had dominated the WCC. They denounced the system of international trade and named the inadequacies of modernization and technology as the determining causes of the growing pauperization of Third World countries.

This meeting underscored that only the Third World countries could break the system of social domination that oppresses them and that they could do this through an active political fight aimed at the seizure of power. The opulent countries, which had been thought of as part of the solution, were now considered to be the cause of the problem. Development was no longer thought of as adequately perceiving or profiting from scientific technological aid, but as overcoming the conditions that cause underdevelopment.[128] By the fourth World Assembly of the WCC at Uppsala in 1968, however, the discussions were being dominated by the idea of revolution as the focus of the mission of the church.

ISAL (*Iglesia y Sociedad en América Latina* — Church and Society in Latin America) was another forum in which Latin American Christians developed their new awareness of the need for liberation. According to José Míguez Bonino:

> [ISAL] partly imported as an extension of the ecumenical interest in the problem of development . . . was born in a conference in Huampani (Peru) attended by people from Protestant churches concerned with social problems. Successive meetings in 1966, 1967, and 1971 marked the rapid transformation of ISAL's conception of itself, its relation to the churches, and its role in Latin America. In the first few years (1960–1965) the analysis of the situation, which at the beginning oscillated between a developmentalist and a revolutionary approach, gained greater consistency, adopted the "Sociology of Dependence" and made a clear revolutionary and socialist option. This ideological clarification was followed in the years 1966-68 by a transformation in the theological perspective, veering from a predominantly Barthian theology to a "Theology of God's transforming action in history" greatly indebted to Paul Lehmann and Richard Shaull.[129]

Hugo Assmann and Julio de Santa Ana, two other important Latin American liberation theologians, affirm Míguez Bonino's point of view.[130] Thus in both the WCC and the ISAL contexts we can discern a clear dependence on the tools of the social sciences, clarification of one's ideological commitment, and a reorienting of the theological task consistent with its new awareness of the Latin American reality. Cleary indicates that in many Latin American countries the "majority of its [ISAL's] members were Catholic," suggesting that a great deal of interaction and cross-fertilization was occurring between progressive Christian thinkers from the Catholic and Protestant traditions:

> One of the great innovations of the [Medellín] Conference was the inviting of non-Catholic observer-delegates. ... At first it was the intention of the Roman Commission for Latin America to limit the participation of non-Catholics to plenaries, but as it turned out the non-Catholic observer-delegates were authorized to participate in all sessions. Their presence proved to be highly beneficial for the proceedings and brought humanism in Latin America to an entirely new level.[131]

Therefore, the Protestant contribution, through such theologians as Rubem Alves, José Míguez Bonino, and others, played a significant role in the development of LALT.

Against the background of the social reality of Latin America and the context of both Catholic and Protestant forums, the Christians of Latin America struggled through and evolved several important intuitions that specifically stimulated LALT and are significant to this study. These intuitions are:

1. The incorporation of a methodology that included analysis of facts, reflection, and recommendations into the comprehensive task of the theologian
2. The incorporation of a "from-the-bottom-up" approach to its analysis of the Church
3. The incorporation of the tools of the social sciences (social analysis) into both the study of the theology by theological students and the work of the theologian
4. The incorporation of liberation into systems that dominate human life.

In addition to these intuitions, it is clear that in the 1950s and 1960s progressive Christian intellectuals and theologians were emerging who would elaborate these basic intuitions into a more systematic theology of liberation for Latin America.

All the factors discussed here—victorious revolutions, radicalized mass movements, and an increasing awareness of the exploited and oppressed— provide an important element in any description of the development of LALT. Any attempt to comprehend its evolution must take into account its development against the background of:

1. The historical role of Christianity, especially the Catholic tradition, in Latin America
2. The economic and political factors that constitute the social matrix of Latin America
3. The radicalization of popular movements of liberation

4. The struggle for Christians to be Christian in Latin America as defined by these particular contours.

The struggle to be Christian and reflect on the meaning of Christian faith in a revolutionary situation were the forces that compelled the development of LALT.

The Emergence of Latin American Liberation Theology in the 1960s: Its Immediate Antecedents

Against the historical backdrop, one must discern the immediate antecedents to the development of LALT. Again, as we have already indicated in the case of BTUSA, the antecedents to the development of LALT are:
1. The failure of development theories in the fifties and sixties to produce change in Latin America
2. The awakening of a new Christian conscience and identity in Latin America
3. The victory of Cuban revolutionaries in 1959
4. The emergence of popular movements.

First, the failure of the development model in Latin America meant that the continent was characterized by internal and external exploitation. This situation led to frustrated aspirations among the masses of Latin America. Second, Vatican II, Medellín and the development of ISAL signaled the awakening of a new awareness among Christians in Latin America of the need for the church to participate in transforming the world. This process led to a new perception of the world and a revitalized dedication to engage in committed praxis for liberation. LALT follows after engagement in the praxis of liberation. Third, the victory in Cuba marked the reality of success and led Latin Americans to the concrete belief that revolutionary transformation was possible. Fourth, the development of popular mass movements throughout the continent reflected the will of human beings to resist oppression and to engage in the struggle for change. The Christian community found itself in a context that required a theological response. LALT was born out of this circumstance.

BTUSA and LALT: Some Common Themes

Having separately considered the historical contexts and antecedents of Latin American Liberation Theology and Black Theology in the United States, one must evaluate them in the light of common themes and differences. These commonalities and differences may bear clues that can shape our further study. Black Theology in the United States was the contemporary expression of a radical black Christian tradition which historically had fought against racism. Thus BTUSA maintains its continuity with the black radical tradition by rejecting white theological domination and affirming black religious and cultural sources as primary for defining a liberating tradition of theology. Black theologians theologize out of the context of their encounter with white racism in North America.[132] This reality is consistent with the history of the United States, where racism continues to be one of the most insidious aspects of its society. The experience of racism by black people shapes the black theological enterprise in the United States in a fundamental manner. This experience constitutes the core of BTUSA's point of departure. For BTUSA, the central ideological enemy is white racism, which means that each theological category or doctrine must be scrutinized from that perspective and through that filter, for, as Gayraud Wilmore has written: "Black theology, explicating the faith that Jesus Christ came to liberate the captive masses of the world, has played a crucial role in unmasking the radical sin of Western Christianity ... the ideology of white supremacy."[133] Thus BTUSA derived from the dialectical interaction between the Bible and the experiences of blacks as they struggled to affirm their humanity and to achieve liberation.

On the other hand, Latin American Liberation Theology emerged in order to provide a critique against Euro-American and European domination of the Latin American continent by means of the colonial and neocolonial enterprise. Latin American theologians sought to challenge the economic structures which perpetuated the exploitation of their countries by the "developed" nations.

For the Latin Americans, there was an irreducible connection between external domination (by superpowers), at the socio-economic, political and theological level, and internal domination (by the neocolonial class). Their experiences and analysis suggested to them that the socio-economic factor was the foundation for the continued exploitation of their nation, as well as for the class conflict in their societies.[134] Therefore, a socio-economic critique of Euro-American domination became primary for defining a theology of liberation, and class analysis became the focus of their definition of the oppressed. Gustavo Gutiérrez, for example, showed LALT's perspective when, in the published text of the first EATWOT meeting (Tanzania 1976), he declared:

> Nationalism and racism are more clearly understood in the context of class inequity; so too the economic and political control of multinational corporations over poor countries.[135]

While these two liberation theologies (BTUSA and LALT) can be viewed as having emerged from oppressed communities, it should also be evident that significant contextual differences have shaped them.

Both Latin American and North American black liberation theologians acknowledge that all ideas, including theological discourse, are socially conditioned and subject to ideological exploitation in order to sacralize the status quo. It is therefore necessary to expose the conscious, or unconscious, ideologies that sustain oppression, while clearing the ground for the creation of a new and more efficacious theology leading to the transformation of the social orders that dominate human life. Thus, ideological suspicion is a necessity within the framework of both theologies.

Black theologians emphasize an analysis based on the historical reality of racism in North America and an affirmation of the worth of black humanity. Black culture and religion were affirmed in the face of a society that had negated all that could be identified with blackness. The goodness of black existence was affirmed as grounded in the reality and work of the black Christ who represented God's affirmation of the humanity of black people.[136]

According to Vincent Harding, the black God of black theology is to be found in the empowering movement of Black Power in the United States.[137] Black Theology not only addressed itself to questions of anthropology and Christology, but issued a challenge to the churches (white and black) to be true to the liberating presence of the black Christ in the struggles of the black poor masses. Dominant ecclesiological structures and definitions were called upon to account for their unfaithfulness to God the liberator, and liberation was defined in such a manner that the hope of the oppressed community was not simply future oriented but had significance for present struggles for liberation. The reality of black struggle and concurrent affirmation of black selfhood would be an instrument in redefining these traditional theological categories: salvation, liberation, Christology, ecclesiology, pneumatology and eschatology.

Latin American theologians emphasize an analysis of society that views the economic factor as the determinative element in defining oppression. The principal contradiction in their experience is neocolonialism and class exploitation. Thus, Latin Americans make class analysis their point of departure. The power of the poor to determine their own future is an expression of their belief that God has taken option for the poor. White "progressive" or modern bourgeois theology seeks to answer the questions of nonbelief in the light of modernity; liberation theology distinguishes itself as a theology which seeks to address itself to the problems raised by those who have been designated as nonpersons: the oppressed. In discussing the starting point of liberation theology in Latin America, Gutiérrez writes:

> We seek to call attention to the historical and concrete conditions of the situation of the poor and the exploited. For it is from their place in society that these nonpersons call us to account, and this is why their questioning goes to the economic, social, political, and ideological root of the society that marginalizes them.[138]

The implications of this choice for the task of theology are far-reaching. If theology arises out of the contradictions of life experienced by nonpersons, then the wretched of the earth become the primary focus of the theological task. The Christian community must follow Jesus Christ the liberator into a commitment to the dispossessed, for it is a prerequisite of our commitment to the biblical God who historically has taken sides with the exploited.[139] The church must reevaluate its commitment in order to clarify whether it is the church that serves the interests of the dominant class or whether it is to be the church of the poor.

Significant Divergences

Black theologians in the United States, however, view race, not class, as the key to understanding their context, while Latin Americans view class, not race, as the key to analyzing their situation. What, theologically, does this difference in context and analysis mean for BTUSA and for LALT? Alfred Reid, a Jamaican, has suggested that this divergence is extremely significant when, in the context of the São Paulo meeting of EATWOT, he said, "We have used the words 'people' and 'the poor' over and over again. Do we mean the blacks, the Indians, the women?"[140] The existence of this question suggests that there are significant theological differences between the worldviews that shape BTUSA and LALT. At the same time, BTUSA and LALT have manifested important commonalities that point to a theology of liberation that takes seriously both perspectives.

CHAPTER TWO

Black Theology (USA)

A Theology of Religio-Cultural and Political Liberation

Black Theology (USA) emerged as a theology of liberation dedicated to the religio-cultural, socio-economic and political liberation of the African-American poor, but it did not explicate a comprehensive understanding of the linkage between these diverse dimensions of the struggle.[1] As a result, BTUSA, in its early stages, stressed religio-cultural and political liberation and did not elaborate an explicit critique of the economic order. There are several underlying assumptions implicit here that are of significance.

First, while BTUSA emphasized primarily religio-cultural and political liberation in its earlier stages, that does not mean there was no commitment to economic liberation. BTUSA, from its inception, had inherent within it an attitude of radical opposition to racist political and religio-cultural structures, as well as to economic structures, although it did not explicitly evolve an integral analysis of the relationship among the economic, political, religious and cultural spheres. It is here that the encounter with the Latin Americans is of critical importance. At stake is a solution to the question of whether one's political and theological commitments flow from one's economic or class position.

The context, time and identity of the early black theologians shaped in a fundamental manner the issues that were emphasized. The late sixties was a time that required an emphasis on black culture and religion as a fundamental aspect of liberation, and BTUSA had a distinctive emphasis on the religio-cultural and political dimensions of the problem of racial oppression, but there is within the black radical tradition itself a call for radical transformation of the economic structures which is muted in the earlier writings of BTUSA.

The basic question that BTUSA sought to answer was: What does the Gospel of Jesus Christ have to do with the oppressed of the United States whose oppression flows from the fact of their racial identity as black people? BTUSA was the specific consequence of black resistance and evolved as an affirmation of black religio-cultural sources as instruments in the power struggle against a racist society.

As early as 1969, black churchpersons issued a call to the black churches to recognize the specific vocation of liberation. This call, issued by the National Committee of Black Churchmen [sic] in Oakland, California, defined the call as:

> political in the sense that it seeks radically to change, by whatever means are necessary, the racist structures which dominate our lives; cultural in the sense that it seeks to identify, recreate, unify and authenticate whatever traditions, values and styles of life are indigenous or distinctive to the black community; and theological in the sense that we believe God—however He chooses to reveal himself today to oppressed peoples in America . . . —who has chosen black humanity as a vanguard to resist the demonic powers of racism, capitalism and imperialism, and to so reform the structures of this world that they will more perfectly minister to the peace and power of all people.[2]

At the heart of BTUSA's project is a radical break with white theological interpretations of Jesus Christ, the Church, eschatology and liberation. Further, BTUSA affirmed the culture, theology and political traditions of African-American people as essential to the struggle against the "institutionalized violence and racism of white America."[3]

Overt racism was the result of individual acts against other individuals, while covert racism involved more subtle acts of racism that were perpetuated by the whole white community against the black community. BTUSA developed a critique of racism, theologically, which manifested a clear recognition of the theological, cultural and political dimensions of institutionalized racism, while at the same time failing to explicate the linkage of the economic factor to the other dimensions of black existence.

We will critically evaluate the contributions of James Cone, Gayraud Wilmore and Deotis Roberts to the development of BTUSA, as they reflect this inherent ambiguity concerning theology, culture and politics and their relationship to economics.[4] Specifically, the theological categories of Christology, ecclesiology, liberation and eschatology will be the common thread through which we will interpret these three black theologians as they sought to respond to the basic question: What does the Gospel of Jesus Christ have to do with the struggles of the black oppressed people of the United States?

The diversity and debate among the emerging black theologians of the 1960s provided the context for interaction and dialogue, which are necessary for the molding of new ideas. Over the past twenty years, Cone and Roberts have been the most consistent and productive in the systematic development of a black theological tradition in the USA. Wilmore has contributed by providing leadership in institutionalizing the concerns of Black Theology in NCBC and the Black Theology Project of Theology in the Americas, as well as proving himself to be a productive scholar of black religion. Each of these three has provided a distinctive emphasis to BTUSA and has demonstrated an appreciation of the need for dialogue with other liberation traditions.

The Radical Break with White Theology and the Affirmation of Black Religion as the New Context of BTUSA

In the social and historical context of the struggle against racism during the 1960s, it was James Cone who first announced the radical break with white theology.

James Cone, the writer of the first published text on BTUSA, *Black Theology and Black Power* (1969), precipitated the break with white theology when he declared that the Black Power Movement represented God's active engagement in the liberation struggles of the black oppressed in the USA.[5] Cone's rejection of traditional white interpretations of theology, in favor of a theology articulated from the perspective of oppressed black people, reverberated through theological circles. His productivity represents his attempt to consistently and systematically pursue the establishment of a new foundation for theological discourse. His work, more than that of any other black theologian, represents the paradigm shift from a theology defined exclusively by white theologians to a theology that seeks to be accountable to the oppressed black community.

Cone wrote:

> It is my thesis that . . . Black Power, even in its most radical expression, is not the antithesis of Christianity, nor is it a heretical idea to be tolerated with painful forbearance. It is, rather, Christ's central message to twentieth century America. And unless the denominational church makes a determined effort to recapture the man Jesus through a total identification with the suffering poor as expressed in Black Power, that church will become exactly what Christ is not.[6]

Cone's claim that Black Power is an authentic expression of the Gospel affirmed his belief that the Christian faith, as the praxis of liberation, was accountable to the oppressed black community, whose experiences of suffering had revealed Jesus Christ as God's liberating power in the world.[7] Gayraud Wilmore, in assessing Cone's contribution, indicates that

> no one before Cone had so clearly summoned us to break with white Christianity. Cone gave the black church the first glimmering of a constructive theological program, which celebrated a distinctive Afro-

American ethnicity and, at the same time, was grounded in the Biblical message of human liberation.[8]

According to Cone, whose grasp of the significance of Black Power was unambiguous, Black Power meant the right of self-determination for black people: the right to shape their own future and destiny.[9] Cone describes the struggle for theological identity as he sought to relate the Christian faith to the black struggle for freedom, Martin Luther King, Jr.'s assassination, riots in America's cities and the Black Power Movement, in his book *My Soul Looks Back*. According to him, his journey was a struggle for both his "Christian and black identity."[10] Like many black Christians in that period, Cone experienced an inner conflict between a concrete commitment to struggle for the freedom of black oppressed peoples and a Christian identity.[11] Again Cone's language was unambiguous: "If Christ was not to be found in black people's struggle for freedom, if he were not found in the ghettos with rat-bitten black children, if he were in rich white churches and their seminaries, then I wanted no part of him."[12]

Authentic Christian faith, according to Cone, was the praxis of faith in the black struggle for life and freedom in the United States. Thus, Black Power was the embodiment of the liberating Gospel of Jesus Christ calling the church to faithfulness in its commitment to Christ. Traditional theological categories had to be redefined in order to manifest the theologians' accountability to black enslaved peoples.

Cone argued that any theology that is to be derived from the experiences of the black oppressed must define its sources and norms in such a manner as to affirm the religious and cultural identity of the oppressed. Cone therefore defines the sources and norms of BTUSA as being rooted in black existence and locates the starting point of black theology in black enslavement and oppression.[13]

Although Cone posits the black condition as the starting point of Black Theology, he does not reduce theology to the sum total of black oppression, because its norm is Jesus Christ, the Liberator. Cone therefore rigorously defends the Christian character of Black Theology by indicating that Black Theology is the explication of the meaning of the Gospel of Jesus Christ in the light of black suffering. Cone's work reveals his concern to utilize black cultural and religious sources in his theology.[14] He acknowledges that his theology is conditioned by his experiences in the black community and the socio-political significance of racism when he writes:

Black theology differs in perspective, content and style from the Western theological tradition transmitted from Augustine to Barth. My theology will not be the same as that of my white colleagues at Union Theological Seminary because our experience is different. They did not know about Macedonia A.M.E. Church and the black spirit.[15]

The sources and norms of BTUSA, then, would be grounded in the black experience, an important source of Black Theology. According to Cone,

> There is no truth for and about black people that does not emerge out of the context of their experience. Truth in this sense is black truth, a truth disclosed in the history and culture of black people. This means that there can be no Black Theology which does not take the black experience as a source for its starting point.[16]

Close scrutiny of the black experience of suffering and oppression, as it is found in the prayers, sermons, songs, poems, folktales and slave narratives, would provide Black Theology with its raw material. Through his attention to Black Theology's sources — the black experience, black culture, black history, Scripture, God's revelations, and tradition — Cone discovered a persistent witness to human dignity and transcendence that testified to God's presence in the black struggle against racism. This was the *pneumatos* (God's spirit), a liberating presence which created and sustained the will of a dehumanized people to struggle against those institutions that perpetrated their destruction.

Another major source of Black Theology is the Bible. Cone, more than any other black theologian, has attempted to demonstrate the biblical basis for the claim of Black Theology that liberation is at the heart of the gospel message.[17] For Cone, the transcendent reality to which blacks bear witness in their prayers, tales and sermons is "none other than Jesus Christ, of whom the scriptures speak."[18] Because the Bible is the witness of God's revelation in Jesus Christ, then "the black experience requires that scripture be a source of Black Theology."[19]

Cone acknowledges the dialectical character of theological speech as it seeks to relate the witness to the truth in black culture and history to the truth of the biblical witness and Christian tradition. God's revelation in Jesus Christ is not a concept but the living parousia (presence) of the liberator erupting through the culture, religion and history of the oppressed in their struggle for liberation. There is and always will be a dynamic process between the testimony of the Scriptures, Christian tradition and the witness to Christ's presence in the culture and history of black oppressed people.

While traditional theology had ignored the social context in general, and black oppressed experiences in particular, as a factor in theology, Cone indicated that since the emergence of the discipline of the sociology of knowledge, any claim to theological objectivity is ludicrous. Cone responded to his critics who claimed that he was too closely linking Christianity with the ideology of Black Power by locating himself as a theologian whose interests are conditioned by the context and experiences of suffering black humanity. Theology, Cone asserts "is always related to historical situations, and thus all of its assertions are culturally (and contextually) limited."[20] Because theology, as human speech, has no theological existence independent of social existence, theologians should consciously articulate their understanding of their own socio-economic, political and cultural location in the world if they are to comprehend their own activity.

Cone rejects any attempt to invoke biblical revelation as the "objective" ground for theological claims and demonstrates that the biblical message itself is transmitted out of the social and cultural conditions of particular historical contexts. Biblical revelation is related to the particulars of the historical situation of the Hebrews.

> Black Theology's answer to the question of hermeneutics can be stated briefly: the hermeneutical principle for exegesis of the Scriptures is the revelation of God in Christ as the liberator of the oppressed from social oppression and the political struggle, wherein the poor recognize that their fight against poverty and injustice is not only consistent with the Gospel but is the Gospel of Jesus Christ.[21]

Therefore, Black Theology is socio-political because God has shown an option for the cause of the downtrodden and because the black experience has been one of gross oppression. God's story is connected to the black story precisely because Jesus Christ, the "oppressed one," has demonstrated that God's concern for humanity is central to the claims of Christian theology. Thus, Black Theology, according to James Cone, challenged the role that white racism plays in the Christian community and sought to recover the Gospel from white culture:

> A culture which equated the authority and omnipotence of Euro-American white men with the authority and omnipotence of God himself, a culture which for almost two thousand years created deity in the image of the white man and gave God the attributes of Caucasian idealization.[22]

Cone's efforts to engage in the reconstruction of theology reflect his commitment to ground BTUSA in the language, experiences and traditions of black people. His radical "No!" to the theological interpretations of white society is simultaneously attended by a persistent affirmation of the importance of the cultural and religious traditions of black people in sustaining the struggles of black people.[23]

Although Cone's work manifested a radical no to white theological definitions and an affirmation of black religious and cultural traditions, his earlier work, embodied in *Black Theology and Black Power*, and in *A Black Theology of Liberation*, was constructively criticized by others in black theological circles as reflecting too much of his white theological training and not enough of a grounding in the history and culture of black people. Cecil Cone, Gayraud Wilmore and Charles Long specifically challenged Cone to utilize black sources.[24]

Gayraud Wilmore has played a decisive role in the development of BTUSA, and his contribution is specifically significant at this juncture. Wilmore's many contributions to the development of BTUSA can be summed up by his continued insistence that the God of white Euro-American religious tradition is not the God of the black masses. Like Cone, he has affirmed the need for a Black Theology that challenges a white culture which created God in its own white image. Like Cone, Wilmore supports the necessity of rejecting white theology as racist. In addition, Wilmore contends

> the African inheritance of the Black Diaspora, the suffering we have experienced, and our historic struggle for survival and liberation have produced an Afro-American religion that cannot be limited to what white believers called Christianity. Black religion transcends the institutional black churches. It exists in the corporate ethnic consciousness, folkways, and culture of the oppressed masses of black folk where it has produced what I have called a "pragmatic spirituality" which can be discerned and documented in our 350 year struggle for liberation.[25]

Wilmore's strength lies in the priority that he places upon a return to the religious and cultural sources indigenous to the African-American experience. "This heterodox theology, emerging from the 'more or less Christian' black religious experience, then, can become the basis of a liberating theology."[26] Wilmore's distinctive contribution to the development of BTUSA is to be found in his continued emphasis on black religion as the context for a Black Theology that would be true to blacks in diaspora throughout the world. He queries black theologians, particularly Cone, when he writes,

> Is Black theology simply the blackenization of the whole spectrum of traditional Christian theology, with particular emphasis on the liberation of the oppressed, or does it find in the experience of the oppression of black people, as black, a single religiosity, identified not only as Christianity, but with other religions as well?[27]

J. Deotis Roberts has been a major contributor to the advancement of Black Theology. His several published works, *Liberation and Reconciliation: A Black Theology* (1971), *A Black Political Theology* (1974), *Black Theology Today* (1983), *Roots of the Black Future* (1980), and *Black Theology in Dialogue* (1987), represent his attempt to elaborate the significance of BTUSA for the Christian community. His work is of particular significance in this context as a foil against which to evaluate the contributions of Cone and Wilmore. This function should not be taken to imply that his work is not important in itself. His work plays a significant part of the Black Theology story in the United States but, in addition, it serves to highlight the shadings that define the work of Cone and Wilmore.

Roberts added significantly to BTUSA by asserting that "black theologians must . . . let the experiences that blacks have had with life under difficult social circumstances, provide their myths and the symbols for theological discourse."[28]

Wilmore encouraged Cone to evolve a foundation for BTUSA that is grounded in an affirmation of the religio-cultural sources of the black experience, in such a way that the discourse of theology would reflect the diversity of black religious traditions. Therefore, Wilmore explains, black theologians must turn to the black community as their primary source for theological insights, and in so doing come to an appreciation of black faith as a folk religion informed by not only the black church, but by an experience which constitutes institutionalized churches, as well as mass-based nationalistic movements and religions.[29] Wilmore encourages black theologians to establish credibility with the masses since,

> To the extent that . . . [BTUSA] . . . draw their main strength from the masses, they will foster the rationalization of certain elements of black religion toward the pursuit of freedom and social justice. [Our] theological roots . . . must go down into the soil of the folk community if they are to maintain their credibility.[30]

Wilmore, Cone and Roberts affirmed the need to reject white theological definitions and to assert the distinctive theological contributions that had emerged from African-American religio-cultural tradition. It was these African-American traditions that had provided black slaves with the resources for the liberation struggle.

They had come to understand, as did Malcolm X and others, that racism had enveloped American society in such a way that it had distorted their perceptions of themselves and of one another. A radical negation was necessary for a break with old patterns of theologizing, and then the constructive project would begin. White racists and racism were the enemy, and the weapons of combat were to be found in the affirmation of black existence. Black liberation could not be achieved independent of an affirmation of blackness: black culture, black existence, black religion, black history, black past and the black Christ.

The Way of Jesus Is the Way of the Black Messiah

Despite the internal debate about the essential character of black religion, Cone, Roberts and Wilmore agree that the pneumatological presence of God among black people in the United States is to be found in the way of the black Messiah. Cone set the parameters of the discourse by positing that in racist white America, God's revelation in Jesus of Nazareth was best represented in the Black Power Movement. The empowering presence of God, testified to in the biblical witness and encountered on the plantation, was the same presence which enabled the black oppressed to struggle for their freedom.

According to Cone, Jesus Christ was the subject of Black Theology because he was the truth that encountered black slaves and enabled them, against hopeless odds, to know that they were human and to have a vision of freedom that transcended their historical experiences. The persistence of black rebellion was a testimony to the presence of the one who empowered oppressed people to hope for that which was beyond the horizon of their experiences: freedom. Cone explains:

> How could black slaves know that they were human beings when they were treated like cattle? How could they know that they were somebody when everything in their environment said that they were nobody? How could they know that they had a value that could not be defined by dollars and cents, when the symbol of the auction block was an ever present reality? Only because they knew that Christ was present with them and that his presence included the divine promise to come again and take them to the New Jerusalem.[31]

Cone is careful to anticipate the criticism that Jesus Christ, in Black Theology, is too closely aligned with the ideological and political aspirations of the black freedom movement of the sixties. According to Cone, there are theological grounds for the assertion of the black Christ. He writes,

> The affirmation of the black Christ can be understood when the significance of his past Jewishness is related dialectically to the significance of his present blackness. On the one hand, the Jewishness of Jesus located him in the context of Exodus, thereby connecting his appearance in Palestine with God's liberation of oppressed Israelites in Egypt.[32]

On the other hand, Cone continues,

> The cross of Jesus is God invading the human situation as the Elected One who takes Israel's place as the Suffering Servant and this reveals the divine willingness to suffer in order that humanity might be liberated. The resurrection is God's conquest of oppression and injustice, disclosing that the divine freedom revealed in Israel's history is now available to all ... It is in the light of the cross and the resurrection of Jesus in relation to his Jewishness that Black Theology asserts that "Jesus is black."[33]

Since the black community's experience in the United States has been characterized by suffering and oppression, and since its persistent witness has been to the presence of the suffering one among them, then Jesus Christ is black.

Understandably, this 1969 assertion gave rise to a cloud of protest in theological circles. Indeed this was the same century in which Karl Barth had sounded the alarm against identifying God's activity with human self-interest and ideologies. Gayraud Wilmore observes that Cone bore the brunt of white theological criticism that blackness of skin was not an acceptable basis of Christian theology.[34] However Cone was tenaciously systematic in defense of his position. His designation of Jesus Christ as black represented both Christ's symbolic and literal identification with the black oppressed of the land.[35] For Cone, "the focus on blackness does not mean that only blacks suffer as victims in a racist society, but that blackness is an ontological symbol and a visible reality which best describes what oppression means in America."[36] Christ is black because the biblical God who identifies with the poor of the land and the Israelite slaves in Exodus is the same Christ who "enters our world where the poor, the despised, and the black are disclosing that he is with them, enduring their humiliation and pain and transforming oppressed slaves into liberated servants."[37]

In regard to his persistent emphasis on blackness, Cone's work reflects his concern with establishing a black theological discourse accountable to the predicament of black people in America. His affirmation of the black Christ was not a new insight, as it had been lifted up previously by Marcus Garvey, for example.[38] However, Cone's systematic application of the black Christ to theology represents an immense contribution:

> because Black Theology's Christology is based on the biblical portrayal of Jesus Christ and Jesus' past and present involvement in the struggle of oppressed peoples, it affirms that who Jesus Christ is for us today is connected with the divine future as discussed in the liberation fight of the poor. When connected with the person of Jesus, hope is not an intellectual idea; rather it is the praxis of freedom in the oppressed community.[39]

Wilmore affirms Cone's emphasis on the symbolic significance of the black Christ in a world defined by white idealizations.[40] Wilmore writes:

> To speak of Christ as the black Messiah is ... to invest blackness in Western civilization, and particularly in the United States and South Africa, with religious meaning expressing the preeminent reality of black suffering and the historical experience of black people in a racist society. But more than that, it is to find in the mystery of Christ's death and resurrection a theological explanation of all suffering, oppression and an ultimate liberation. To speak of the Messiah figure in terms of the ontological significance of the color black is to provide both black people and white people, if the latter are open to the

possibility, with a way of understanding the relevance of the person and work of Christ for existence under the condition of oppression, and to call both the black and white church to the vocation of involvement in the liberation of the oppressed in history.[41]

Wilmore contends that the meaning of the cross is as a signification that the Oppressed One who is revealed in Jesus Christ is God's identification with those who are oppressed, both as a radical affirmation of the humanity of the oppressed and as a basis for the hope of a liberated future.

For Wilmore, Jesus is "the Oppressed One of God" who came to dehumanized blacks as the black Messiah. The black Messiah's cross and resurrection manifest "God's identification with the conflict and oppression of man's sin and finitude, man's blackness," as well as "the grace and judgement" that gives "the hope of liberation and reconciliation beyond lightness and darkness."[42] Like Cone, he presupposes the particularity of Jesus the Jew, who is called the Christ, about whom in each new context Christian theologians must always speak of as one who is scandalously particular. Thus, for Wilmore, as for Cone, Jesus is the black Messiah: a symbolic and literal resource in the struggle for freedom. Wilmore's contribution is in his insistence that BTUSA utilize black religio-cultural sources, despite the theological complications endemic to such an enterprise.

Concerning the black Messiah, Roberts declares that BTUSA must indigenize its understanding of Christology, since "The Americanized Christ, as created by the majority group in this country, is found in all artistic presentations of him to be a WASP."[43]

With Cone, Wilmore and Cleage, Roberts believes that it is necessary to create new cristological images that represent the black experience and "make Christ and his message speak directly to the black man."[44] He rejects Cleage's attempt to make Jesus Christ a literal black man in ancient Palestine, but is prepared to contextually acknowledge the need for a black Messiah. He writes:

> The visualization of Christ as black may enable the black man to have a real encounter with himself and God through Christ. The black man has in the black Messiah a savior. He discovers his own dignity and pride in a self-awareness that is rooted in black consciousness.[45]

For Roberts, Jesus means freedom. He grounds this claim in the traditional Christian claim that there is continuity between Jesus of Nazareth and the Christ of faith. Roberts argues that a Christology true to the cause of black freedom must be grounded in the black church and provide the black church with "a theology of social change and political action."[46] Jesus, according to Roberts, is God's historical revelation as the Savior. The Jesus of history cast his lot with the oppressed in his own situation and therefore,

Roberts contends, has special significance for a powerless, oppressed black community.

This is the good news: *that God, through Jesus, was on the side of the oppressed.* The Jesus of history who is the liberator of the oppressed is the Messiah who concretely brings deliverance and hope to men and women. According to Roberts, the notion of a black Messiah will be of "psycho-cultural" significance as the one who "leads us to a new self-understanding . . . [and] . . . helps us to overcome the identity crisis triggered by white oppression of blacks."[47] Roberts recognized the significance of the black Messiah as a religious and cultural manifestation of the liberating God who delivers the black oppressed from the debilitating cultural and psychological affects of white racism. In doing so, Roberts's work manifests a common thread with Cone and Wilmore: The stress on the black religio-cultural traditions was an important aspect of the struggle to liberate black people from the self-hatred that had been nurtured by a racist society.

The strength of Roberts's position lies in his emphasis on Black Theology as a political theology of liberation. According to Roberts, the African worldview is one that conceives of life as a whole. Therefore, the economic and political lives of the people are integrally interwoven with their religious rituals, and Black Theology, as political theology, "will overcome quietism and privatization of religion and open up the possibility of a secular/sacred merger as well as a personal/public ethics."[48]

While the white Christ is alienating to blacks, the black Messiah provides us with a basis of hope and liberation but, in Roberts's view, it is the universal Christ who reconciles us to our brothers and sisters. Jesus frees black minds from the debilitating consequences of white oppression, and the universal Christ reconciles all humans.[49] Roberts writes:

> The Jesus of the disinherited sets us free. The Jesus who breaks through the color line reconciles all men . . . We cannot fully know Jesus in the role of reconciler until we know him in his role as lib-erator. The way to a knowledge of Christ as reconciler passes through his "liberator role."[50]

Roberts, with the other black theologians, asserts the continuity of the historical Jesus and the Christ of faith as integral to the faith of the black church.

The christological interpretations of Cone, Wilmore and Roberts reflect the commonalities that define the black theological enterprise: the rejection of white christological interpretations and an affirmation of the black Messiah. Derived from the dialectical interaction between the biblical witness and the black experience, the black Messiah is God's presence, which motivates the black oppressed to hope, to fight to transcend their oppression and to seek freedom. There are several intuitions present in BTUSA that are of relevance here. First, black theologians (USA) are persistent in rejecting white definitions and articulating their christological insights within the context of the black experience. Second, black theologians (USA) have consistently established the black experience as a primary point of reference in their theological work. Thus, their insistence on deriving their theological intuitions from the religio-cultural traditions of the black oppressed. Third, black theologians (USA) affirm the priority of the struggle to demystify and critique the cultural, religious and theological supports of white racism. Fourth, black theologians (USA) articulate a christological perspective that acknowledges the importance of culture and religion in confronting the psychological affects of racism on black people. Malcolm X, the Black Muslims and Black Nationalists had issued a challenge to the black Christian community that had stimulated black christological development.[51] Thus the way of the black Messiah was through the religio-cultural and political struggle for black power.

The Challenge to the Churches' Identity and Mission

BTUSA evolved to challenge the apostasy of the white churches, as well as to critique the contemporary black church for having lost its sense of rootedness and vocation. The challenge to white churches was issued because historically the white churches in the USA, with few exceptions, had succumbed to the racist values and practices of American society. Due to the failure of white Christians in this regard, Black Muslim nationalists, for example, could argue quite persuasively that Christianity had failed for the black community.[52]

BTUSA intended to demonstrate that the failure of white Christians to enflesh Christian faith was due to their apostasy, rather than to some inherent deficit within Christianity. Amid the turmoil of the 1960s, black clergy, laypersons and theologians had returned to study the historical black church and found an authentic, living black faith. Again, black theologians would evolve a theological interpretation of the church's identity and mission which was grounded in black religio-cultural sources.

Christian identity, insofar as it is grounded in the memory of Jesus Christ, is inextricably linked with the "least of these." In the case of the United States, the least of these were black people. Therefore the Christian community's identity must take seriously the testimony of black religio-cultural traditions to the God who will fight the battles of the oppressed of the land and ensure justice and righteousness for all.

Cone contends that faith in the biblical Christ is not simply the affirmation of belief in him but an engagement in the concrete political praxis of liberation in each situation. Faith emerges from the struggling black underside and can be measured by one's concrete commitment to the struggle for liberation. Christians, therefore, both discover and sustain their Christian identity as they engage in the praxis of the liberating movement of the black Christ in the struggles of oppressed black people. Whites must become black in order to remain faithful to Christ, the foundation of the church.

Ecclesiologically, then, the church finds its identity clarified and discovers its mission in its commitment to blacks in the United States. The mission of the church is to take the side of black people in their historical struggle for liberation, which, by itself, is a testimony to God's sustaining presence among them. For Cone, Jesus Christ is the basis of relating faith to the praxis of liberation and justice. Accordingly, he writes:

> By becoming human in Jesus, God connects faith with the social, political, and economic conditions of people and establishes the theological conclusion that we cannot be faithful to the Creator without receiving the political command to structure creation according to freedom.[53]

According to this perspective, there can be no discussion of evangelism or mission without reference to the social, economic and political conditions that constitute black existence. In this regard, Cone's critique is directly applicable to the idea, rampant among American Christians, that Jesus Christ came to spiritually liberate souls. For African-Americans — and here Cone and the other black theologians have tapped into the deep African past — the physical and spiritual worlds are but two intimately related dimensions of the same universe.[54]

Wilmore deepens Cone's insights with his investigation of the history and evolution of the black church in his text, *Black Religion and Black Radicalism*. According to Wilmore, ecclesiological structures and entities, insofar as they are defined by the black Christ, will reflect a reorientation of priorities. The black church in modern America, in Wilmore's mind, needs to hear the challenge of BTUSA, whose task is: "to lift up the gates of the black Christian church to that divine intervention and let the King of Glory come into our congregation and communication, and perhaps through them, into the white churches and American society in general."[55]

The contemporary black church, despite the events of the 1960s, needs to recover its dedication to the way of the oppressed black Messiah whose presence lies in the black community, often beyond the doors of the churches. The challenge of black ecclesiology, according to Wilmore, is to explicate how the survival and liberation of African-Americans living in a racist society has evolved a different perspective on the meaning and mission of the church.[56]

There are two dimensions of black religion which warrant mention in this context. First, Wilmore asserts the black church's distinctive theological understanding of religion as intersecting all aspects of human life.[57] Wilmore explains the evolution of the peculiar "genius" of the black religious tradition as flowing from the African roots, as its integral understanding of religion and political activism.[58]

Second, Wilmore indicates that black Christians, unlike their white counterparts, did not draw a sharp distinction between the secular and the sacred. He argues that it is the distinctive African tendency to view the profane and the sacred as integral parts of one whole. Black churches, according to Wilmore, were indeed cultural and political centers that coordinated the diverse dimensions of African-American life, and African-American spirituality was manifested in the churches' commitment to the political struggle for freedom.[59]

Roberts's ecclesiological perspective is informed by his understanding that the task of Black Theology must be grounded in the black church, an institution that "has been not merely an ark of salvation, but a hospital for the sick, a haven for the lonely, an agent of social action and change."[60]

The ecclesiology of Roberts's brand of Black Theology would affirm the priestly and prophetic role of the historic black church as it functions in the survival and liberation struggles of black people. The black church plays both a priestly role—as it provides a context for the survival of the black community—and a prophetic role—as it challenges the racist structures of American society. Roberts acknowledges the historical role of struggle in which the church has been in the forefront, but he challenges the black churches in the present, since:

> If the impact of the black church is to continue we must take seriously the tradition to which we belong. It is a heritage with a deep spirituality which has brought healing to a long-suffering people ... Its priestly tradition has brought meaning and healing to us as persons, but the black church has produced prophets as well as priests. Therefore, the black churches as institutions have been agents of social change for the [wholistic] liberation of black people.[61]

Thus the black church is understood to function not simply as a religious institution, but as an agent for political and social change. Even as he recognizes the socio-political function of the black church, however, Roberts wants to ensure that the black church upholds its spiritual function. He writes: "The power of the black church is not merely a material power. It is spiritual. It is anchored in a community of believers who serve and work under the Lordship of Jesus Christ."[62]

There are several consequences of Roberts's ecclesiological formulation. First, he conceives of the task of Black Theology as a function of the black church. While he is willing to value the input of the broader black religious community, Roberts is careful to define black theological reflection within the context of the black church community. Thus black theologians must be grounded in the life of the black church.[63] Roberts elaborates this claim by writing:

> Black theology is to be church theology. The black churches have preserved the African temperament of black religion. It is logical that

black religious and cultural nationalism will find a strong ally in the black church . . . The black church is the one master "political" institution under black control. As a political, economic, social and cultural institution it is unrivaled, and it has deep historic roots in the aspirations of black people for liberation from all types of bondage.[64]

Second, Roberts concedes the black churches' role in sustaining the religio-cultural particularity of African-American people, while at the same time recognizing its role as an instrument for socio-political struggle. Third, Roberts conceives of the church as an institution that provides a prophetic word to society and the world.

This brief analysis of BTUSA's ecclesiology is ample evidence that a reinterpretation of the meaning and mission of the church was evolved by the black theologians, grounded in the black experience. Cone, Wilmore and Roberts are representative of the black theologians in the United States in three critical ways. First, they link Christian identity with the Oppressed One (Jesus Christ) and with the oppressed ones in the United States context. This is a revolutionary claim in a society where Christian identity was often identified with the white power structures.

Second, based on their investigation of black history, they affirm an indissoluble link between Christian faith and political action. For example, against the white religious leaders in Birmingham, Dr. King had declared that Christian faith was not authentic unless it was materialized in a commitment to justice and freedom. Cone would later assert that the Black Power Movement was the way of Jesus Christ in a racist society. Despite white theologians' insistence that Jesus Christ must be distinguished from all ideologies, Cone established a methodological basis for linking Christian faith and political action.

Third, and here Wilmore's contribution has been indispensable, the black churches were reminded of their historic vocation of black liberation, and the white churches confronted with their unfaithfulness. Holistic liberation was the mission of the church.

Liberation: The Mission of the Gospel of Jesus Christ

The concept of liberation lies at the heart of Black Theology's interpretation of God's project in history. The theme of liberation (deliverance) in the biblical record resonates with the concept of freedom in the African-American community. Liberation, therefore, cannot be reduced to abstract spirituality but must be connected to the struggle for economic, political and social liberation. Cone asserts that God's deliverance in the biblical text is always linked to the political and social realities of the day. God's liberation defined by the black Christ is the project of freeing blacks from all of those conditions which sustain their enslavement and dehumanize them. The proclamation of God's liberation in all the breadth and depth of the biblical teaching is fundamental to the gospel for the oppressed. In making this claim, Cone, on the basis of his understanding of the biblical record and the black experience, is positing the notion that liberation is all-encompassing and holistic, despite the fact that popular American Christian views limit the meaning of salvation to justification, forgiveness and spiritual regeneration. From Cone's perspective, the Black Power Movement points to the "complete emancipation of black people from white oppression by whatever means black people deem necessary."[65]

Because the African-American worldview is integral, it follows that liberation is holistic. According to Wilmore:

> The African attitude literally created the image of the preexistent God in the freedom of the religious imagination and opened human life to the influence of divinity that flowed out of history and the natural world. The liberation of the whole person—body, mind and spirit—from every internal and external constraint not deliberately and purposely elected was the first requirement for one who would be possessed by the Spirit.[66]

Wilmore is persistent in his effort to demonstrate the African-ness of this perspective. Rather that the dichotomized spirituality of Euro-American Christianity, BTUSA should focus on the black religious tradition's emphasis on a religion that extends into and is connected to every aspect of human existence. Black Christian faith is intimately related to and involved with the social, economic and political conditions that define the lives of black people. He observes:

> Christianity alone, adulterated, otherworldly, and disengaged from its most authentic implications—as it was usually presented to the slaves—could not have provided the slaves with all the resources they needed for the kind of resistance they expressed. It had to be enriched with the volatile ingredients of the African religious past.[67]

One of Roberts's distinctive contributions to BTUSA emerges at the point of his development of the notion of liberation. According to Roberts, liberation and reconciliation are two dimensions of the Christian faith, with reconciliation as the final goal and hope of the Christian community. In this context, liberation is the consequence of the recognition that "the God who sets us free from the enslavement of sin is the one who promises an abundant life to the whole man [sic]."[68] Liberation, for Roberts, is holistic insofar as it is linked with reconciliation. The driving force behind Roberts's work is his intention to establish a theological basis for the ethical principles that should motivate the Christian. While white Christians have been lacking in the application of Christian faith to the problem of racism, the black

Christian must apply the love ethic of Jesus in the particular context of a society where they have been dehumanized. Roberts observes:

> Love in the Christian context . . . is to be applied horizontally as well as vertically. In fact, it cannot be genuine Christian love if it is not ethical as well as spiritual. There can be no unilateral expression of love between man and God which does not include the brother. Furthermore, the expression of love must be particular, concrete, and personal.[69]

Black Theology, if it takes its point of departure from the black perspective, must be liberational in content and must be an advocate of wholeness. According to Roberts, "the African and biblical outlook" lends endorsement to a comprehensive view of the individual in the context of community, and affirms the value of a religious perspective which is concerned with the whole person, and from which all of life is affirmed.

While Cone, Wilmore and Roberts express a commitment to holistic liberation as the content of their theologies, none provides a comprehensive analysis of the causes of racism that includes a specific critique of the economic order: How would Black Power, in capitalist America, lead to holistic liberation?

BTUSA: Eschatological Hope and History

BTUSA is thoroughly eschatological because of its emphasis on a hope for the Kingdom of God which impinges into the historical circumstances of the black oppressed and motivates them to hope in the midst of hopelessness and to struggle despite great odds. Proleptic eschatology, based on the promise of God in the Bible and inspired by the Gospel which will destroy evil, provides a vision of the future and releases the power of the future in the present.

James Cone indicates that "It was the expectation of the future of God, grounded in the resurrection of Jesus that was the central theological focus of the black religious experience."[70] The significance of the future was birthed in the slave churches as black people struggled to survive, and it remains central even today. What was the force of that future expectation upon the lives of black people? How did it effect the life of the church? Or, to put the question in theological terms: What was their eschatology?

The adjective *proleptic* best describes the eschatology of black religious experience. The word is best defined as "the end occurring ahead of time." Black eschatology

> involves the kind of perspective that enables blacks to say no in spite of the military power of their oppressors . . . Christ's death and resurrection have set us free. Therefore it does not matter that whites

have all the guns and that, militarily speaking, we have no chance of winning. There comes a time when a people must protect their own, and for blacks the time is now.[71]

The fact of the continued struggle for liberation among blacks is a testament to the presence of the Transcendent One in the struggles of blacks. The will to struggle on against great odds and to reject the definitions of white society is a testimony to the proleptic presence of God's Kingdom in the black community. The black eschatological perspective, which according to Cone is reflected particularly in black spirituals, bear witness to a "transcendent element of hope which elevated black people above the limitation of the slave experience, and enabled them to view black humanity independently of their oppressors."[72]

Wilmore's understanding of eschatology is deeply influenced by his appreciation of the African background. He writes,

In both African and Afro-American religion the idea of the next world, which is to say the Kingdom of God, is not some highly mystical, spiritualized realm that floats over the real world and has no connection with it. It is peopled with the ancestors who are ever near, with people we have known and loved, and it contains the things of this world wonderfully transformed. In that important sense it is the criterion of the present world, a model of perfection which stands in judgement upon it.[73]

Here again, Wilmore contends, is found the African tendency toward connectedness rather than bifurcation. There is otherworldliness in black religion, but Wilmore believes that it is only a part of the picture, since the otherworldliness of black religious expressions often served as a shield for intensely "this-worldly" oriented activity. The eschatological vision of the Kingdom of God functions as a motivating factor in the ongoing, present struggles for life and freedom. The authentic faith of the black religious experience, "brought together this world and the next in a creative tension," and Wilmore cites Martin Luther King's "I have a dream" speech as an authentic expression of a black tradition which understood the eschatological significance of the black struggle for freedom.[74] Belief in God's future was an affirmation of the future of black existence and its enduring struggle to achieve its goal of total liberation.

The eschatology of Roberts's theology parallels the work of Cone and Wilmore in recognizing that the dualities of traditional Western theology do not adequately describe the black perspective on eschatology. The future of Christ the Liberator impinges dynamically upon the present as God's power which frees dehumanized people. The future hope of the Kingdom is both realized and unrealized in the present. Heaven, as a future reality, is integrally connected to present activity on earth. Future and present, sacred and secular, heaven and earth, faith and ethics are dualities that are held in dynamic tension within the framework of Black Theology.

The eschatology of BTUSA reflects the black theologians' commitment to unearth their theology from black religio-cultural sources. Thus the spirituals and sermons from the black religious experience are one source of black eschatology. Albert Raboteau has provided an important contribution to the work of BTUSA in his book *Slave Religion*. What was the future like for black oppressed slaves? In answering this question, we will demonstrate BTUSA's dependence on black sources for its eschatology.

Perhaps the word *reversal* is the best description.[75] Heaven was for them to be a reversal of the present order. In the present they had no home, but in heaven they did. "My Lord! Po' mourner's got a home at las'. Mourner's got a home at las'."[76] In the present they were enslaved, but in heaven freedom awaited. "And before I'll be a slave, I'll be buried in my grave, and go home to my Lord and be free."[77] Moreover, the easy freedom of the white slaveholder would be reversed. Frederick Douglass claims "slaves knew enough of the orthodox theology of the time to consign all bad slave holders to hell."[78] That is, the future eschaton meant judgment by a just God: "You shall reap what you sow."

The future meant mercy for them and retribution for their masters. In fact, sometimes they were very specific about the reversal of the present order of exploitation, saying that in the life to come there will be black and white people, but the white people will be slaves and the black people will have dominion over them.[79] However, the most basic and commonly expressed aspect of the reversal in the spirituals and conversion stories is that God will turn death into life, a life of freedom and justice.

It is this future reversal, which Cone calls the "transcendent future," that "aroused discontentment and made the present subject to radical change."[80] It provided an excited vision of what was to come, which released the power of the future into their lives, bringing not only strength to survive but courage to strive toward their freedom. The eschaton was not for the slaves an opiate, precisely because it functioned proleptically. The "transcendent future" was also a "transcendent present."[81] The "home over yonder" and the "promised land" in the spirituals were, for the slaves, both an otherworldly promise and a "this-worldly" hope for freedom.

In fact, often it is hard to distinguish, when the slaves sang words like "O Canaan, sweet Canaan, I am bound for the land of Canaan," whether they meant life after death or a freed life in the North or back in Africa. One simply has to conclude that both meanings were expressed, that they anticipated the future in the present and that the future was occurring ahead of time, that is, proleptically. This is beautifully expressed in the words of Harriet Tubman when she gained her freedom in the North. "I looked at my hands to see if I was de same person now I was free. Dere was such a glory ober de fields, and I felt like I was in heaven."[82]

That the transforming power of the final future was experienced proleptically by the slaves is most evident in the slave conversion stories from the book *God Struck Me Dead*. The experience of being "struck dead" was a proleptic experience. Certainly for the slaves, with death came the end and the future reversal. In the conversion stories it is as if Jesus transports them from their present strife to the end and they see, hear and feel his act of deliverance. For example, from the story, "Waist-Deep in Death," the passage, "Then God took me off. I experienced death, the way I'm going to die ... I heard groaning while in hell. Then he lead me into the green pastures."[83] The experience of being led through a judgment scene and then arriving in heaven is common. The passage from the conversion story "God Struck Me Dead," is perhaps the most telling.

> The Father, the Son, and the Holy Ghost led me on to glory. I saw God sittin in a big armchair. I saw the Lamb's book of life and my name written in it. A voice spoke to me and said, "Whosoever my Son sets free is free indeed. I give you a through ticket from hell to heaven. Go into yonder world and be not afraid, neither be dismayed, for you are an elect child and ready for the fold."[84]

The future salvation and liberation of the person is truly experienced. The freedom of the end becomes real in the present. And with this proleptic experience of heaven comes the call to go back unafraid into "yonder world," the world of oppression. The experience of heaven, that one is an elect child and free, gives strength to continue in the struggle. The call to go back to do God's will after the conversion experience is also common in the stories.[85] Therefore, the conversion experience was inseparable from the present. Or, as Cone would say, inseparable from history.

This eschatological perspective is reflected in the sermons and life of Dr. Martin Luther King, Jr., in a most poignant manner. King's eschatology is nothing less than the proleptic eschatology of the slave church.

A brief picture of King's vision of the future should be sketched. Similar to the reversal expectation of the slave church, it would be a time when the "lion and the lamb will lie down together" and "every valley shall be exalted and every mountain and hill will be made low."[86] In his now famous "I Have a Dream" speech, King exclaims that the eschaton will bring "justice and freedom" uniting all humanity and destroying the power of sin in the world.[87] His dream is thoroughly eschatological and comes from the hope and promise of God's future found in Scripture.

What is the force of this future for Dr. King? In answering this question we see that Dr. King was a contemporary example and proclaimer of a proleptic eschatology. The force of the future is one that has everything to do with the present struggle for justice. In fact, just as the "promised land" of heaven was equated by the slaves with the present struggle for freedom, so too for King the end of life is inseparable from the present toil for justice. In another speech he stated,

I still believe that standing up for the truth of God is the greatest thing in the world. This is the end of life. The end of life is not to be happy. The end of life is not to achieve pleasure and avoid pain. The end of life is to do the will of God, come what may.[88]

As one struggles for God's will in the present, the very power and reality of the end is experienced.[89]

The eschatology of the slave songs, Martin Luther King, Jr., Cone, Wilmore and Roberts manifests the common threads within the black religious experience. First, black eschatology refers to the present as much as to the future. The fact of blacks affirming their humanity in the face of white society's destructive practices and the black will to fight for freedom are witnesses to the presence of the future of God. The hope of God's Kingdom had everything to do with black slaves trying to escape and Martin Luther King, Jr.'s struggle for freedom, justice and righteousness. Second, black eschatological perspectives inform the persistent hope that in God's future "the wicked will cease from troubling and the weary will be at rest." Justice and judgment would come, as sure as God was God. Further, blacks' view of life and death indicated that their affirmation of the resurrection was a motivating force behind their willingness to sing "before I'll be a slave, I'll be buried in my grave." Death and its threat by whites lost its power in the presence of the hope that issued from their belief in the black Christ. As a consequence, black eschatology was inextricably linked to the historical struggle for life and liberation.

Evaluation

This investigation of three black theologians, Cone, Wilmore and Roberts, as they formulated this new theological tradition, provides some important insights into BTUSA. Black theologians in the United States view racism as the root oppression in the black experience, and as such the issue that defines the shape of their discourse. Racism is the enemy, and racist values, institutions and attitudes are the target. Racism is not simply a sociological or economic problem, but a theological (ideological) one which calls into question the theological (ideological) interpretations of Euro-American society. Since black people, too, have been made in the image of God, then

To place more value upon one individual or group than upon another is to choose the judgement of the creature over that of the Creator who made human beings in his [sic] own image ... Racism is, therefore, self-idolatry, self-glorification, the worship of a particular color of skin.[90]

BTUSA, emerging in the 1960s, is rooted in the prophetic black religious tradition which provided a milieu for the nurture of black humanity. Black theologians therefore agree that black theological discourse must affirm the religious and cultural traditions of African-American people, for these traditions have been important resources in the survival and liberation struggles of the people. Further, black people have utilized their religio-cultural traditions to help them to adapt the Christian religion and to create an interpretation of the Christian faith that reflects their roots and experiences as African people. The black religious experience is the fulcrum of inspiration, meaning, survival and liberation of the people and provides the raw material of a black theological discourse that is accountable to black oppressed people.

This review of the doctrines of Christ, the Church, the eschaton and liberation within BTUSA clearly evidences the black theologians' emphasis on black religio-cultural sources, as opposed to the white theological interpretations of the dominant society. Black theologians assert that BTUSA must address itself to the power relations in the society. Black theology is, therefore, a political theology. Africans view human existence as integrally connected, as a whole.

Despite the prevailing and self-serving tendency of white theological interpretations that sought to distinguish between spiritual and political liberation, black theologians insist that this distinction is a false one. Black theologians critique these dualistic tendencies in white theology because they contribute to the privatization of religion and to false distinctions between faith and politics, religion and ethics. More importantly, BTUSA asserts that theological discourse must challenge the political structures of society as a means of redressing the racial inequities of American society. For Cone, the way of the black Christ in the contemporary period was to be found in the Black Power Movement, which sought to bring about political and economic changes in the land. Thus integrationism, as a specific strategy for enacting the liberational content of Black Theology, was not the answer for African-American people, since it often meant "accepting the white man's style, his values, [and] his religion."[91] Black people must reject this strategy as a presupposition of their struggle, because it led to the destruction of black selfhood.

Nathan Wright contributes a similar point of view in claiming that:

Black power raises, for the healing of humanity and for the renewal of a commitment to the creative religious purpose of growth, the far too long overlooked need for power, if life is to become what in the mind of its creator it is destined to be.[92]

Despite, however, the black theologians' emphasis on the religio-cultural and political dimensions of liberation, and their basic commitment to holistic liberation, they did not evolve a specific description of the economic aspect of black struggle. While references to the need for economic liberation appear in the writings of Cone, Wilmore and the documents of NCBC, there is no explicit elaboration of the notion.

How would Black Power, in capitalist America, lead to holistic liberation? This question was not explicitly addressed. James Cone and Deotis Roberts have acknowledged this failure in the later works of BTUSA. Cone, in his later texts, acknowledges the failure of his earlier work to elaborate the content of liberation in a manner which would entail relating racism to the economic system.[93] Roberts, likewise, acknowledges this failure when he affirms the significance of the dialogue with Latin Americans in his *Black Theology Today* and *Black Theology in Dialogue.*[94]

Despite the liberational content of BTUSA and the contextual nature of its discourse, the black theologians did not provide their discourse with a description of the underlying economic structures that supported racism. It is their encounter with the Latin Americans that provides the dialogical input and challenge for them to deepen their analysis of racism and its relationship to United States capitalist structures. Racism is the product of complex relationships among economic, political and ideological power structures. While BTUSA provided critical input to the black church, challenged prevailing white theological interpretations, named the evil of racism as the enemy, and established new ground for liberation theology in the United States, it failed to be thoroughgoing in the completion of its task. Thus the significance of the Latin American challenge.

CHAPTER THREE

Latin American Liberation Theology

A Theology of Socio-Economic and Political Liberation

Latin American Liberation Theology (LALT) evolved as a response to the cry of an oppressed continent against its political, economic and ideological domination by Europe and North America. In contemporary terms the Latin American continent is seen as a victim of colonial and neocolonial exploitation by the inhabitants of Euro-American societies. Black Theology emerged from a community with a historically grounded identity as the victims of white racism and an identifiable history of radical Christian protest to racial injustice. In contrast, the Latin Americans were struggling with the need to clarify their identity in relationship to the historical role of Christianity in Latin America and neocolonial socio-economic, political and ideological domination by Europe and North America, while at the same time developing a new awareness of their own situation.

There are two fundamental insights basic to any discussion of LALT that are reflected in the following words of Gustavo Gutiérrez:

> From the beginning, the theology of liberation posited that the first act is involvement in the liberation process, and that theology comes afterward, as a second act. The theological moment is one of critical reflection from within and upon concrete historical praxis, in confrontation with the word of the Lord as lived and accepted in faith — that comes to us through manifold, and sometimes ambiguous, historical mediation, but which we are daily remaking and repairing. . . . The second insight of the theology of liberation is its decision to work from the viewpoint of the poor — the exploited classes, marginalized ethnic groups and scorned cultures. This led it to take up the great theme of poverty and poor in the Bible. As a result the poor appear within this theology as the key to an understanding of the meaning of liberation and of the meaning of the revelation of a liberating God.[1]

These two emphases are fundamental to an evaluation of LALT. LALT developed in the process of the attempt by Latin American Christians to respond to a new awareness of their situation and the need to *decolonize* and *Latin Americanize* their churches and theology. Accordingly, LALT has a strongly anticapitalist, anticolonial, and anti-imperialist tradition. The major source of the social, political and economic crises of Latin America could be traced to the pervasive effects of colonialism and imperialism — extensions of the world economic system of capitalism. The Latin Americans focused on the reinterpretation of the meaning of the Gospel from a situation in which the questions were defined by the realities of a crisis caused by capitalist exploitation. Latin America was decisively shaped by the economic influences of capitalism, and thus there came to be an understanding of liberation that viewed the economic basis of Latin American life as primary.

Consequently, due to the existence of pervasive poverty and the Latin Americans' commitment to the poor, on the one hand, and their emphasis on the primacy of class analysis, on the other hand, LALT emerged as a theology of socio-economic and political liberation.

Due to their emphasis on the priority of class analysis, unlike BTUSA, the Latin Americans viewed political and cultural commitments as flowing out of and being shaped by one's economic class. Later, under the stress of both internal and external factors, the Latin Americans would begin to emphasize the religio-cultural traditions of the oppressed in Latin America. Externally, pressure came by way of their dialogical encounter with other liberation theology traditions, particularly BTUSA and the African and Asian theological traditions that emphasized the religio-cultural dimensions of liberation. Internally, pressure came by way of the voices of oppressed cultures, races and ethnic groups within Latin America, who began to query LALT concerning its lack of references to them.[2] Gustavo Gutiérrez, José Míguez Bonino, and Hugo Assmann are three Latin American theologians who will receive particular attention as a means of evaluating the claim that LALT emerged, particularly in its earlier stage, as a theology of socio-economic and political liberation.

Theology of liberation in Latin American, like BTUSA, came into being as Christians sought to understand anew their role in the context of revolutionary struggle against the ruling classes. The central question to which LALT sought to respond was: What is the significance of the Gospel amid a world of suffering, exploitation and oppression endured by workers and poor peasants? In response to this question, the Latin Americans asserted that Christian identity and mission were to be found by means of engagement in liberating praxis on behalf of the oppressed. This is the common starting point for liberation theologies in Latin America: a commitment to the struggles of the poor and the oppressed and to liberating praxis on behalf of the oppressed.

At the heart of the theology of LALT is the desire to liberate theology from its captivity to the theological norms of the Euro-American colonial and neocolonial empire. LALT can be interpreted as a declaration of independence by the Latin Americans as they sought to devise a theology that was accountable to the poor in Latin America. In defining their project in this manner, the Latin Americans established a priority for commitment to the poor.

For Gutiérrez, the most distinctive difference between other theological innovations in the history of the Church and the current development of liberation theology in Latin America is the fact that the poor have erupted into history in such a manner as to disrupt and confront all prior formulations of theology. Further, some Christians have chosen to acknowledge the presence of the poor by incorporating their concerns into the heart of the theological enterprise.

Whereas Gutiérrez views much of nineteenth- and twentieth-century European and North American theology as a response to the needs of bourgeois culture and life, he views LALT as a response to the reality of the poor, the exploited and the oppressed.[3] He distinguished between progressive theology (which he views as theology engaged with modernity), traditional theology (which he views as theology still bearing the mark of the feudal world), and liberation theology (which addresses itself to the problem of the oppressed):

> The theology of liberation begins not with the problematic of the "modern (bourgeois) human being," but with that of the poor and dispossessed—those whom the bourgeois dominators seek to maintain "without a history," while they present their own middle-class society . . . as pertaining to the natural and constant order of things.[4]

He continues:

> "Progressive" theology seeks to answer the questions of the *nonbeliever*; liberation theology confronts the challenge of the *nonperson* . . . The point of departure of liberation theology is not only different from that of progressivist theology, it is in historical contradiction with it . . . Liberation theology is an expression of a dialectical opposition to bourgeois ideology and the dominant culture that comes up out of the popular classes. It is the exploited segments of society, the despised ethnic groups, the marginalized cultures, the persons we may know in their energy and vitality only by looking at them from the underside of history—in a word, those whom the Bible calls "the poor"—who are the historical agent and repository of this new understanding of the faith. The breach of liberation theology with other theological perspectives is not simply theological. It transcends the world of theology strictly so called—the realms of ideas—and enters

the real history, where persons and social groups live in confrontation.[5]

Thus the culture, religion, spirituality and history of the poor become an important context for the continuing development of liberation theology. It is at this point—identification and solidarity with the poor—that we see the beginning of the second stage of the liberation of Latin American theology from oppressors. In the first stage, roughly equivalent to the process of Latin Americanization, Latin American theologians sought to decolonize Latin American theology from its dependence on Europe and North America.

Now, in the second stage, the important work of grounding LALT in the history, religion and culture of the poor of Latin America has just begun. It is here also that we note the glaring absence in LALT, not only of blacks, who constitute a significant portion of the population in some Latin American countries, but also of women and the indigenous peoples of Latin America. The insight concerning an "option for the poor" has led to the rereading of history through the experience of the poor and the reinterpretation of traditional theological categories.

Another important theme in LALT is its approach to the relationship between truth and praxis. José Míguez Bonino describes it well in contrasting "the classical conception of the relationship between truth and practice" and the conception that many liberation theologians affirm.[6] Concerning the classical conception, he writes:

Truth belongs, for this view, to a world of truth, a universe complete in itself, which is copied or reproduced in "correct" propositions, in a theory (namely, a contemplation of this universe) which corresponds to this truth. Then, in a second moment, as a later step, comes the application in a particular historical situation. Truth is therefore preexistent to and independent of its historical effectiveness. Its legitimacy has to be tested in relation to this abstract "Heaven of Truth."[7]

On the other hand, he affirms the conception of truth supported by the liberation theologians:

When Assmann speaks of the rejection of "any logos which is not the logos of a praxis" or Gutiérrez writes about an "epistemological split," they are not merely saying that truth must be applied, or even that truth is related to its application. They are saying in fact that there is no truth outside or beyond the concrete historical events in which men [sic] are involved as agents. There is therefore no knowledge except in action itself, in the process of transforming the world through participation in history.[8]

Míguez Bonino claims biblical warrant for this affirmation of Gutiérrez's and Assmann's position by pointing out that the biblical conception is that truth verifies itself as truth in action. Thus Latin American theologians of liberation have emphasized doing the truth as the appropriate means of verifying the validity of its claim as truth. Theology of liberation, Gutiérrez writes, is "theological reasoning that is verified—made to be true—in a real, fertile involvement with the liberation process."[9]

It is the Latin Americans who remind all theologians that conceptualizations of God are not the most important aspect of theology, but the practice of those idealizations in human history.

Theology, therefore, is a second-order discipline, since it follows the practical activity of the community of faith. LALT, Míguez Bonino points out, "emerges *after the fact,*" as the reflection about facts and experiences which have already evoked a response from Christians.[10] And, Gustavo Gutíerrez asserts:

> Theology is a reflection, a critical attitude. Theology follows: It is the second step. What Hegel used to say about philosophy can likewise be applied to theology: it rises at sundown. The pastoral activity of the church does not flow as a conclusion from theological premises. Theology does not produce pastoral activity: rather it reflects upon it.[11]

Theology is a critical reflection on the practice of the community of faith. The Christian community is called to a definite praxis—that is, to "real charity, love, and commitment to the service of men [sic]."[12] Accordingly, theology is critical reflection on the liberating transformation of the human situation by those for whom Jesus Christ is central. Because the massive suffering and oppression of the times is what gives rise to the crisis for Latin American Christians, then this praxis must incorporate the struggle for liberation of the masses from exploitation. A concrete *commitment* to the struggle for human freedom is prior to theology. Juan Luis Segundo writes, "Any and every theological question begins with the human situation. Theology is the second step. The ultimate criterion . . . is the remedy brought to some sort of human suffering, however temporary and provisional that remedy may be."[13]

Thus a precondition for LALT is the acknowledgment that human sensitivity and political commitment are intimately connected to theological reflection. Segundo demonstrates his liberation methodology by positing that the first step in the hermeneutical circle always includes a definite problem and an act of commitment on the part of the subject to find a solution to the problem. He asserts that a hermeneutical circle in theology "always presupposes a profound human commitment, a partiality that is consciously accepted—not on the basis of theological criteria, of course, but on the basis of human criteria."[14] Thus LALT must engage in clarifying its ideological presuppositions and commitments precisely because of the history of the role of Christianity in Latin America.

Since theology itself is part of the ideological superstructure, the ground must first be broken by uprooting the ideological traps. Hence Segundo declares, "Ideological criteria are logically prior, but in no way alien to theology."[15] If theology is the second step that follows after commitment to the liberation of the disenfranchised, then the first word in theology must be a thorough analysis of the situation. The concept of suspicion is important here and is based on Segundo's hypothesis that the ideologies connected with current social conditions and vested interests are unconsciously ruling our present theological consciousness. It is here that Marxist analysis becomes useful to Latin American theologians. Míguez Bonino writes:

> The option for Marxist analysis is necessary if it is true that every form of praxis articulates — consciously or unconsciously — a view of reality and a projection of it, an analysis and an ideology. This means that reflection on this praxis must necessarily raise the question of the rightness or inadequacy of such analysis and ideology.[16]

Latin Americans ruthlessly affirm the need to opt for this or that concrete political praxis. Marxism was adopted because it was adequate to the reality of Latin America and because Marxist social analysis provided a means for establishing ideological clarity in the midst of a crisis in identity. However, Míguez Bonino and other Latin American theologians immediately want to clarify the sense in which they have assumed Marxism. Míguez Bonino explains:

> Our assumption of Marxism has nothing to do with a supposedly abstract or eternal theory or with dogmatic formulas — a view which is not absent in certain Marxist circles — but with a scientific analysis and a number of verifiable hypotheses in relation to conditions obtained in certain historical moments and places and which, properly modified, corrected, and supplemented, provide an adequate means to grasp our own historical situation.[17]

Latin Americans, according to Míguez Bonino, earlier appropriated Marxist social analysis as a pragmatic instrument for understanding and interpreting their experiences. Several writers have argued that the Latin American liberation theologians have gone through several stages in their appropriation and use of Marxist tools of analysis. While it is evident from a cursory evaluation of the earlier writing of LALT that there was a selective usage of a wide variety of Marxist-oriented analytical tools, the Latin American liberation theologians, in general, were quite clear that it was their commitment to Christian faith that motivated them into their involvement in the struggles for liberation. Hugo Assmann was the theologian who

pervasively employed Marxist views. José Míguez Bonino utilized Marxist
social categories but elaborated his work in a distinctively theological fashion. Gutiérrez's writings, by comparison, contain relatively few references
to Marxism. Arthur McGovern evaluates the Latin Americans' emphasis
on Marxism and concludes that

> If one looks at the bulk of writings by [Latin American] Liberation
> Theologians, Marxism serves, if at all, only as one method of under-
> standing conditions in Latin America ... Writers like Juan Luis
> Segundo and Enrique Dussel use a broad range of social theories and
> theorists in their analyses. Even a theologian like Míguez Bonino who
> stresses the importance of Marxist analysis does not really employ it
> to any extent other than saying it is right in its judgements about
> capitalism.[18]

While earlier LALT writings stressed various elements of Marxist social
analysis, more recent developments have manifested a turn to more "theological" or "spiritual" dimensions of the struggle for Latin America's freedom.

Latin American theologians were not prepared to surrender their Christian identity for the sake of a radical philosophical materialism. They were
prepared, however, to argue that theology must focus on the material needs
of the people and that the truth of the Gospel must be historically verifiable.
The truth of the Gospel is vindicated in liberating praxes where, they
believe, God will surely vindicate God.

The aim of LALT, in view of these emphases, was to remake the whole
of theology, to the extent that it was possible. It was necessary, Segundo
writes,

> to de-ideologize our language and our message about God, the
> church, the sacraments, grace ... in order to get the whole church to
> carry to our people an understanding of our faith both more faithful
> to Jesus' gospel and more capable of contributing to the humanization
> of all people and social classes in our continent.[19]

Another theme of LALT is its emphasis on class analysis. Although it is
true that the Latin Americans could have employed other forms of class
analysis (i.e., Weberian), it is evident that the attraction of Marxist class
analysis for them was based on their perception that the problems of the
Latin American poor are consequences of an exploitative and unjust economic order. This is significant, for Marxist social analysis then becomes
useful in two ways: as a means of understanding and evaluating the real
factors that affect Latin American life, and as an instrument for clarifying
the ideological interests informing one's theological claims.

Furthermore, Latin American liberation theologians, in general, agree that the current economic system of capitalism is unjust and inhuman and that it is necessary to change the current system to one that would be more just and human for the oppressed of Latin America.

Strengths that flow out of Latin Americans' understanding of their situation are: a political commitment, based on social analysis, to involvement in the struggles of the oppressed for liberation; and the development of a biblically grounded theology in light of the prior commitment to the perspective of the poor. A political commitment grounded in historical praxis and informed by a social analysis of the Latin American situation reflects the need for Latin American Christians to be specific, self-conscious and intentional concerning the ideological interests that motivate their theological reflection.

The theologians of liberation in Latin America therefore reorient the context of theology in such a manner that its substance and content is conditioned decisively by their political commitment to the struggles of the nonpersons in Latin America.

We will critically evaluate the theological categories of Christology, ecclesiology, eschatology and liberation in the works of Gutiérrez, Míguez Bonino and Assmann as they engaged in an effort to respond to their basic question: What is the significance of the Gospel of Jesus Christ amid a world of poverty, suffering, exploitation and oppression?

Toward the Liberation of Christology: Jesus Christ the Liberator

In 1973 Hugo Assmann indicated that there were two "fundamental theological gaps" of vital significance for the development of a theology of liberation.[20] In issuing this challenge to the theologians of liberation, Assmann, a Catholic theologian who served as a professor at the Methodist University of Piracicaba in his native Brazil, was articulating the need for Latin American theologians of liberation to evolve a christological perspective that was relevant to the process of liberation in Latin America.

According to Assmann, somewhere between the "vague, general Christology *ad usum omnium,* unrelated to any particular situation [on the one hand] ... and on the other, particular embodiments designed to fit a particular ideological purpose at a particular moment [was] ... a legitimate need for a historically mediated Christology relevant to the basic problems in a given historical situation [Latin America]."[21] Assmann's second "fundamental gap" pertained to hermeneutics and flowed from the first, Christology. According to Assmann, it was necessary to evolve a hermeneutical criteria and methodology that would assist Latin American Christians in mediating between their sacred texts — the Bible, tradition, the magisterium, dogma — and the struggle for the liberation of the oppressed.

Approximately twelve years later, in an essay entitled "The Actuation of the Power of Christ in History: Notes on the Discernment of Christological Contradiction," Assmann was critical of the various Latin American liberation Christologies which evolved during the intervening period, as well as those who continued to emphasize the "christological vacuum" in Latin America.[22]

Assmann's criticism of many liberation Christologies was based on the fact that, according to him, they had attempted to fill the Latin American christological lacuna with many ingenious, and often simplistic, interpretations of Jesus as a revolutionary. On the other hand, he disapproves of those who fail to acknowledge the historical contradictions between the Christ of the oppressor and the Christ of the oppressed, or fail to acknowledge the fact that these conflicts can only be resolved within the dialectic of social reality. Thus, Assmann writes, "the conflict of Christologies cannot be analyzed or resolved apart from the dialectic of socio-political conflicts."[23]

The answer, for Assmann, lies in the development of a liberation hermeneutic that incorporates social analysis and transforming praxis as the objective basis for mediating the contradictions between the Christs of the dominant class and the Christs of the dominated class. According to Assmann, "faith in a Christ the liberator whose liberating power is vitally involved in class struggles and 'takes sides' with the oppressed, inevitably collides with all the Christs of the oppressor classes and the contradiction can only be resolved within the dialectic of socio-economic and political conflicts."[24] Latin American liberation Christology should be developed within the framework that presupposes class struggle as the central contradiction within the Latin American situation.

The intervening years between Assmann's initial and later comments were characterized by an irruption of liberation Christologies in Latin America, as well as the explication of a liberating hermeneutical methodology.[25] The aim of the developing Christologies of LALT is the recovery of Christ from those who have manipulated his image in order to justify domination over the oppressed.

José Míguez Bonino builds on Assmann's call for a distinctive Latin American liberation Christology by asserting that Christologies of Latin America must be analyzed in order that "the Christ of the gospels [might] ... be rescued along with the prophetic tradition and its mighty charge of humanizing potential—by means of a critical and topical rereading."[26]

By defining the Latin American christological enterprise as the recovery of the Christ whose power is mediated through the radical demands of discipleship for transforming praxis, Míguez Bonino points to an active commitment to historical praxis as the means through which to recover the Liberator Christ who transforms history. This new way of doing Christology rejects "any recourse to a facile textual hermeneutics, or a reformulation of doctrines or concepts."[27] Latin American liberation Christology must discover the liberating Christ of the Gospels in the historical project of the struggle for liberation.

According to Míguez Bonino and Assmann, Jesus is Christ the Liberator.

The methodological implications for Latin American liberation Christology is the acknowledgment that the point of departure is determined by both their ecclesiastical location as theologians who presuppose faith in the Gospel, as well as theologians whose social location is defined by a commitment to the oppressed. Hence the point of departure for Latin American Christology is the *historical Jesus*, since he is "the irruption into history of the one by whom everything was made and everything was saved," and as such is the central "hermeneutical principle of faith."[28] Their emphasis on the historical Jesus is an implication of the Latin Americans' insistence that Christology must begin from below. Human history is the location of the encounter with the God of Liberation who is incarnated in Jesus the Christ. Gutiérrez writes:

> Our encounter with the Lord occurs in our encounter with others, especially in the encounter with those whose human features have been disfigured by oppression, despoliation, and alienation, and who have "no beauty, or majesty" but are the things "from which men turn away their eyes" (Isa. 53:2–3).[29]

Jesus of Nazareth, as the *locus classicus* of God's historical revelation, must be the historical point of departure for Christology in Latin America. Jon Sobrino, however, warns against any simplistic dependence on dogmatic formulas, notions of the biblical or kerygmatic Christ, experiences of the presence of Christ among the worshiping community or the teachings of Jesus as the appropriate point of departure for Christology. According to Sobrino, writing on behalf of the Latin Americans,

> We choose to adopt the historical Jesus as our starting point . . . for several reasons. Our Christology will thereby avoid abstractionism, and the attendant danger of manipulating the Christ event. The history of the church shows, from its very beginning . . . that any focusing on the Christ of faith will jeopardize the very essence of the Christian faith if it neglects the historical Jesus . . . We feel that the historical Jesus is the hermeneutic principle that enables us to draw closer to the totality of Christ both in terms of knowledge and in terms of real-life praxis.[30]

But how does the theologian recover this *historical Jesus* without imposing his or her own ideological self-interest upon Jesus of Nazareth? Míguez Bonino acknowledges the difficulty of discovering the real Jesus Christ by arguing that a pluralism of Christologies exist, both in the biblical text as well as in the contemporary context. Further, Míguez Bonino continues, we cannot assume the homogeneity of "biblical images" or "Christs of the gospels" which are recoverable and which will lead us to the Christ who stands behind the message of the Gospel. The only means of avoiding the reduction of Christ to a projection of determinate social conditions, on the one hand, and a "simple transposition of the [so-called] 'Christ of the gospels'" into the present day, is the establishment of a hermeneutical methodology "that respects not only the original historicity of the text but also the singularity of the reader's locus — hence a hermeneutics incorporating careful exegesis and historico-social analysis as well."[31]

Míguez Bonino evidently believes that a hermeneutical method that dialectically engages the historical record of Jesus' life and the historical presence of Christ in the oppressed community will provide the necessary safeguards from the christological mistakes of the Christian theologians of the past.

A critical rereading of the Gospels from the viewpoint of the poor and exploited of Latin America will reveal that Jesus' mission entailed a sociopolitical dimension. Gutiérrez writes of the political dimension of Jesus' mission in three specific contexts: Jesus' relationship to the Zealot movement, his attitude to the religious and political leaders of the people, and his death at Pilate's hands.[32] Gutiérrez is wary of any simplistic parallelism between Jesus and the Zealots, since that approach would violate the integrity of Jesus's life, message and witness.

Despite his concern to carefully explore the complex relationship between Jesus and the Zealots and to distinguish between the Zealots' narrow nationalistic interest and Jesus' universalistic orientation, Gutiérrez discovers in Jesus a revolutionary message and mission. Whereas the Zealots were primarily concerned with their own national liberation struggle, Jesus was concerned with all humanity. Gutiérrez writes: "The justice and peace he advocated knows no nationalistic boundaries. In this he was even more revolutionary than the zealots, who were fierce defenders of literal obedience to the law; Jesus taught an attitude of spiritual freedom toward it."[33]

Jesus' attitude toward the Zealots, Gutiérrez continues, reflected a deeper comprehension of the problem of injustice and oppression, as well as a different understanding of God's Kingdom. Thus, Gutiérrez concludes, Jesus rejects any political/religious Messianism "which does not respect either the depth of the religious realm nor the autonomy of political action . . . The liberation which Jesus offers is universal and integral; it transcends national boundaries, attacks the foundation of injustice and exploitation, and eliminates politico-religious confusions, without therefore being limited to a purely spiritual plane."[34]

The second context in which Gutiérrez evaluates the political aspects of Jesus' life is his relationship to the political and religious leaders. Essentially, Jesus' relationship with the political and religious leaders is one of confrontation. This confrontational stance is determined by Jesus' belief that the primary benefactors of God's Kingdom would be the poor and the oppressed.

His beliefs and actions bring him into confrontation with: the Herodians, who are the internal oligarchy of a dependent nation; the Sadducees, who are the religious hierarchy threatened by Jesus' proclamations, which questioned their religious skepticism, legalistic religiosity and privileged status; and the Pharisees, who although they reject Roman domination, console themselves with "a complex world of religious precepts and norms of behavior which allowed them to live on the margin of that domination."[35] In contrast to these powerful groups, Jesus proclaimed a prophetic religion that could only be authentically realized on the basis of a commitment to the oppressed and the needy, in a holistic liberation.

In the third context, Gutiérrez explores the fact of Jesus' death at the hands of the political authorities. Gutiérrez is inclined to the view that Jesus was sentenced to death due to the religio-political implications of his message. Gutiérrez contends:

> Before the justice of the power groups of the Jewish people and the Roman oppressors, Jesus was guilty precisely because he challenged their legitimacy, in the name not of some partisan option, but of a message of love, peace, freedom and justice. This message undermined the very bases of religious formalism, unjust privileges, and social injustice which supported the order of the power groups of the Jewish people and the Roman authority.[36]

Gutiérrez concludes that Jesus' life and preaching therefore reflect a profound commitment to social transformation that extends to all spheres of human existence and which is universal in its intention. Further, the struggle for transformation occurs amid a conflictive history which is defined in a fundamental way by class struggle. Jesus Christ, then, is the bearer of a gospel that motivates Christians to contend, amid the conflict, for socio-economic and political liberation. The historical Jesus is interpreted in the context of biblical history where the Exodus motif and prophetic faith consistently emphasized radical discipleship in the struggle for justice, peace, love and freedom. This is the way of Jesus, the Christ.

It is not enough, however, to exegete the biblical texts in order to discover the Christ of liberation. Míguez Bonino, Gutiérrez and Assmann believe that the danger of simplistic reductionism can only be avoided by means of a hermeneutic that incorporates historico-social analysis of the situation and the historical presence of Christ in the oppressed community. A historico-social analysis of the Latin American situation reveals the existence of class struggle and a pluralism of Latin American Christologies. The existence of diverse Christologies in Latin America is especially significant when considered within the context of the economic and political self-interests of different class formations in Latin America. A rereading of the history of Latin America, the Latin Americans argue, will help us to understand the evolution of various Christologies that shape the popular Christologies of Latin America.

In Latin America, the Christologies of the dominant classes must be distinguished from the Christologies of the oppressed classes. Popular Christology in Latin America is dominated by the division between the perspectives of the oppressed and the oppressor. Pedro Negre Rigol states:

> If we examine the Christological consciousness of the masses, the proclamation of a Cristo Libertador contrasts profoundly with the images of those other "Christs" of the people, which are prisoners of Catholic colonialism or of Protestant neocolonialism. The former are the dolorous and defeated Christs of Good Friday or the monarchical ones of the Spanish Empire; the latter are pietistic, sentimental Christs, prisoners of private religion and its uncritical ideology.[37]

The ideological entrapment and manipulation of images of Christ is a primary reason for the Latin Americans' insistence that all Christologies be subject to review in light of an a priori commitment to the struggle for liberation and to the priorities of the historical Jesus. The Christs of the masses can be classified in several ways. First, there are the images of Christ that pacify the oppressed: dead, powerless, distant, suffering Christs who have been defeated.[38] This image tends to encourage a fatalistic resignation among the oppressed because it does not empower them to fight to change their circumstances. As Hugo Assmann put it:

> The dolorous Christs of Latin America, whose central image is ever the cross, are Christs of impotence — an impotence interiorized by the oppressed. Defeat, sacrifice, pain, cross, impotence, powerlessness, is accepted "undigested," recognized in advance and submitted to. Defeat is not perceived as a temporary reversal to be overcome in struggle. It appears as an inevitable necessity, as a condition for the privilege of living.[39]

While Gutiérrez acknowledges the fact that this image (the dolorous Christ) is subject to manipulation by the oppressor, he also recognizes the subversive potential of a Christ whose power for liberation comes to us through those who suffer. Gutiérrez claims:

> We must recover the memory of "the scourged Christs of America," as Bartolome de las Casas called the Indians of our continent. This memory never really died. It lives on in cultural and religious expressions. It lives on in resistance to ecclesiastical apparatus. It is a memory of the Christ who is present in every starving, thirsting, imprisoned, or humiliated human being, in the despised minorities, in the exploited classes (see Matt. 25:31–45). It is the memory of a Christ who not only freed us, he meant us to remain free.[40]

A second image of Christ in Latin America is the celestial-monarchic image of Christ which was associated with the Spanish Conquistadores of King Ferdinand of Spain. This image, the product of both European and Latin American indigenous cultures, has played a role in subjugating the people to the authority of the political and religious leaders. This Christ is the Christ of established power, which encourages "a subjugation that has no need to struggle."[41] This image of Christ has often been an instrument of pacification utilized by the dominant classes to sustain their exploitation of the poor. Since the Latin American church has often been the church of the aristocracy, church has been a primary instrument for espousing uncritically an image which is triumphalistic and supports the status quo.

A third image of Christ that emerges in any analysis of popular Latin American Christologies is the marginalized Christ. This Christ is the one who suffers and dwells with the weak ones, and whose missions were announced when he said:

> The Spirit of the Lord is upon me, because he has anointed me to preach good news to the poor. He has sent me to proclaim release to the captives and recovering of sight to the blind, to set at liberty those who are oppressed, to proclaim the acceptable year of the Lord [Luke 4:18–19].

The Christ of marginalization is derived both from Scripture and from the popular images of Christ among the people. Christ in this context is the epiphany of the liberating God who takes sides with the oppressed against injustice and exploitation and empowers the poor to fight for liberation in history. This is the reason the Latin American liberation theologians have committed themselves to analyzing popular religion, in order to discover the presence of Christ the Liberator within the histories of the poor. Thus, the importance of Míguez Bonino's emphasis on the need for a hermeneutical method that employs both careful exegesis and historico-social analysis in light of the interpreter's singular focus on the liberation of the oppressed. The priority of a hermeneutical methodology that manifests a preference for the liberation of the oppressed illuminates the Latin Americans' belief that any christological approach must always presuppose the humanizing intentions of the Gospel. Indeed, Gutiérrez's often-quoted phrase has indicated "the subject of theology is not Christ, but liberation."

In summary, then, LALT is dedicated to the recovery of Christ the Liberator. This recovery project is dependent on:

1. The establishment of a hermeneutical methodology that utilizes both a historico-critical analysis and rereading of the gospels
2. A social analysis of the situation
3. A reassessment of the pluralism of christological perspectives which characterize both the Bible and Latin America, in the light of an a priori commitment to the poor and the oppressed

4. Engagement in liberating praxis within the dialectic of social history.

Since theology is the second act, the Latin Americans have derived an understanding of Jesus Christ the Liberator as one who took sides with the poor and the oppressed against the dominant classes of Latin American society. The Christian faith, therefore, entails a continual renewal of interpreting the gospel traditions in such a manner that it becomes the good news of God's liberation for the oppressed, and the church becomes an enduring witness to God's future victory. But the Christ of liberation has emerged in the conflictive history defined by class struggle. Assmann's comment concerning the Christian encounter with Christ reflects his dedication to a Christology which is defined according to the insights of the Latin American liberation theologians. He declares:

> The Christian discovers and adheres to Christ here and now, to the Christ who is present and contemporaneous in the brethren, above all in the oppressed; this should become for the Christian the first meaning of the expression "historical Jesus," that is Christ in present history, however much the discovery of this contemporaneity of Christ may evidently demand the confrontation with the Christ in his former life and actions.[42]

Ecclesiogenesis: The Church in the Struggle for the Poor[43]

LALT has emerged in Latin America as a consequence of participation in revolutionary activity by members of the Christian community and their subsequent effort to understand the meaning of their faith in this new situation. Gutiérrez comments that this participation

> constitutes the most important fact in the life of the Latin American Christian community. It gives rise to a new way of being a human . . . and believer, a new way of living and thinking the faith, a new way of being summoned, and summoning, into ek-klesia, church, the assembly of those called together for mission.[44]

As a consequence of their commitment to transforming praxis on behalf of the poor in Latin America, and consistent with a theology which emerges from pastoral praxis on their behalf, Latin American ecclesiological formulations have begun to evolve new ways of being the church. Indeed Gutiérrez is persuaded that it is necessary to radically revise what the church is and what the church needs to be. He observes:

> What is called for is not simply a renewal and adaptation of pastoral methods. It is rather a question of a new ecclesial consciousness and a redefinition of the task of the church in a world in which it is not

only present, but of which it forms a part more than it suspected in the past.[45]

Involvement in the liberation process elicited new questions within the Christian community: What does it mean to be a Christian? How can the church truly be the church in a situation characterized by exploitation and oppression? How, and to what, is the church bearing witness? These questions reflect the dual crises that confronted Latin American Christians in recent Latin American history. On the one hand, there was the need to clarify the role of the Christian community in the Latin American situation and to choose where the Christian should stand. On the other hand, there was profound ambivalence concerning the supporting role that Christianity had played in both the colonial and the neocolonial period. What did it mean to be the church in Latin America? Liberation entailed the continual need to clarify the meaning and mission of the church. "On the one hand," Míguez Bonino writes:

It is necessary to unmask the fact of class struggle as it takes place within the church and insofar as the sociologically measurable entity that the church is becomes or remains a part of the system of oppression, to "combat the church" and work for its overthrow. On the other hand, the struggle for the poor discovers within the ecclesiastical institution . . . the factors of alienation and oppression that operate as a part of the religious life itself.[46]

Consequently, Míguez Bonino rejects the static ecclesiologies based on a "set of foundational doctrines, structures, or norms" and affirms the existence of a situation in which "theological upheaval is accompanied, reflected and forwarded by an ecclesial fluidity which makes traditional confessional criteria and institutional crystallization largely irrelevant."[47] He concurs with Gutiérrez that the fundamental sociological and theological discovery of the oppressed of Latin America has necessitated a reconceiving of ecclesiology. He affirms:

The people become "a theological locus," the meeting place where Christ himself has promised to be present, the privileged sanctuary and sacrament of this presence. If the church is where Christ is, do not the poor become constitutive of the mystery of God?[48]

The true church in Latin America, Míguez Bonino affirms, is the church that stands with the Servant-Christ who stood for others, and above all, the poor.

Gutiérrez establishes the conditions for the discussion of the meaning of the church in a divided world when he rejects any discussion of the idea of Christian unity, for example, which simplistically glosses over the real divisions in Latin America. He criticizes the notion of unity as a myth in need of redefinition.[49] He contends:

> The church is in a world divided into antagonistic social classes ...
> It is not possible to speak of the unity of the church without taking into account its concrete situation in the world.
> To try piously to cover over this social division with fictitious and formalistic unity is to avoid a difficult and conflictual reality and definitively to join the dominant class.[50]

He challenges the Christian community to acknowledge the fact of class struggle and its implications for a divided church, and to recognize that in a revolutionary situation "neutrality is impossible."[51] To acknowledge the reality of class struggle is to recognize the need to choose sides in the historical conflict between the dominated and the dominators. The universality of Christian love of all persons, according to Gutiérrez, will remain an abstraction unless it is translated into liberating praxis within the conflictive dialectic of human history. Gutiérrez is simply explicating the implications of Assmann's earlier christological insight: the inevitably conflicting theological perspectives that distinguish any divided society can only be resolved within the dialectic of social history. A church that chooses sides is one that makes an option for one ideological perspective or the other, despite the theologians' reluctance to reduce the Gospel to an ideology. Nonetheless, Gutiérrez and Míguez Bonino's liberation theology rejects the notion that the church of the conservative must understand itself as both "the church of the conservative and the progressive, the reactionary and the revolution, [the rich and the poor,] of the right and the left."[52] Consequently, the church must take sides with the oppressed, since neutrality implies support of the status quo, and since the Gospel demands radical discipleship for the God who has opted *for* the oppressed.

Implicit in Gutiérrez's redefinition of the ecclesiological task is an implicit criticism of traditional approaches to ecclesiology as being abstracted from the historical context of the praxis of the community of faith. Consequently, the new meta-criterion of the church's identity and mission is defined as liberating praxis on behalf of the oppressed. For Assmann, Míguez Bonino and Gutiérrez, the definitive criterion of the true church is the development of a revolutionary consciousness and commitment to the struggles of the poor. There are several insights that result from the Latin Americans' redefining the contours of ecclesiology that are significant. First, the discovery of the poor has led to the uncentering of the church away from the traditional ecclesiocentrism and toward the world of the oppressed. Rejecting any dependence on a narrow dualism between church and the world, Gutiérrez argues that the church finds its true identity and mission insofar as it is converted to the world. Gutiérrez contends:

the church must turn to the world, in which Christ and his spirit are present and active; the church must allow itself to be evangelized by the world ... the church is not a non-world; it is humanity itself attentive to the Word. It is the people of God which lives in history and is oriented toward the future promised by the Lord.[53]

Míguez Bonino grasps the full meaning of Gutiérrez's elaboration of the church as an historical institution when he states "the church holds the meaning of human history."[54] Míguez Bonino deepens Gutiérrez's insight when he notes that God's saving action in the world, to which the church must bear witness, lies in the struggle for the liberation of the poor, which is "pioneered and carried forward by social classes and revolutionary movements among which Christians are a minority, while the churches are largely indifferent if not hostile to them."[55] Thus, Míguez Bonino concludes, Gutiérrez's interpretation of the insights of Vatican II suggest that "the secular struggle for the liberation of the poor discloses the meaning of the church."[56]

While he supports Gutiérrez in his explication of this point, Míguez Bonino believes that it is dangerous to rest the definition of the Church on a primarily "extra-ecclesiastic" viewpoint, since he wishes to safeguard the autonomy of the Church (as it defines itself), as well as the human struggle for liberation. Míguez Bonino proposes an understanding of the Church and the world that emerges from a more unitary understanding of God's project in the histories of creation and redemption. He states:

If creation—and human reality within it—is seen as a static, ready-made thing, the Christian dispensation might appear as a purely restorational device (the two-story view) or as an independent supra-historical realm (the two-kingdom idea). But if we take seriously the dynamic dimension inherent in the covenant-prophetic theology, the picture is altogether different. Creation is the installation of a movement; it is an invitation and a command to man to create his own history and culture, creatively to transform the world and make it into his own house. ... Faith in Christ is not, therefore, a step beyond humanity, but toward it. "We are not men in order to be Christians, but Christians in order to be men." In this soteriological order, the Church has a distinct but provisional and subordinate place. It is commissioned to proclaim [word and act] God's salvation in Jesus Christ.[57]

The creational and soteriological intentions of the biblical message are therefore set within its proper context: "a single humanity created by God in order that it might grow toward full maturity."[58]

Subsequently, the heart of the church's witness is a fellowship which is primarily determined by the poor. The resultant evangelization by the poor challenges the church to find its identity and mission in concrete historical praxis toward liberation. This means, Gutiérrez, Míguez Bonio and Assmann would concur, that the battle for a new ecclesiology is a conflict for the true church. The confrontation between concrete historical options reflecting the class divisions in Latin American society will call the Christian to make specific choices, and will call the corporate church to make known its commitments. This is the context in which unity or disunity must be resolved. Míguez Bonino writes: "To belong faithfully to the church means to claim our place within this field and to engage in the struggle for a true, faithful, historical obedience."[59]

The truth of the Gospel of Jesus Christ the Liberator, therefore, is to be contended for in the midst of the concrete historical situation where men and women must choose between the two faces of the Latin American church: the church of the rich and the powerful, wherein the poor are alienated and oppressed; or the church that emerges from the histories, cultures and struggles of the poor.

A second insight that emerges with Latin American liberation ecclesiology is the notion that the church is called to be the sacrament of history.[60] Whereas the first insight proposes the reorientation of the church away from the dominant classes and in the direction of the poor, the second insight highlights the essential character of the church's witness. LALT ecclesiology affirms that the church which springs from the poor is the locus of the anticipatory presence of that which God intends to accomplish — liberation — and a witness to God's liberating action in the world. Therefore, the material manifestation of the church's witness to the reign of God — the central message of Christ the Liberator — lies in the church's identification and solidarity with the struggles of the poor.

Accordingly, Míguez Bonino contends:

> The church is itself when it witnesses to God's saving activity in Jesus Christ, that is, when it makes clear God's renewed authorization, commandment, and liberation to man to be human, to create his own history and culture, to love and to transform the world, to claim and exercise the glorious freedom of the children of God.[61]

Within the Latin American situation, there has been eruption of new ecclesial structures which represent these ecclesiological insights. Specifically, the development of basic Christian communities is considered by the Latin Americans as one manifestation of their dedication to reinvent the church.[62]

The primary distinction characterizing this process is the fact that, in this case, the church — base communities — are the oppressed, organizing themselves for the liberation struggle. While the institutional church is viewed as being accountable to the magisterium, this new ecclesial phenomenon is accountable to the poor and oppressed community in Latin America.

It is evident that the earlier emphasis on the notion of *class struggle* by the Latin American liberation theologians contributes to the reorientation of their *ecclesiological interests*. Leonardo Boff, a Brazilian Catholic theologian, has observed that the central contradiction which these new ecclesial formations seek to address is the problem of class division based on capitalist structures. Boff states:

> When it comes to identifying the causes of the miseries they suffer, the members of the basic communities see the main one—not the only one, but the main one—as the capitalist system. But worse than the system itself is its individualistic spirit of accumulation, its social irresponsibility, and its insensitivity toward human beings.[63]

Conflict between the economically privileged and the disfranchised masses, grounded in the existence of an unjust economic system, determines the shape of any ecclesiology within the historical conflict between the church of the rich and the poor—the "haves" and the "have nots." As a result, the ecclesiology of LALT defines itself, in Míguez Bonino's words, "as a conflict for the true church, as the confrontation of concrete historical options embraced as the obedience that faith is, 'within which context the church becomes accountable to' the presence of the suffering Christ in the poor."[64]

Finally, then, the church finds its identity, nature and mission, as it makes a preferential option for the poor and stands against a model of the church favored by the dominant classes that sacralizes the oppression and exploitation of the poor. This choice is determined by maintaining the christological center of the church while at the same time redefining the meaning of the church in terms of the presence of the poor.

The emergence of the basic Christian communities from the poor represents the converging interest of the poor classes, and constitutes a challenge to the church of the dominant class.

Eschatology: Between Faith and History

Traditional Christian eschatology in Latin America Liberation Theology is also transformed in order to better serve the liberation struggle. Hope and faith in the establishment of the Kingdom are reinterpreted in the light of the need to materialize such commitments within the dialectic of historical contradictions within the economic order. Under the dual influences of Marxist insights concerning history and the rereading of the biblical and Christian traditions from the perspective of the oppressed, traditional approaches to eschatology are either rejected or revised.

According to Míguez Bonino, for example: "the ardent expectation of the total transformation of the world and the advent of the kingdom of God was soon replaced in (historic) Christianity by a spiritualized and individualistic hope for immortal celestial life."[65] Consequently, there emerged the two-world framework which is especially significant, as Míguez Bonino distinguishes between: "this present, temporal, earthly one which had a preparatory, contingent, and even at points negligible value, and the eternal one which is the true realm of life, fulfillment and happiness, the goal for the Christian."[66] This traditional bifurcation—temporal and eternal, *civitas dei* and *civitas terrena*, religious and political—must be rejected in favor of "one singular God-fulfilled history," according to Gutiérrez. Whereas, for instance, the Marxist vision of utopia continually encourages historical action and values human history, the Christian vision, under the influence of these traditional dualisms, tends to "lead to accommodation to present conditions . . . empties history of meaning and value and relativizes [immediate and provisory stages and achievements]."[67]

The challenge of LALT, within the sphere of eschatology, is to evolve an understanding of eschatology that rejects the two-world conceptual framework in the light of both biblical and historical considerations; develops a more adequate understanding of the intrinsic connection between eschatological expectations and historical action; and describes the historical mediation through which Christians can participate in bringing God's reign to fruition.

In accordance with a reinterpretation of biblical and Christian theology from the perspective of the underside, the Kingdom of God—the vision and goal of Christian faith—is defined as being organically linked to human liberation struggles.[68] By rejecting the traditional two-story approach to history, the liberation theologians are able to view God's creation and redemption as two dimensions of one singular historical project. As the final document of the São Paulo, Brazil (1980), meeting of the Ecumenical Association of Third World Theologians indicates, "The coming of the kingdom of God's final design for his creation is experienced in the historical processes of human liberation."[69] The Latin American theologians are careful not to reduce the utopian vision of God's reign to historical liberations. They contend:

> On the one hand, the kingdom has a utopian character for it can never be completely achieved in history . . . The kingdom pervades human liberations, it manifests itself in them, but it is not identical with them. Historical liberations, by the very fact that they are historical, are limited, but are open to something greater . . . Historical liberations incarnate the kingdom to the degree that they humanize life and generate social relationships of greater fraternity, participation, and justice.[70]

Under the dual influences of a commitment to "the poor" and a new interpretation of the meaning of the Christian hope, the Latin American liberation theologians have sought to redefine their eschatology.[71]

Some important new eschatological insights are noteworthy here. First, Christian faith is experienced in its most authentic sense, historically, when the community of faith identifies in solidarity with the journey of the poor in liberating praxis. Jesus Christ—the poor one who is God's presence in the poor—and his message of the Kingdom elicit a response of faith and hope which is symbolized in historical action within the political plane of class struggle. Within the political struggle, faith and hope are the expressions of the ultimate vision of God's reign in the present. As God's actions are historically embodied within the one stage of conflictive human history, then there can be no separation of history vis-à-vis the classical dualisms of traditional theology. Míguez Bonino argues that any such separation is in fact inconsistent with the biblical perspective.[72] Concurring with Gutiérrez, Míguez Bonino stresses the singular character of history and thereby legitimizes any emphasis on the political character of Christian eschatology.[73] He contends: "Every attempt to separate the political from the religious areas . . . is artificial . . . We must stress the political character of this history, i.e., as action and word embracing the total life of the people and of peoples as collective entities and the reality of power."[74]

Faith is the gracious gift of a liberating God that illuminates and motivates the poor to engage in liberation struggles as material concretions of eschatological hope.

Therefore, according to Gutiérrez, the Christian eschatological vision is a utopian vision that entails a critical questioning of things as they are (status quo); defense of the oppressed; and a political strategy or plan for societal transformation. The Kingdom of God as a promise of a transformed future is a disquieting prophetic message that confronts the status quo— the oppressive rulers of this age. Rather than being a sacralizing message to human society, the Gospel of the liberating Christ raises critical questions about the existing societal and ecclesial structures, especially as they contribute to the oppression of the poor.

Second, and here again we are confronted with the specific contribution of liberation theology, the reign of God is understood as God's promise to defend the poor and the oppressed and to vindicate their rights as humans. The defense of the oppressed is a primary criterion for any theology of liberation in Latin America.

Third, the historical concretion of the presence of God's reign is manifested where the Christian commitment to God is expressed in political action that leads to societal transformation and the liberation of the oppressed. Where is the Kingdom of God to be found? The reign of God is found where faith and hope open history to the promise of God by struggling for liberation, a new humanity and new life in the Spirit.

The historical mediation of Christian participation is found where men and women are motivated to engage in liberating praxis. Hugo Assmann, who had difficulty in articulation of the nature of the specifically Christian contribution to liberation struggles, finally concludes by stating his belief that:

> the Christian formula "love = death–life," kept on a historical and existential plane, can become the key to the series of radical conundrums that impose themselves daily on those who live entirely for others. Perhaps this is the best way to understand the specifically Christian contribution to liberation.[75]

The possibility of affirming a positive relationship between God's Kingdom and the human historical liberation struggle confirms the Latin Americans' understanding of faith in God as a call to active engagement in human affairs on behalf of liberation and "makes it possible for the Christian to invest his life historically in the building of a temporary imperfect order with the certainty that neither he nor his effort is meaningless or lost."[76]

Closely linked to Latin American liberation eschatological perspectives, and buttressing their view of history, is the fundamental understanding of liberation as entailing a dynamic linkage between historical projects of liberation and God's comprehensive project of salvation. The notion of liberation in LALT is understood as holistic and comprehensive.

The Dialectic of Salvation and Liberation

Fundamental to LALT's concept of liberation is the notion of the Kingdom of God. God's relationship to the work of creation and redemption is best captured in the biblical symbol of the reign of God, where emphasis is placed on the empowering presence of God in history and God's intention to transform history (*historicity*), on the one hand, and the *totality* of God's sovereign rule over all history, on the other hand. All areas of human existence stand under the call and judgment of God for transformation.[77] From the viewpoint of faith, then, history is not merely profane history that is opposed to sacred history, but is itself an essential unity in the Kingdom of God. Salvation and liberation, two distinct yet mutually interrelated moments of the same history, are dialectically linked within and under the reign of God.[78] This fact explains Gutiérrez's claim that the ultimate meaning of historical liberation can be "grasped in all its depth only when one knows that this liberation leads this same history out beyond itself, to a fullness that transcends the scope of all human doing or telling."[79]

While the historical struggle for liberation finds its ultimate meaning within the larger context of God's salvific intentions, the Latin Americans are careful to reject the crude reduction of salvation to historical liberation. Within the one "Christo-finalized" history, the liberation process receives its fullest meaning when it encompasses the totality of human existence.[80] *Liberation* is the central focus of this tradition of theology, which views the total liberation of humankind and of the whole created order as God's intention. Gutiérrez and Assmann agree in their writings that the term *liberation*, to use Gutiérrez's words, refers to "three levels of meaning of a single, complex process, which finds its deepest sense and its full realization in the saving work of Christ."[81]

Assmann writes: "The term 'liberation' can be applied on three levels: the political liberation of oppressed nations and social classes; the liberation of mankind throughout the course of history; and liberation from sin, the cause of all evil, preparing the way for a life of all mankind in communion with the Lord."[82] Both Assmann and Gutiérrez explicitly define their meaning for the term *liberation*, because they are concerned about its misuse, especially in religious circles. Gutiérrez, on the one hand, writes that a comprehensive description of liberation is necessary because:

A comprehensive view of the matter presupposes that all the aspects can be considered together. In this way two pitfalls will be avoided. First, idealist or spiritualist approaches, which are nothing but ways of evading a harsh and demanding reality, and second, shallow analyses and programs of short-term effects initiated under the pretext of meeting immediate needs.[83]

Continuing in the same direction, yet placing stronger stress on the historical character of the liberation process, Assmann writes:

The precise term "liberation" subverts the magical and proclamatory structure of "action through the word" (Ger.: *Worttat*) and replaces it by "the word of action" (Ger.: *Tatwort*). It aims at the historical growth of liberty as a political reality, and it contradicts the semantic bases of the vague liberal idea of rights to freedom.[84]

The genius of liberation theology in Latin America, Míguez Bonino has observed, "is not to have discovered these three levels of meaning but to have started from their *unity* as the fundamental point of departure."[85] In accordance with their rejection of traditional theological dualisms, the Latin Americans assert an essential unity of "sociopolitical struggle, human maturity and reconciliation with God."[86]

The concept of liberation in LALT entails emphasis on three dimensions of the liberation process within the unity and totality of God's salvific will. The first dimension of liberation is the historic struggle for socio-economic and political liberation. The second dimension of liberation is the struggle to transform the consciousness of humans whose existence and identities have been defined by oppressors, and the third dimension of liberation refers to liberation from sin and the need for reconciliation with God.[87]

The intrinsic linkage of these three levels of liberation is derived from the modern enlightenment and a rereading of eschatological history (Scriptures) from the perspective of the poor. Gutiérrez admits the significance of enlightenment thinkers in his discussion of the important differences between the concepts of *development* and *liberation.*[88] Underlying LALT's conception of liberation is a philosophical anthropology (description of human existence) and approach to metaphysics which was originally refined within the context of the modern enlightenment.[89]

Thus it must be noted that the struggle for liberation presupposes:

1. The existence of divisions and conflict within the dialectic of social history
2. Revolutionary praxis in order to transform those structures which sustain alienation and oppression
3. The ultimate resolution of historical conflict in the establishment of the Kingdom of God, where men and women are freed from sin and are reconciled to one another.

In discussing the basic unity of these three levels of liberation, Jon Sobrino has observed that LALT has utilized an anthropology of concrete totality, in distinction to the other philosophical approaches utilized by classical theology.[90] In contrast to the classical metaphysical approach, which is grounded in an intellectual anthropology consisting of the theoretical affirmation of God's transcendence by way of analogic predication, or the existentialist approach, which consists of an anthropology that views human existence as responsible for itself as it is accepted in commitment amid the ambiguities of life, LALT views the human subject as a concrete reality. This subject pursues his or her cognitive and existential transcendence to God in and through concrete social history, amid social contradictions and historical conflict, consequently, the emphasis on historicity and praxis. God's transcendence is not simply an object of theoretical contemplation requiring an act of cognition, nor is it simply a call to personal repentance and salvation, but it is a call to concrete historical transcendence of sin and evil on the basis of faith in the eschatological hope in the definitive reign of God in the future.

Therefore, LALT rejects the traditional emphasis on the separation of the supernatural and natural worlds, or secular and divine spheres, and affirms that God's work of redemption is applicable, relevant, and operative throughout all dimensions of life in the world. Thus liberation is not simply otherworldly but entails a this-world project and the concrete need for liberation in it. Hence the diverse spheres of activity for Christians, where political involvement becomes a necessary aspect of Christian life and work.

Of particular relevance in this context is the fact that the concept of liberation in the works of Gutiérrez, Míguez Bonino and Assmann is derived from a commitment to a specific liberating praxis. At the heart of their understanding of liberation is the acknowledgment that social conflict characterizes the human situation where neutrality is impossible. Theology of liberation situates its point of departure as being derived from the perspective of the struggles of the poor and in the context of class struggle. The assumption of orthopraxis as the ultimate criterion of theological language means that "theology is not an effort to give a correct understanding of God's attributes or actions but an effort to articulate the action of faith [and] the shape of praxis."[91]

Hence, given the presuppositions of LALT, liberation is a comprehensive term that articulates three mutually interpenetrating levels of meanings which achieve historical materialization within the class conflict of Latin America and entail specific options for or against the poor. Gutiérrez acknowledges that liberation encompasses "economic, social, and political processes which put them [liberation theologians] at odds with wealthy nations and oppressive classes."[92] Liberation is *cultural* (breaking away from European post-enlightenment cultural formations), *political* (breaking away from the power of the Euro-American economic empire and its petit bourgeois supporters) and *economic* (breaking with the capitalist world order and creating a new socialist society), and achieves its full meaning when viewed within the framework of God's liberation of men and women from sin and its effects.[93]

Underlying the concept of liberation in Míguez Bonino, Assmann and Gutiérrez is the presupposition of historical conflict between the privileged and the poor, grounded in the historical reality of economic dependence and exploitation. Nevertheless, a cursory review of the notion of liberation within their writing suggests that for LALT, liberation is constituted of a complex web of separate and yet related strands of the human struggle to achieve holistic liberation.

Evaluation

In sum, this investigation of LALT, by means of a consideration of the Christology, ecclesiology, eschatology and concept of liberation in Gutiérrez, Míguez Bonino and Assmann, has revealed the fundamental significance of a critique of the economic order for this theological enterprise. In its initial stages, LALT developed primarily as a theology that emphasized the socio-economic dimension of liberation. This suggests that the Latin Americans were primarily in dialogue with Marxist economic and philosophical theory rather than with the religions and cultures of the poor, for and about whom they were presumably speaking. Gustavo Gutiérrez acknowledges this when he remarks:

We shall not have our great leap forward, into a whole new theological perspective, until the marginalized and exploited have begun to become the artisans of their own liberation — until their voice makes itself heard directly, without mediation, without interpreters — until they themselves take account, in the light of their own values, of their own experience of the Lord in their efforts to liberate themselves. We shall not have our quantum theological leap until the oppressed themselves theologize ... for they are the bearers of this hope for all humanity.[94]

Therefore, Juan Luis Segundo's two stage description of the development of LALT would seem an adequate description of a theological tradition, albeit radical, that emerges among Christian middle-class intellectuals who are primarily involved in a dialogue with sociology, philosophy and economic theory.

Segundo detects the need to acknowledge Gutiérrez's insight and explains the need for this shift in emphasis when he indicates that LALT has evolved through two stages.[95] According to Segundo, LALT emerged, in its earlier stage, out of the university, where middle-class Christian students had raised questions concerning Christianity's role in the suffering and oppression of Latin Americans. In this context, Christians experienced suspicion concerning the link "between oppressive and inhuman behavior [by oppressors] and a similar oppressive and inhuman understanding of Christian faith."[96] Thus, the importance of class analysis emerges as a means of evaluating one's commitments. In the second stage, LALT recognized the need to relate its suspicions to the facts of the histories of the victims of oppression, and therefore, the turn to religo-cultural traditions of the oppressed. The published work of Gustavo Gutiérrez clearly shows this evolution. While his earlier work, *A Theology of Liberation,* reflects a sophisticated socio-economic and theological discussion LALT, it is his later work, *The Power of the Poor in History, We Drink from Our Own Wells* and *On Job,* which shows a plumbing of the religio-cultural traditions of the oppressed in Latin America. Due to the influence of BTUSA and other liberation traditions, as well as from the oppressed in Latin America, LALT turned to a careful consideration of the religions and cultures of the poor.

Class conflict is the fundamental contradiction to which the Latin Americans sought to respond. Their reinterpretation of Christology, ecclesiology, eschatology and the concept of liberation were decisively determined by their conviction that the root cause of injustice, exploitation, and poverty in Latin America could be traced to the economic structures of the Euro-American capitalist order.

Meanwhile, certain fundamental cultural and religious questions that characterized the Latin American situation were left unaddressed. Also, almost completely absent was any reference to the problem of racism; the primary contradiction to which black theologians sought to respond in the United States. Any discourse which seeks to evaluate BTUSA and LALT in relationship to each other must, as a means of determining the specific reasons for them, explore their differences and similarities. This exploration will also contribute to a dialogical encounter, which would be mutually beneficial.

It is evident, on the one hand, that LALT depends upon the conviction that the poor in Latin America are somewhat similar to Marxist definitions of oppressed classes, the Latin American poor with the proletariat. It is not equally evident why a more sophisticated analytical framework was not utilized to deepen their understanding of the problem of poverty in Latin America. Even as they emphasized the importance of a scientific means of verifying the problem of oppression in Latin America, they were not comprehensive in their description of the problem. If the poor in Latin America are most often blacks, Indians and women, then the Latin Americans' description of the "poor" has been inadequate. How are the theological insights of the poor being incorporated into LALT? These are questions which still seek an answer. While it is clear that LALT has revised its theological perspective, it also is evident that there is still need to evolve a more comprehensive understanding of oppression, as well as liberation.

On the other hand, BTUSA's emphasis on the religions and cultures of African-American people, while important, needs to incorporate economic analysis into a more comprehensive view of the dynamics of oppression in the United States and the world. The historical concretions of the vision of the Kingdom of God require coherent and comprehensive analysis, as well as strategies for specific action strategies. In either case, a deeper appreciation of BTUSA's and LALT's commonalities and differences will provide each tradition with helpful tools for their respective liberation struggles, and BTUSA and LALT can complement each other in the advancement of their mutual commitment to the liberation of the oppressed.

CHAPTER FOUR

BTUSA and LALT

What Can They Say to Each Other?

Introduction

BTUSA and LALT reflect two different trends within the tapestry of liberation theology traditions. On the one hand, BTUSA emerged, historically, as a theology which emphasized the significance of the religio-cultural traditions of African-American people and stressed the primacy of race in determining the identity of the oppressed. On the other hand, LALT emerged as a theology that reflected its interaction with the philosophical traditions associated with the European Enlightenment, Marxism particularly, and which stressed the primacy of class in determining the identity of the oppressed.[1] Understandably, these contextually and methodologically defined differences would be manifest in any enterprise that purports to analyze LALT and BTUSA in relation to each other. We will evaluate the similarities and differences between these two liberation theologies by investigating the history of their encounter as a backdrop against which to scrutinize their mutual approaches to Christology, ecclesiology, eschatology and liberation.

The History of a Dialogical Encounter: From Suspicion to Mutual Support

Black theologians and Latin American theologians encountered each other for the first time in Geneva, Switzerland (May 1973), at a meeting intended to introduce liberation theology to the World Council of Churches.[2] This encounter was an important beginning to the conversation for Latin Americans and black North Americans.[3]

Although the meeting was organized to develop a dialogue between European and liberation theologies, both black and Latin American theologians were more interested in sharing with each other than with the Europeans. Hugo Assmann articulated the problem of their future dialogue when he stated that he felt that "incommunication" similar to that which he felt concerning non-Western persons in Latin America.[4] He indicated his commitment to honest dialogue when he asserted:

> We Latin Americans are still in the early stages of our search for Latin American identity. If you look in my library you will find books by German authors, Italian authors, Marx, Moltmann, etc. There is something false in this . . . something which is not Latin American. I would say to my friends in Black theology: I don't know how this dialogue with you can be improved, but it is more important than European theology for us Latin Americans. I don't want to destroy the connection with you. But I do want to reach a state of tension with you — a third kind of tension which is found more and more in the third world.[5]

In this statement, Assmann clearly acknowledged a source for the tension that would characterize the initial stages of this dialogue. However, he went on to affirm the need for a dialogical process as a means of encouraging alliances among those who represent the "poor and oppressed world" — persons from the First World as well as the Third World. It is these persons, Assmann asserts, who are "our real friends."[6] Cone acknowledged the difficulty of dialogue by pointing out that the question of social context was most significant because if LALT continued to define itself in relationship to Europe, and blacks dwelt in the world of the oppressed, communication would be nearly impossible. Concerning the claim of Black Theology that God is black, he went on to assert, "the more the question is explained, the more you realize that communication is not possible . . . because we live in two worlds: the world of the oppressed and the world of the oppressors; the world of the Black and the world of the white."[7] According to Cone, "Blacks left the Geneva symposium feeling that the dialogue between Latin American theologians and us had already begun to move from indifference (created largely by lack of knowledge) to mutual support."[8]

In some ways, this judgment was premature, for as we shall see, change is not easy to implement. Before we move on, however, it is important to highlight the important issues, as they surfaced at Geneva in 1973, that will shape our study of these two liberation traditions. There was an acknowledgment by both parties of the need for constructive dialogue between these two liberation theologies.[9] The group also recognized that the dialogue process would be difficult and full of tension, but that an alliance of Third World theologies of liberation could occur only by means of such tension-filled dialogue.

The next time the two encountered each other in a conference context was in August 1975 in Detroit, Michigan, at the first meeting of Theology in the Americas. The records of this meeting indicate that the real intention of the meeting was to introduce Latin American liberation theology to North Americans. In his opening address, Sergio Torres, a Chilean liberation theologian, acknowledged that some issues had emerged in the process of preparation for the conference, but he nevertheless proceeded to establish the structure of the conference as a North American response to the Latin American challenge.[10] The small number of blacks invited to participate led black theologians to conclude that here again the dialogue between black theologians and Latin American theologians of liberation was being marginalized on behalf of an encounter between Latin Americans and white North Americans.[11] At this meeting, the black theologian Herbert O. Edwards was given the opportunity to present a paper. In it he argued that the dimension of racial oppression was indispensable to understanding the particularity of the historical reality of the United States.[12] According to the interpretation of John Eagleson and Sergio Torres, who reported the taped recording of the proceeding:

> The Latin Americans, in particular, asked whether the Black theological reflection failed to emphasize sufficiently the necessary change in the overall system that produces racial, economic and cultural exploitation. Their feeling was that the insistence on racial oppression detracted from the global struggle.
>
> The Black theologians responded that racial oppression cannot be identified with any other kind of oppression and that the Latin Americans cannot comprehend the historical and sociological roots of Black oppression.[13]

Coming out of that conference, blacks felt that the Latin Americans were blinded by their own racism. The Latin Americans felt that blacks were blinded by their identity with and participation in capitalist North America. Suspicion of each other thus became a panic ingredient in the process of dialogue. Cone identified the source of black suspicion when he wrote:

> It was assumed by most Latin Americans and white North Americans that race oppression can best be understood in the context of class analysis ... the reason for our resistance to the Latin American emphasis on class analysis was our deep mistrust of the white religious left in North America whose past and present behavior in our communities contradicted the public affirmations of their solidarity with the struggles of poor people for freedom.[14]

Cone posited another reason also:

In addition to our distrust of the white religious left, we were also concerned about the failure of most Latin Americans to be open to the suggestion that they might have something to learn from our struggles for justice in the U.S. and from theologies emerging from those struggles.[15]

The relevance of Cone's words concerning this basic mistrust was borne out when Theology in the Americas sponsored its second major convocation in 1980, also in Detroit.[16] The structure and process of this conference were planned with the purpose of establishing coalitions organized around regional concerns within the United States, without any significant movement in the direction of fostering dialogue and alliance building among Third World persons at the conference.[17] The structure and process were subverted at the meeting by the formation of a coalition of interethnic and indigenous peoples, which empowered the restructuring of the organization in such a manner as to engender ongoing dialogue and alliance building among these groups. It is important to note that in his address at this 1980 conference, Gustavo Gutiérrez made his affirmation of that process clear:

Why do we sometimes have this impression that the Latin American theologies are more accepted by some groups than are Black, Indian, or Asian theologies of this country? Why?

Maybe it's because Latin America is a little farther away. But I must say clearly that we cannot be recognized theologians in this country if our sisters and brothers in this country are not also recognized.[18]

At least for Gutiérrez, to share theologies emerging from among the poor meant having the poor present to speak for themselves and focusing the dialogue between Latin America and North America on those who are actually oppressed. According to Cone, by 1977 the emerging hostility had been reduced by two of the more open Latin Americans, Sergio Torres and Gustavo Gutiérrez.

Subsequently, black theologians from the United States have been involved in an ongoing dialogue process with the Latin Americans in the context of the Ecumenical Association of Third World Theologians (hereafter referred to as EATWOT). This organization was formed explicitly for the purpose of fostering communication among Third World theologians.[19] James Cone, Enrique Dussel and Sergio Torres trace the beginnings of EATWOT to conversations which occurred in Louvain, Belgium, among some Latin Americans, Africans and Asians, in 1974.[20] Concerning the dialogue initiated in 1973, Cone, a consistent participant in the process, wrote:

The dialogue has been characterized by the attitudes of indifference, hostility, and mutual support. Although these three attitudes have

been present among some Latin and Black theologians during the
entire period of our dialogue, there have been occasions in which one
of the three has dominated the consciousness of most of the participants.[21]

These attitudes have all been a part of the history of the EATWOT
process, from its first major meeting in Tanzania, August 1976, to its most
recent in Nairobi, Kenya, 1992. Despite the fact that in 1973 some of the
Latin Americans had already accepted black Americans as a part of the
Third World, there was continuing discussion about the question of their
inclusion and participation. In Tanzania, according to Cone,

> Latin Americans were vehement in their rejection of North American
> Blacks as members of an association of third world theologians. They
> wanted to limit its meaning . . . to persons born and presently living
> in Asia, Africa and Latin America. But Africans (and some Asians)
> were even more vehement in their insistence on the inclusion of North
> American Blacks, because Africans said the black world is one. They
> contended that the third world referred to the condition of depend-
> ence, a situation of exploitation and oppression.[22]

The final communique of the Tanzania meeting confirms Cone's position
when it identifies membership of the association as being "for members of
the dispersion from Africa, Asia and Latin America involved in some form
of doing theology."[23]

At the second meeting of EATWOT, in Accra, Ghana (December 1977),
the Africans encouraged the participation of North American blacks by
inviting eight black delegates.[24] In Sri Lanka (January 1979), the Asians
limited the number of non-Asian participants to a few fraternal delegates.
At the meeting, James Cone was invited to be a member of EATWOT.[25]
Asians, Africans and black Americans supported one another in their resistance to the Latin Americans. By 1979 the Latin Americans in EATWOT,
now sufficiently aware of their lack of attention to the issue of race, planned
a conference to be held in Jamaica as a preparatory stage to the fourth
meeting of EATWOT in Brazil the next year. The significance of this meeting lies in the fact that it reflected the growing awareness of each other's
realities through an effective dialogue process, and movement from igno-
rance to knowledge could lead only to openness. Cone wrote, concerning
this tension-filled dialogue:

> We have moved from indifference and hostility to serious dialogue
> on race and class with the expressed purpose of supporting each oth-
> er's theological projects. I hope that we can keep sharply before us
> the history of our eight years of dialogue so that we will not be

tempted to make the mistake of the past and thereby create hostility and indifferent attitudes toward each other.[26]

Liberation theologies emerge from the victims of oppression, who often have few resources for encountering each other. It is not surprising, therefore, that suspicion and mistrust had to be overcome in order to foster a deeper engagement. The preparatory meeting previously mentioned was held in December 1979, in Jamaica, and sponsored by the Latin American membership of EATWOT. Although the purpose of the meeting was to prepare the Latin Americans for a serious discussion of racism at the São Paulo meeting of EATWOT (1980), Cone noted that, "Most blacks left Jamaica having grave doubts about the possibility of Latin American liberation theologians taking racism seriously."[27] This attitude was present also in the EATWOT meeting in São Paulo, Brazil, where Africans, African-Americans and Afro-Caribbean participants noted the absence of blacks and Indians at the meeting and expressed concern that their absence was reflective of an oppression that emerges primarily from the existence of racism.[28]

Cornel West, a philosopher of religion who was a North American black participant in both the Jamaica consultation and São Paulo dialogue, addressed the heart of the matter when he wrote:

The cultural gap between Europeanized Latin Americans on the one hand, and Blacks and Indians on the other, holds not only at the level of evangelization in the Comunidades de Base or of the mobilization of political parties, but also at the level of armed struggle.[29]

Despite these moments of suspicion and conflict, the black theologians from the United States and the Latin American liberation theologians in EATWOT have been committed to an ongoing dialogue which has proven to be supportive of learning and growth for both black and Latin American theologians of liberation.

The São Paulo meeting of the Ecumenical Association of Third World Theologians (1980) had merely confirmed the doubts of black theologians, though Cone suggests that the initiatives in the direction of integrating racism and sexism are indications that there may be hope in the future.[30] He concludes his assessment of the São Paulo meeting:

Despite their advances on racism and sexism at São Paulo, there was little evidence that Blacks, women, and indigenous populations made any significant impact on the nature of Latin American liberation theology. . . . It seemed that the concerns of Blacks, women, and the indigenous people were peripheral for most Latin Americans, and their conspicuous absence from the plenary sessions during the discussion of these issues confirmed this suspicion for many non-Latin American participants.[31]

EATWOT has held several meetings since São Paulo, and the final statements of the conferences (New Delhi [1981], Geneva [1983]) reflect a deepening appreciation of the problem of racism.[32] The final statement emerging from the Geneva meeting states:

Racism has two aspects. The first and most evident is the dehumanization and subjugation of persons because of their color and physiognomy in order to exploit their labor. But the second aspect goes beyond rational economic exploitation and takes the form of an odious ideology. Whites project phobic characteristics onto persons of color, dehumanizing themselves in the process. Racist ideology has penetrated the dominant theologies, which in turn have legitimized it.[33]

The Latin American liberation theologists themselves have acknowledged the earlier shortcomings of their analysis of oppression in Latin America, have organized specific processes for incorporating the issues of race and culture within EATWOT and have organized ongoing constitutions that will facilitate input from blacks and indigenous people.[34] Another aspect of this deepening awareness is to be seen in the Latin Americans' turn to the culture and spirituality of the poor in Latin America. An important part of this commitment has been manifested in the continuing existence of specific projects within Latin America organized around black and indigenous peoples.

James Cone, the most consistent North American black participant in this dialogical encounter, has observed that "the Latin Americans have come a long way since Geneva 1973," and is hopeful that the future will be one of deepening understanding and appreciation of the common ground between these two liberation traditions.[35]

A crucial part of the history of the encounter between BTUSA and LALT has been the role of Cuban theologians, and Gustavo Gutiérrez and Sergio Torres. At a conference on "Evangelization and Politics" held in Matanzas, Cuba, in 1979, it has been reported by Cone that "the most significant and fruitful dialogue between Latin and Black theologians occurred."[36] Although this was not the first encounter between BTUSA and Cuban theologians, Cone indicates that the level of openness on both sides was greatly enhanced by the active involvement of the Cubans, who "have developed a slightly different methodological approach to both theology and race, an approach open, if not similar, to black theologians."[37] Cone explains this phenomena by stating:

Cuban theologians ... take the race question seriously, and this is due to the fact that black people are taken seriously in the context of the larger society. The Cuban revolution affected deeply the relations between blacks and whites, and the positive consequences are found in the openness of Cuban people to face head-on the race question in their society.[38]

The Cubans, Cone declares, have been influential on this question because the Latin Americans view Cuba as a concrete symbol of liberation and therefore "are naturally open to hearing what the Cubans have to say."[39] The Cubans' openness to the contributions of African-Americans was manifested in their continuing dialogue with the members of the Black Theology Project, particularly in 1984, when a theological homage to Martin Luther King, Jr., was sponsored in Havana, Cuba. During the encounter between the representatives of the Black Theology Project from the United States and Cuban clergy, laypersons and theologians, a common commitment was affirmed to a theological perspective that supports the various liberation projects against oppression.[40] Concerning the question of race in Cuba, José Carniado, the Director of the Department of Religious Affairs of the Cuban government, noted that while legislation had been passed outlawing racial discrimination since 1959, it had been difficult to eradicate racism from the point of view of culture.

The members of the Black Theology Project have also been a part of an ongoing process of dialogue with Latin Americans through an encounter in Brazil in 1988 with theologians, activists and laypersons active in the struggle against racism in Brazil.

This brief review of the history of the encounter between BTUSA and LALT confirms the view that there are important commonalities that distinguish these two schools of liberation theology. This dialogue is the primary reason that an encounter earlier characterized by suspicion has been turned into one in which mutual support and trust exist.

The Latin Americans, on the one hand, would naturally have been suspicious of any theology emerging from North America, because North America represented the imperialist extension of neocolonialism into Latin America. Their suspicion would be further strengthened if the theologians in question, black theologians, did not appear to have a critique of the economic structures that were responsible for the dependence and underdevelopment of Latin America. On the other hand, black theologians from the United States would have been suspicious of any theology emerging from Latin America, espoused by "white" Latin Americans, which subordinated the race question to class struggle and depended on philosophical and theological categories that had their origin in Europe. Although it was immediately evident to both BTUSA and LALT that important commonalities existed between them, it was also evident that significant differences would have to be negotiated in their work together. The history of their encounter itself—from suspicion to mutual support—will be the backdrop against which we will evaluate similarities and differences in their approaches to the theological task. Clues to the response to the question, "What can BTUSA and LALT say to each other?" can be discerned not only in their dialogue, but by scrutinizing the similarities and differences in their theological methods and contexts.

Methodological Similarities and Differences

A distinction between "methodological" and "contextual" similarities and differences is utilized to point out those similarities and differences which respectively can be attributed to theological method, on the one hand, and to contextual differences, on the other. Methodological choices are indissolubly linked with the historical context out of which they emerge. Nevertheless, this distinction between methodological and contextual similarities and differences will provide the basis for a discussion of the nuances between BTUSA and LALT. What are the methodological similarities and differences of BTUSA and LALT?

BTUSA and LALT affirm the need to define a new methodological approach to the theological task that rejects the theological methodologies of the dominant Euro-American theological traditions.[41] While they acknowledge the necessity of revising concepts that appear in the dominant theological tradition, BTUSA and LALT assert the need to make theology accountable to the victims of oppression. Therefore, BTUSA and LALT agree that the central focus of the Gospel is liberation. They affirm that liberation is the aim of God's activity in history.

Thus, theological method must be revised in the light of the struggle for liberation. Liberation is holistic, extending to all dimensions of human existence. The theological enterprise is to be reoriented, so that the quest for socio-economic, political and cultural liberation is conceived as an essential aspect of the Christian message. In order to be accountable to the underside — the poor, the oppressed and the marginalized — those who dominate the oppressed should not be the ones to determine the theological methods of BTUSA and LALT.

Even though theologians in both camps agree that liberation is the central focus of the Gospel, there has nevertheless been some disagreement concerning the exact meaning of the term. In its earlier stages, BTUSA stressed the religio-cultural dimension in the political struggle for liberation. Derived from African-American religio-cultural sources, liberation was viewed holistically. Nevertheless, BTUSA did not earlier stress a coherent critique of capitalism. Later, under the influence of its critics, both internally (the increasing class tensions within the black community) and externally (LALT), black theologians began to stress the relationship between oppression based on race and the capitalist economic structures of American society. The reason for the black theologians' lack of emphasis on the socio-economic dimension is grounded in its context.

LALT, in its earlier stages, stressed the socio-economic dimension of the political struggle for liberation. Its definition of liberation was derived originally from its discourse with Hegel, Freud, Feuerback and Marx—the masters of European philosophy whom Latin American theologians had studied in Europe.[42] While they, like BTUSA, also depended upon the Bible, which was influential in leading them to affirm holistic liberation, they nevertheless did not develop a comprehensive view of liberation that extended into the religio-cultural dimensions of racist oppression.

While Gutiérrez, Míguez Bonino and Assmann all acknowledge the importance of cultural liberation from the hegemony of European ideas, sensibilities and values, scrutiny of their work suggests that the task of grounding LALT in Latin America is a development that was emphasized later. Due to the challenge of both the poor in Latin America and BTUSA, some Latin American liberation theologians have begun to look carefully at the religions and cultures of the people, and to view race as an indispensable element of their social analysis.[43] The reason, though, for LALT's lack of emphasis on the religio-cultural traditions of the oppressed, and race, is grounded in its context.

Another aspect of BTUSA and LALT that manifests methodological similarities and differences lies in their respective Christologies. BTUSA and LALT agree that the God of the Bible identifies with the poor and the oppressed. God's ultimate work for the oppressed is that God historically has opted to be with them in their suffering and to struggle with them for liberation. The concept of God, in BTUSA and LALT, is one that reflects a divine affirmation of the humanity of the poor and oppressed ones of the world and legitimates their struggle as central to God's redemptive activity. This God is made manifest in the suffering and oppressed one (Jesus Christ), who sides with the oppressed ones in history and is their liberator. Emphasis is placed, christologically, upon the explication of a gospel which shows that in Christ God is revealed as the one who is the liberator of the oppressed, a co-sufferer alongside the oppressed and a co-creator of the new society.[44]

Gutiérrez's challenge to recover the "scourged Christs" in popular Latin American religion and BTUSA's emphasis on the black Christ are indicative of the common christological interests of black theologians and Latin Americans who presuppose a prior commitment to the oppressed. In specific methodological terms, the norm of BTUSA and LALT is Jesus Christ the Liberator. Despite the designation of this theological norm, the Latin Americans and black theologians insist that the context for verifying this claim is not to be found in dogmatic formulations, but in the praxis of liberation christological images of the poor. The Latin Americans' earlier efforts reflected an inability to face the poor to allow them to speak christologically. Alfred Reid, a Jamaican delegate to the São Paulo (1980) meeting of EATWOT, raised this question when he said:

We have used the words "people" and "the poor" over and over again. Do we mean the blacks, the Indians, the women? The cultures of the

Indian nations are absolutely fundamental in the hemisphere. Are we satisfied that they speak in our liturgy and theology? Not—please note—not that they are spoken for, or spoken about, but that they speak for themselves and speak to all of us as we speak to them . . . but are you convinced that the church has really learned from them? . . . It is our belief that "the people" and "the poor" need to be defined more concretely and specifically.[45]

Again, this deficiency in LALT can best be understood in relationship to the context that shaped its development.

A third methodological context for observing similarity and difference is found in BTUSA and LALT's common commitment to the use of social analysis in theology. Due to the a priori commitment to the oppressed community, which entails ideological suspicion, BTUSA and LALT affirm the use of social analysis as a means of clarifying ideological presuppositions and commitments, as well as a means of mediating between religious commitment and concrete praxis. BTUSA, from its inception, asserted itself as a theology that rejected white theological norms and affirmed the history, culture and experience of the victims of white racism—black people. Ideological suspicion, while not a term utilized by the earlier black theologians, was clearly present in their unwillingness to allow the rules of theology to be set by whites.[46]

Thus, the framework, albeit unspecified, of social analysis that was to inform BTUSA was definitively shaped by its perspective on race. Black Power, as the contemporary manifestation of the black Christ in the struggle for black liberation, was the radical affirmation of the worthiness of black humanity, history and culture, and highlighted the significance of this history for authentic Christian existence.

While LALT currently would affirm its a priori commitment to the religio-cultural traditions of the oppressed in their situation, their initial insistence on the priority of class analysis was problematic from the perspective of blacks, native peoples and women, who themselves constituted the oppressed in Latin America. The Latin Americans' initial insistence on the primacy of class analysis subordinated the problems of gender and race oppression to class analysis. Again, the methodological similarity—the commitment to the use of social analysis—is also reflective of the differences between these two theologies.

The eschatological dimension of BTUSA and LALT is a fourth area in which similarity and difference are to be seen. Both acknowledge a unitary view of history in which the *civitas dei* is inextricably linked with the *civitas terrena*. But, here again, while LALT's description of its eschatology demonstrates its dependence, not only on the Bible, but on Hegel, Kant and Marx, BTUSA evolves its description, primordially, from the African worldview, which views God's actions as always historical and which rejected the classical dualism of nature and spirit, profane and sacred. For black theologians, religion and politics were a part of the same web of social existence. The Latin Americans' explication of the eschatological significance of Christian faith suggests that Hegel's insight that "growth comes through struggle" is of decisive significance for them. Despite the fact that both agree on the necessity of linking God's Kingdom with human struggle, the evolution of their respective traditions reflect in, the one case, emphasis on truth derived from the stories of the poor, and in the other case, truth derived for a particular philosophical description of human existence.

Lastly, both BTUSA and LALT agree that liberating praxis is the meta-criterion by which theological commitments are evaluated, and seek to challenge the church to measure its practice in relation to it. Two inter-related consequences are: the highlighting of praxis as the context for evaluating the truth of one's theological claims and practices, and the issuance of a challenge to reform ecclesial structures or to create new ones.

Theology of liberation, Gutiérrez has noted, is "theological reasoning that is verified — made to be true — in a real, fertile involvement with the liberation process."[47] The liberationists' claim that Christ is the liberator is to be actualized within the historical dialectic of struggle between oppressor and oppressed. Although the Latin Americans elaborated this insight earlier than the BTUSA, black theologians also affirm this methodological point. Further, and here we note both similarity and difference, the evolution of basic Christian communities in Latin America evidences the ecclesiogenesis that arose from the need to develop new ecclesial structures responsive to the needs of the poor and oppressed.[48]

Within the predominantly Catholic Latin American situation, the emergence of a church of the people, in contrast to a church of hierarchy, is an indication of a willingness, at the popular level, to reorient the values and structures of the church. While black theologians acknowledge the need to revise the structures of the church in order to make it more sensitive to the liberation struggle, BTUSA emerged from a strong tradition that has for 200 years defined its historic vocation as the liberation of black people. While Latin Americans are essentially creating new structures, black theologians are able to refer back to a distinctive black Christian interpretation of faith and to a historical Christian community.

The methodological similarities and differences disclosed in these two theologies suggest that BTUSA and LALT can complement each other's projects as they continue to dialogue with each other and come to a greater awareness of each other. Furthermore, our investigation of the methodological similarities and differences and the history of the encounter between BTUSA and LALT indicate the necessity of scrutinizing differences and similarities that have been contextually determined.

Contextual Similarities and Differences

BTUSA and LALT are both liberation theologies that emerged in contexts of political struggles against exploitation and oppression. They are both committed to transformative praxis that would change the socio-eco-nomic, political, religious and cultural inequities in their societies. It is the Latin American theologians' position that the gross inequities which engen-der poverty, dependence and underdevelopment in Latin America can be traced to their basic cause: neocolonial imperialism as the extension of the capitalist world economy, and the inevitable class division which results from it.

In the USA, black theologians contend, the gross inequities and oppres-sion of the black community can be traced to its fundamental cause: white supremacy and its partner, racism. Although both traditions acknowledge the need for political liberation, the difference over their respective empha-ses on class and race has been a source of tension in the past and continues to be an area in which both BTUSA and LALT need to do further work together. This important difference is a consequence of the historical con-text of each theology and is indispensable to any discussion of continued dialogue and cooperation. Despite James Cone's positive assessment that the dialogue in EATWOT has led from indifference to mutual support,[49] both theologies have affirmed the necessity of plumbing the experiences of the oppressed in order to unearth the instruments of liberation. Yet the black and indigenous contribution to the published writings of LALT is somewhat scarce. Again, both have noted the importance of class analysis and economic critique of capitalism, yet this emphasis is still relatively minor in the published writings of the black theology movement in the United States. James Cone has noted that this is the main question that has emerged in their dialogue with each other. He writes:

> The main question has been: What is the relationship between race and class oppression? Because the Latin Americans are Marxists, they emphasize class oppression, almost to the exclusion of race oppres-sion. In as much as black theologians live in the white racist society of North America, with a heritage of two hundred years of white capitalist oppression, it is not likely that they will ignore cultural oppression as imputed by white racism.[50]

While important contextual similarities exist between BTUSA and LALT, it is evident that their differences on this issue must be accounted for and can contribute to a common enterprise of liberation.

Two differences that have been accentuated are (1) BTUSA's emphasis on the religio-cultural dimension relative to the liberation struggle and its relative inattentiveness to the development of a comprehensive social anal-ysis of the relationship between racism and capitalist structures, and (2) LALT's emphasis on the importance of Marxist analysis and its relatively inadequate attention to the issues of the cultural manifestations of racism.

BTUSA's stress on the religio-cultural traditions of African-Americans is based on the fact that blacks have derived instruments from these traditions that have historically contributed to their struggle. BTUSA, from its inception, was antiracist and sought to reject theological categories that supported white supremacy. BTUSA, like other forms of black radicalism, emerged to challenge the racist institutions, values, and sensibilities that had defined black existence.

Concomitantly, BTUSA affirmed its independence from white theology, as well as its commitment to the distinctive contributions of a black faith perspective that defined itself according to the black liberation struggle. Thus, BTUSA stressed from the beginning its connection to and affirmations of the history, religions and cultures of African-American people. James Cone, for example, is insistent that there can be no Black Theology of liberation that does not take seriously the history, culture and religion of oppressed people.[51]

The assertion that "Jesus Christ is black" is the theological affirmation of the importance of black life. BTUSA referenced its interpretation of the meaning of the Gospel to a long history of activism that integrated the black freedom struggle and the Gospel in a distinctive and dynamic way. Thus, when black theologians encountered the perspective of the Latin Americans, which tended to downplay the culture and religion of the people, it was not surprising that they would be cautious and suspicious. Those who view their religio-cultural independence as crucial to their struggle will be cautious vis-à-vis dialogue partners who are not explicit in their commitment to such values. Due to the context of white North American racism and BTUSA's development as a challenge to white racism, it was inevitable that emphasis would be placed on the religio-cultural dimension of liberation.

The lack of attention to the development of a social analysis that linked racism to a critique of capitalism is not so easily accounted for, although this too is contextually grounded. It should be noted, however, that it would be inaccurate to say that Black Theology was bereft of social analysis.[52] Black theologians, in asserting a radical antiracist stance, employed the dominant paradigms of the black community.

In proposing a black nationalist Christian perspective, Albert Cleage was appropriating one of the two prevailing ideologies that dominated the black communities' response to white racism.[53] In arguing for "participation at all levels of the life of our nation," those who affirmed the Black Power Statement of 1966 betrayed their integrationist tendencies.[54] Both the nationalist and the integrationist response to white exercise of racist power had limitations.[55] Cone's later words capture the point well: "We need to do more than try to be assimilated into white American society or to separate ourselves from it. Neither alternative is possible or even desirable. We need a broader perspective."[56] Any analysis of the structures of racist domination based on race exclusively was insufficient to comprehend racism in the modern world.

In 1973, black theologians and Latin American liberation theologians encountered each other and began an association that would decisively influence the directions that their respective traditions would take in the future. It was during this period that some black theologians began to turn to a substantive critique of capitalism and to explore Marxist analysis as a viable tool for understanding socio-economic reality. This fact raises the questions: Why did black theologians begin to critique capitalism only at this point? Why did it take so long? Was it their encounter with Latin American liberation theologians, along with their vision of the new society, that forced them to sharpen their tools of analysis? Why have black theologians, generally, remained disengaged in the development of critical thought vis-à-vis the capitalist economy of the United States? Have black theologians evidenced a broadening of their perspective on the nature and extent of oppression? These are some of the questions we must explore in order to grasp the direction of Black Theology at present.

In 1976, the National Conference of Black Churchmen issued a statement on Black Theology that affirmed:

Black Theology does not shrink from the exploration of socialistic alternatives to the idolatrous worship of the dollar, the chaotic individualism and corroding materialism of the American economic and political system. Black Theology affirms that "the earth is the Lord's" and opposes any politics which are based on a theory of adherence to absolute self-interest, the precedence of private to public ownership, and the ascendancy of the profit motive and property rights over the public good.[57]

The following year, in Atlanta, in a statement accepted by the National Conference of the Black Theology Project, black theologians asserted:

Exploitative, profit-oriented capitalism is a way of ordering life fundamentally alien to human value in general and to black humanity in particular. Racism and capitalism have set the stage for the despoliation of natural and human resources all around the world. . . . and political power systems that prevent us from managing the reality of our everyday lives.[58]

At that same meeting, James Cone presented a paper in which he claimed:

Black theologians and church people must now move beyond a mere reaction to white racism in America and begin to extend our vision of a new socially constructed humanity for the whole inhabited world. We must be concerned with the quality of human life not only in the ghettoes of American cities but also in Africa, Asia and Latin America. Since humanity is one, and cannot be isolated into racial and national groups, there will be no freedom for anyone until there is freedom for all.[59]

From 1975 onward, it was evident that some black theologians had begun to push beyond mere criticism. It is evident from these statements emerging out of NCBC and the Black Theology Project that black theologians were moving beyond mere criticism and were addressing the major deficiency in their theological work that had been noted by Latin American liberation theologians: the lack of critique of capitalism and imperialism. The easy inference has been that encounter with the Third World outside United States borders has been responsible for the broadening of the perspective of Black Theology. But is this so? Why, for instance, did black theologians, in their commitment to recover the radical black tradition, not recover the radical anticapitalist posture in the black community? Why did black theologians not follow through on the anticapitalist stance of some of the young radicals in the Civil Rights and Black Power movements? What can account for BTUSA's cautious attitude toward Marxist social analysis as a means of comprehensively linking race and class exploitation with a critique of capitalism? It is true that the encounter with the Latin Americans and with their explicitly Marxist social analysis compelled the black theologians to consciously clarify their analysis of oppression, but it is also true that the black community had, all along, within it resources that would facilitate such an analysis. The real question is: Why had black theologians not explored those possibilities prior to that encounter?

The answer to these questions is that there are contextual reasons for BTUSA's initial inability to critique capitalism, as well as the black theologians' initial suspicion concerning the Latin Americans' stress on the primacy of class analysis.

First, the black theologians' inability to develop an explicit critique of capitalism based on Marxist analysis is grounded, contextually, in the fact that Black Theology evolved among black clergy and activists who had been trained in American universities and seminaries where, until recently, Marxist ideas were marginalized and devalued. American society, in general, had developed a deep-rooted anti-Marxist stance that extended into its educational institutions. Many of the clergy involved in the early Black Theology movement would not have been widely read in Marxist theory, or would have assumed an anti-Marxist stance derived from the broader society. It is worth noting that Martin Luther King, Jr., did encounter Marxism, had read and evaluated it, and determined that it contained basic insights into the weakness of capitalism and challenged the Christian conscience, but had rejected its emphasis on metaphysical materialism, ethical relativism and totalitarianism.[60]

Second, the black theologians' inability to develop a critique of capitalism based on Marxist analysis was based in their unclarity concerning a coherent vision of the new society. Cone expresses his belief that:

The failure of black preachers and theologians to incorporate Marxist class analysis into their theological discourse and church projects is due partly to their assumption that the problem of racism can be solved in the United States without a socialist transformation in the political economy. Apart from racist practices of social, economic and political institutions, most blacks have assumed that American society is essentially just and consequently has the best of all possible political systems.[61]

The two prevailing ideologies which shaped the African-American community's political commitments—integration and nationalism—have not generated a coherent analysis and critique of American society that incorporated race, class and imperialism. As noted earlier, the latter portions of the lives of Martin Luther King, Jr. and Malcolm X hint, tantalizingly, at the possibilities of a rapproachment in perspectives that might have reshaped the black liberation movement of the 1960s.

Nevertheless, BTUSA did not, initially, follow through on this possibility. It is evident that the radical Black Power activists of the sixties were critical of capitalism and affirmed the right of black self-determination, but this was not supported by a coherent social analysis. "The Black Manifesto," for example, clearly indicated that:

> There could be no separation of the problems of racism from the problems of our economic, political and cultural degradation . . . Ironically, some of the most militant black nationalists, as they call themselves, have been the first to jump on the bandwagon of black capitalism. They are pimps, black power pimps and fraudulent leaders, and the people must be educated to understand that any black man or Negro who is advocating a perpetuation of capitalism inside the United States is in fact seeking not only his ultimate destruction and death but is contributing to the continuous exploitation of black people all around the world.[62]

But the anticapitalist vein was not pursued further in the writings of the black theologians publishing at the time. What did it mean for NCBC to support in principle the demands of the National Black Economic Development Conference, in light of the anticapitalist posture taken in the manifesto? At the third annual convocation of NCBC in Oakland, California, a statement was issued that called blacks to an unequivocal commitment to the wretched of the earth, and hoped that "through them the world might be saved from the selfishness, greed and subjugation which has characterized the centuries-old hegemony of the white, Anglo-Saxon, European civilizations of the West."[63] These statements clearly indicate that, at least as early as 1969, black religious thinkers were making the connections between racial oppression in the United States, capitalist exploitation, and

American imperialism in Africa. This should have indicated to black theologians the need for a more comprehensive social analysis.

The same questions can be raised about the black theologians' failure to give substantive meaning to Black Power. It was evident to many that blacks needed to have control over their lives, but barring a mass return to Africa by blacks or the division of the country in order to create a black nation, the precise content of Black Power was ambiguous. For many, Black Power meant black capitalism, and black capitalism simply meant a preservation of the status quo, except that blacks would control a larger piece of the pie. The distinction between cultural liberation and socio-political liberation was not clarified.

Black Power meant self-determination and control over the institutions, values, and sensibilities of the black community, but it was never clear how that would be achieved in a "pluralistic" society in which blacks were a minority—a society where hegemony of monopoly capitalism was complete. These issues should have demonstrated to black theologians the need for a more profound social analysis in light of the inadequacy of their inordinate dependence on race analysis, prior to their encounter with Latin Americans. As it was, the Latin American theologians stimulated investigation into an area that BTUSA had been hesitant to explore, since black theologians, too, were caught in the web of assumptions to which Cone has previously referred.[64]

Third, BTUSA was based on the black experience, which has historically viewed as suspect any ideology or viewpoint that did not incorporate their primary concerns as a central component of its perspective.

Blacks have always known that the fabric and structure of American society were not right. It is not surprising, therefore, to find black men and women calling for this unjust society to be transformed. As early as the late nineteenth century, leaders such as Reverend Ransom, James Holly, George Woodbey, and Peter Clark were espousing the tenets of socialism as a viable option for black revolutionaries and using economic analysis as a critical tool. Holly understood the economic deprivation that blacks experienced as a consequence of capitalism. He wrote:

> There is no Gospel morality in our organized modern industry, and therefore offerings from such ill-gotten riches are made as if God could be bribed by the mammon of inequity. But such gifts, amassed by grinding the face of necessitous poor, and heartlessly wrung out of the blood and sweat of careworn toilers, are already smitten with the curse of heaven in answer to the sighs and groans of the oppressed laborers that mount up sighs, crying for vengeance on the capricious oppressors.[65]

Blacks participated in meetings and demonstrations organized by white socialists. This was not due to any specific programs, however, but to the fact that blacks were looking for any group that would take up their cause. In fact, common goals and shared strategies were not to emerge; white American socialism foundered on the race question. As Phillip Foner has written:

> The failure of American socialism to exert any influence in the black community is manifest in the fact that the histories of the First International in America lists not a single Negro member and only a handful of activities associated with blacks. Given the isolationist tendencies of the German-American Marxists, the absence of guidance from their theoretical leaders, and the chasm between the European-born urban radicals and the recently emancipated Southern-born blacks, it is probably hardly surprising that the issues crucial for blacks in post-Civil War America were never of any major concern for American Marxists.[66]

Peter Clark, "the first black American to identify himself publicly with socialism," resigned after a long and distinguished career in the Socialist Labor Party because "the welfare of the Negro is my controlling political motive, but the SLP rarely concerned itself with the welfare of the Negro."[67] Clark remained a socialist, but was content to wait until there arose a socialist movement that would make the interests of blacks primary. Rev. George Woodbey also wrote extensively on socialism and the struggle for black freedom.

Although black thinkers could see that blacks could gain a great deal from a transformation of society, they viewed the socialist cause with suspicion because its actions did not follow its rhetoric. This suspicion was borne out when socialist workers refused to allow blacks into white unions and union organizers made the pragmatic choice to deny social equality in the South rather than antagonize white Southern workers.

For blacks, the "Negro question" always assumed primary importance. For Marxist ideologues, the "Negro question" was first an economic question and only secondarily a race issue, and it became crucial only when black socialists forced the issue to the fore. There were, Foner states, "constant efforts made by black reformers to get their white co-workers to reject and oppose racism, both within the reform movement itself and throughout society in general."[68] These efforts often failed.

These struggles are reflected in the continuing attempts by black intellectuals to formulate ideological alliances that would contribute to the struggle for black freedom. The writings of Richard Wright, W. E. B. DuBois, and others embodied a shifting back and forth between the ideologies that were available to them. Foner points out that DuBois tried to explain why socialists had not earned more support from blacks:

> Again and again, he mentioned that in their platforms and literature the socialists referred to the Negro only "vaguely and as an after-

thought." He added rather bitterly, since this was hardly the first time he had made the point: "If American socialism cannot stand for the American Negro, the American Negro will not stand for American socialism."[69]

DuBois, though sympathetic to socialism, saw that the primary concern of black Americans was their freedom and well-being, and knew that they would not support any movement that did not approach this concern with utmost seriousness.

In *Rebellion or Revolution?* Harold Cruse, a leading black social critic, scrutinizes internal debate among blacks concerning ideology, and posits that black intellectuals were unable to free themselves from the white ideas prevalent in the dominant culture. He argues that black socialists follow their white companions in not taking their socialist ideas more meaningfully in relationship to the particularities of American society:

American Marxists have never been able to understand the implications of the Negro's position in the social structure of the United States. They have no more been able to see the Negro as having revolutionary potentialities in his own right, than European Marxists could see the revolutionary aspirations of their colonials as being independent of, and not subordinate to, their own. Western Marxism has no adequate revolutionary theory for the Negro. The belief of some American Marxists in a political alliance of the Negroes and whites is based on a superficial assessment of the Negro's social status: the notion that the Negro is an integral part of the American nation in the same way as is the white working class. Although this idea of Negro and white unity is convenient in describing the American multinational and multiracial makeup, it cannot withstand a deeper analysis of the components which made American society what it is.[70]

Marxian socialism leaves questions centrally important to blacks unanswered. What guarantee do African-Americans have that socialism would assure racial equality any more than capitalist democracy does? Would socialism mean the assimilation of the African-Americans into the dominant racial group? According to Cruse, "The failure to deal adequately with the Negro question is the chief cause of American Marxism's ultimate alienation from the vital stream of American life."[71]

The fact that socialist thinkers have consistently bypassed the cultural issue in America has contributed to the distrust that exists today. For blacks, the problem of racism is at the central core of the American problem. Marxist persistence in subsuming this issue led to continual infighting among both white and black socialists, and has created insurmountable difficulties for blacks who espouse socialist ideas but simultaneously see the need to particularize Marxist ideology for the American social context.

Blacks have been reluctant to commit themselves to socialism as a viable option because of this persistent myopia on the part of white American socialists. This has been especially true due to the marginal status of blacks and the fact that the need to survive dictates that they assume a certain degree of pragmatism when living in America. Thus, with the rejection of socialism by the dominant society, it becomes even more difficult for blacks, who are living on the very edge of American social reality, to involve themselves in another marginal group that seems to have little hope of success. BTUSA's initial inability to evolve a coherent social analysis and suspicion concerning the inadequacies of Marxist analysis is contextually based on a historical experience of the inadequacies of the white American socialist movement with regard to racism, and the need to find a framework that viewed race as a central component within itself.

Fourth, the history of the communist movement in America has consistently reflected an inability to separate the movement from the racist tendencies of American society. Pro-white biases informed the racial perspective, practices and strategies of the Socialist Workers Party.[72] Therefore, blacks have evolved a suspicion of Marxism based on their historical experiences of these movements.

The fifth reason for BTUSA's indifference to Marxist analysis is based on the marginal status of both the black community and Marxism in America. A marginalized and oppressed people are not likely to look for the instruments of liberation in another marginalized group. Cone affirms this when he asserts that: "The negative attitude toward Marxism in the black community and church is . . . linked with the anticommunist attitude of the white church and the marginal status of Marxism in American society."[73]

The sixth reason for black theologians' indifference to Marxist analysis must be attributed to the class character of black religious thinkers, who invariably were a part of the black bourgeois class.[74] Despite this weakness, however, James Cone, the most prolific black theologian, is quite insistent that black theologians need to begin to utilize Marxist social analysis as a useful instrument in the black struggle for freedom. His more recent work reflects his own commitment to the development of a comprehensive analytical method that incorporates an analysis of the diverse aspects of the problem of racial oppression.

Another reason for black unwillingness to view the Marxist perspective as a valuable instrument of liberation has been set forth by Manning Marable in his discussion of factors that shape black political commitments. He writes:

> The language of black politics has always been conditioned by the idiom of the church. Opposition to Marxism and socialism often comes from black preachers and those most influenced by them. Atheism could never be popular among a peasant and working-class people

whose nationality and identity were forged in part through faith in churches and a just God.[75]

All these reasons have militated against black willingness to trust Marxist/socialist revolutionaries, and are fundamental in black theologians' mistrust of Latin American liberation theologians. This, however, does not alleviate the responsibility of black theologians to develop an adequate analysis of monopoly capitalism in the United States. It is at this point that Cone has rightly stated:

I reject dogmatic Marxism that reduces every contradiction to class analysis and thus ignores racism as a legitimate point of departure in the process of liberation. There are racist Marxists as there are racist capitalists, and we must struggle against both. But we must be careful not to reject the Marxists' social analysis simply because we do not like the vessels that the message comes in. If we do that, then it is hard to explain how we can remain Christians in view of the white vessels in which the Gospel was first introduced to us.[76]

Racial oppression will always be the point of departure for those who experience its debilitating consequences. To acknowledge the interconnectedness of racism with other forces of global exploitation will enhance BTUSA. The Latin American liberation theologians have been persistent in challenging black theology in this regard.

In summary, BTUSA's emphasis on the primacy of race, and its insistence that liberation theology must evolve the instruments of liberation from the experiences of oppressed people, is a consequence of its contextual grounding in the racist United States. Concomitantly, BTUSA's initial suspicion concerning the Latin Americans' emphasis on the primacy of class analysis and Marxism, as well as its inability to incorporate a critique of capitalism within a coherent social analysis, are additional consequences of the influence of its context.

Similarly, the Latin Americans' emphasis on Marxism, the primacy of class analysis and the earlier inability to incorporate the experiences of the poor blacks, natives and women in Latin America into their theology was contextually determined. Why did not the Latin Americans give attention to the problem of race in their earlier writing, given the presence of great numbers of blacks and natives in Latin America? The answer to this question lies in an investigation of the context from which LALT emerged and in scrutiny of the Latin Americans' use of Marxist analysis. In order to evaluate the Latin Americans' appropriation of Marxism and its role in defining their emphases, it is necessary to inquire specifically into the nature and extent of the LALT commitment to Marxism.

Any discussion of LALT appropriation must acknowledge that Latin American liberation theologians have undergone some significant changes in their perspective on Marxism. Gutiérrez, Míguez Bonino and Assmann all utilized Marxist categories in their earlier writings, with varying degrees of emphasis, but, as Arthur McGovern has noted in his analysis of their work, it is Assmann who seemed most Marxist.[77] In response to the question, How do liberation theologians use Marxist analysis? McGovern responds:

> For all the controversy over use of Marxist analysis in liberation theology, I have yet to find any specifically Marxist studies of Latin America that serves as guides to liberation theology analysis. One finds in Gutiérrez and others many references to dependency theorists and the use of ideas of earlier Marxist writers . . . But at this point I have not found in liberation writings any references to detailed contemporary works of analysis by Latin American Marxists. One does find, on the other hand, Marxist concepts and insights used as "heuristic" principles to challenge prevailing, traditional ways of thinking.[78]

Latin American liberation theologians' commitment to the popular struggles of the poor and the landless engaged them in the practical work of coalition building with Latin American revolutionaries, some Marxist, in such a manner as to stress the ambiguity and contradictions within their common commitments to build a just society. The Sandinista movement in Nicaragua stands as a case in point. The rise and fall of the Sandinista movement reflected both the potential for creative engagement between people of faith and Marxist revolutionaries and inherent contradictions which acknowledged that the movement itself was an attempt to achieve economic, political, cultural and moral hegemony within a society.[79] The internal debate within the Sandinista movement reflected these contradictions. Giulio Girardi correctly notes, "The debate over the relations between Sandinism, Marxism, and Christianity is not merely intellectual, but rather is part of an underlying struggle for a new hegemony, a new culture, a new society."[80]

The Latin Americans' focus on Marxism emerged within the fabric of the historical situation within Latin America, where Christians and revolutionaries found themselves asking similar questions, fighting in similar battles, confronting a common enemy and being committed to the same popular movements.

The failure of the Soviet experiment with communism, Cuba's present problems, and the Sandinistas' fall from power is mute testimony to the ambiguity of history. Nevertheless, in Nicaragua, at least, those of the Sandinista front (a coalition of Marxists, Sandinistas and Christians) still view themselves as the vanguard of the people's movement in the ongoing struggle to create a just society. This is the context for evaluating LALT's appropriation of Marxist ideas.

It has already been noted that Latin American liberation theologians have incorporated Marxist insights into their sociological studies of Latin America. Gutiérrez, for example, came to view the poor as a social class, an important step in Marxist analysis.[81] Segundo has asserted that proper verification of the claim that Christian praxis is liberating can be observed only when one applies a methodology that historically verifies the truth of that claim in action (historical praxis).[82] Míguez Bonino points out that a means of scientifically verifying the content of one's praxis with respect to its rightness and adequacy is a necessity in light of the coaptation of religion and theology into the ideological superstructures of those who dominate society.[83]

These are all intuitions of Marx's historical materialism applied to the study of the social organization of human life. In addition, the Latin American liberation theologians came to view their homelands as characterized by dependency and underdevelopment, as well as by its organization into social classes. The record makes it evident that Marxist insights are pervasive in Latin American theology, but what, specifically, constitutes the Latin Americans' commitment to Marxism? This question is significant, especially if one is to assess fairly the Latin American liberation theologians' ability or inability to explain adequately the problem of the absence of references to the problem of race in their theology.

At the first meeting of Theology in the Americas in 1975 (Detroit 1), there was an extensive discussion of Marxism and theology by the Latin Americans.[84] Gregory Baum, citing a distinction made by Yves Vaillancort during the discussion, writes, "Marxism can be understood (1) as a philosophy, (2) as a plan of political action, and (3) as an instrument of social analysis."[85] In his assessment of the manner in which Latin American theologians utilized Marxism in Detroit, Baum writes:

> The Christians gathered at Detroit did not speak of Marxism as a philosophy. For them the dynamic of history was ultimately revealed by God in the history of Israel and the person of Jesus Christ — even if they should hold that this dynamic moves through class conflict and dialectical reconciliation. Nor did the participants generally speak of Marxism as a plan of action, except for a few members from Latin America who were discussing the strategies of liberation in their countries and the search for suitable political allies. The constant references to Marxism at the Detroit Conference understood it almost exclusively as an instrument of social analysis.[86]

A review of the literature of LALT suggests that Baum's assessment is correct, although one must acknowledge the difficulty in separating the philosophical foundations of Marxism from its application, either as a plan of political action or as an instrument of social analysis. Baum contributes to understanding LALT with his insight:

The Latin American theologians . . . showed that Christian theology, in an attempt to come to an understanding of its historical situation, must engage in a social analysis that brings to light the sins of the world, that is, the contradictions within the inherited system and the oppression which they produce. While there are a variety of Marxist social theories, it is possible to define a social analysis as "Marxist" if it focuses on the economic system as the key factor of oppression, if it makes class analysis the central and indispensable element for understanding the social situation, in terms of the interests of the class that owns and controls the major industries.[87]

There are at least four reasons why these theologians utilized Marxist social analysis as one of their primary dialogue partners. Míguez Bonino hints at the first reason when he asserts that their assumption of Marxism had to do with:

A scientific analysis and a number of verifiable hypotheses in relation to conditions obtained in certain historical moments and places and which, properly modified, corrected and supplemented, provide an adequate means to grasp our own historical situation.[88]

For instance, Míguez Bonino writes that the concept of class struggle is used because "it is recognized as a fact."[89] Thus, plainly stated, Latin American theologians utilized Marxist social analysis because its description of the facts of the Latin American situation was the most adequate and correct description available. For them, Marxist social analysis went a long way toward explaining the problems of Latin Americans. Hence Marxist social analysis was taken up as the instrument that could most adequately describe the Latin American situation. These insights into the Latin American situation — dependency and underdevelopment — have wide support in the literature of Marxist analysis.[90]

The second reason Latin Americans utilized Marxist socialist analysis was the fact that the prevailing development models had failed. This is related to the first reason, but it is another aspect of what has already been stated. Dependency theory sees development and underdevelopment as connected. Class analysis explains the manner in which external dominance is maintained by an oligarchy supported by a military apparatus. Both old (agricultural) and new (industrial) oligarchies are intimately tied to the world capitalist system and assist in perpetuating its dominance. The elitist group of internal oppressors maintains national political power or controls to correspond with the interests of capitalists. According to Edward Cleary:

The fact that this analysis derives from Karl Marx and his followers does not deter liberation theologians. They accept these explanations as factual or at least as better explanations of reality than those provided by structural functionalism in American sociology or Keynesian economics. For many Latin Americans such theories are bankrupt.[91]

Marxist instruments of social analysis were utilized by the Latin American theologians because of the failure of other descriptive instruments to adequately capture the essence of Latin American reality.

The third reason Latin American theologians of liberation used Marxist analysis is explained by Westhelle:

The dependency model began to be conceptualized simultaneously with the penetration of Marxism, as a philosophical system, into the academic milieu of many Latin American countries during the '60's. Quite obvious is the importance that Marxism had in reshaping the intellectual situation in Latin America, and in providing the social sciences with a broad theoretical reference whose explanatory power and exuberant analytical resources could hardly be surpassed.[92]

It must be remembered that many of the articulators of LALT studied in European universities where, unlike North American universities, dialogue between Marxism and the social sciences was pervasive. At this time, Marxist ideas had begun to infiltrate and shape the contours of social sciences in Latin America. Sociology of knowledge became extremely useful in the work of analyzing the social mechanisms that govern the formation of ideas in general and theology in particular.

The fourth reason for the Latin Americans' use of Marxist analysis was the natural affinity found between progressive Christian ideas and the aims of Marxism. In other words, Gutiérrez's recognition that the poor are an oppressed social class is a decisive one. Marxists have argued that any revolutionary theory, Christian or Marxist, requires a scientifically verifiable method of measuring its validity. Thus the liberative content of a transforming Gospel must be verified in concrete historical praxis. To know the truth of reality (ultimate reality/God) is to do the truth in concrete transformative action. Míguez Bonino indicates similarities in the Marxist and Christian understanding of humanity in relationship to work. On the one hand, Míguez Bonino writes on Marx's point of departure, "Man is to be basically and radically understood as a worker, as the being who appropriates, transforms, and humanizes the world through his work and who himself comes to his own identity, becomes man through this same work."[93] On the other hand, for Christians, Míguez Bonino writes:

Whether one deals with the creation stories, with the law, or with the prophetic message, there seems to be in the Bible no relation of man to himself, to his neighbor, or even to God which is not mediated in terms of man's work. His dignity is located in his mission to subdue and cultivate the world. His worship is related to the fulfillment of a law in which the whole realm of his economic and political activity is taken up.[94]

Likewise, Míguez Bonino contrasts the estranged character of workers from their work and the similar estrangement found in Pauline texts between "the works of the law" and "the works of faith." For this reason Míguez Bonino asserts, "the Christian will therefore understand and fully join the Marxist protest against the capitalist demonic circle of work-commodity-salary."[95] According to Míguez Bonino, the view of humanity that emerges in Marxist discussions is also basic to biblical anthropology, especially on the emotion of the human being as worker.

The transition from the biblical idea of the poor and the Marxist view of oppressed classes is less obvious. Nevertheless, Míguez Bonino, agreeing with Gutiérrez, can affirm that the notion of the poor,

> insofar as it refers to the oppressed and disinherited—is a pre-scientific, simply empirical designation arising out of direct observation of a situation of oppression and injustice. When Christians in Latin America denounce the hard and moving realities of hunger, unemployment, premature death, exploitation . . . they are . . . moving at the level of empirical observation and ethical and religious judgment. This is no doubt also present, although in a humanist form, in Marxism.[96]

The analytic mediations between Christianity's "the poor" and Marxism's "oppressed class" are twofold and necessary for Míguez Bonino:

> A revolutionary theory . . . (1) . . . purports to give a rational, verifiable and coherent account of the causes, dynamics, and direction of the process and (2) it offers a corresponding rational, calculated, organized and verifiable strategy for overcoming the present situation.[97]

Hence, the Christian and the Marxist, both revolutionaries, can work together on the basis of this parallel. Generally then, Marxist analysis was adopted by Latin American theologians of liberation who recognized these affinities, while acknowledging the difficulties of moving too quickly toward reducing the two visions of human life to one.

The fifth reason for the Latin Americans' appropriation of Marxist analysis stemmed from their concern for ideological clarity in Latin America where, historically, Christian commitment had not been a commitment to the poor and the oppressed. The crisis in identity for Latin American Christians was precipitated by the historical role of the Latin American churches, both Catholic and Protestant, as supporters of the status quo and as extensions of colonial and neocolonial domination. Christian religion—as institutions and values—were viewed as a part of Euro-American hegemony over Latin America. Thus, the application of an analytical method that required concrete historical verification of one's commitment to the Gospel was viewed by the Latin Americans as a necessary prerequisite for liberation.

What, then, was taken over from Marxism? This is of critical concern, especially when attempting to discern the Latin Americans' perspective on race, culture and ethnicity. As has already been suggested, the Latin American liberation theologians were primarily interested in Marxist social analysis as a scientific study of the structures, mechanism, values and sensibilities that constitute domination in Latin America. It is evident that their perspective recognizes the profound problems inherent in capitalism as an economic order. Further, Latin Americans were committed to a revolutionary transformation in Latin America that would lead to socialism.

It is also clear that Marxist intuitions informed the Latin Americans' perspective on ideology, truth and praxis. What is not true, though it has often been claimed, is that Latin American theologians have uncritically integrated Marxism into the Christian faith and, as such, have emptied Christianity of its distinctive content. It is not the adoption of a dogmatic, orthodox Marxism that defined their relationship but, as Míguez Bonino puts it:

A scientific analysis and a number of verifiable hypotheses in relation to conditions obtained in certain historical moments and places and which, properly modified, corrected, and supplemented, provide an adequate means to grasp our own historical situation.[98]

The Latin American liberation theologians assumed a method of analysis that laid bare the internal and external apparatuses of domination as they function within monopoly capitalism. They recognized the problems inherent in orthodox Marxism and insisted on the Latin Americanization of Marxist ideas. Gutiérrez, for example, cites José Carlos Mariátegui, a Peruvian Marxist, who wrote:

Marxism was not a body of principles which can be rigidly applied the same way in all historical climates and all social latitudes ... Marxism, in each country, for each people, works and acts on the situation, on the milieu, without overlooking any of its modalities.[99]

Continuing in this manner, Gutiérrez cited Fidel Castro, who stated in 1968, "Marxism needs to develop, to become less rigid, to interpret today's realities objectively and scientifically, to behave as a revolutionary force and not as a pseudo-revolutionary church."[100]

The most decisive intuition drawn from Marxist analysis is that class struggle is the primary, determining factor relative to the organization of human society. According to Latin American theologians, the conflict between the poor and the rich is a fact of Latin American life that could best be understood through economic analysis. Segundo, however, reflects the sophistication with which Latin American theologians of liberation approach Marxism when he identifies two problems concerning the possibility of collaboration between Marxist sociology and liberation theology:

1. The problem of Marx's perspective on religion, which Segundo judges to be inconsistent
2. Marxists' application of Marx's economic determinism.[101]

Concerning Marx's perspective on religion, Segundo notes that Marx simply appears to have an antireligion bias, which allows him to view religion as "nothing but an error" and designate its abolition as a precondition for the revolution.[102] His point is that Marx, without a clear reason for doing so, treats religion differently from other ideological forms: art, law, philosophy, and so on. Concerning Marx's economic determinism, Segundo reasons that whereas Marx was ambiguous in his own texts, Engels refuted a rigid economic determinism by stressing that "neither he nor Marx had ever spoken in terms of purely economic determinism; that they had referred to the economic element as ultimately the determining factor but not as the only determining factor on superstructure."[103]

The Latin American position on Marxism acknowledges the fact that the basic contours of the LALT assumption of Marxism is shaped decisively by a commitment to the economic base as primary, though not exclusive. Thus, economic analysis of class conflict was decisive both in its analytic mode and as a contribution to a revolutionary strategy for social transformation. The question that is really relevant is whether or not the Latin American liberation theologians have, in fact, adopted orthodox Marxism's "economic determinism" in such a manner that it excluded the possibility of viewing race as having vital relevance to the social ordering of Latin America. The question might be put differently: Is the Latin American liberation theologians' inability to incorporate racism into their analysis of oppression in Latin America a product of their adherence to an analysis based on "economic determinism"? The answer to this question can be given only after a thorough discussion of Latin American perspective on race, an issue to which we will turn shortly.

This survey of the Latin Americans' use of Marxist analysis was intended as an examination of their Marxist assumptions in order to establish a framework for entering into the discourse concerning economic analysis and racism. Racism in general and reference to other races in particular is a dimension all but absent from the discourse of Latin American liberation theologians until their encounter with black theologians from North America and Africa, as well as Asian theologians. The Latin Americans' appropriation of Marxist categories only partially explains the absence of reference to race or ethnicity in their writings. The inability to incorporate the issue of race is partly determined by the racist assumptions that influence the ideological superstructure of Latin American civilization, and the theologians who were the articulators of LALT were inevitably conditioned by those assumptions.

First, black North American theologians, with their uncritical attitude toward the capitalist economic structures that perpetuated the external and internal domination of Latin America, were viewed as lacking in any serious commitment to holistic liberation in Latin America. Because North Americans were participants in the benefits of an economic system that fosters imperialist exploitation and appeared not to be critical of that system, it seems quite understandable that the Latin Americans would be suspicious of black North American theologians.

Secondly, the Latin American theologians of liberation were alienated from their own Latin American homelands. Inasmuch as most of the Latin Americans producing liberation theology were of European background, their alienation from both Europe and Latin America produced an ambivalent attitude within them toward the nonwhite peoples and cultures of Latin America.[104] This explains Assmann's feeling of "incommunication" with Black Theology, the Latin Americans' inability to appropriate the black and indigenous cultures and religions of Latin America, their failure to be thorough in their project of Latin Americanization, and their continued dependence on the intellectual sources and categories of Europe.

Any attempt to understand the Latin Americans' appropriation of Marxist categories and dependence on them must be viewed against the background of the historical process in which the Latin American theologians of liberation began to decolonize their theological traditions. In this respect it is important to note that Latin American Christianity differs from the Afro-American religious tradition in that the latter has had an anticolonial theology since slavery, whereas the former has just recently begun to formulate its own anticolonial tradition.

Thirdly, the Latin American theologians' primary dialogue partner in the process of developing LALT was Marxist social analysis, which viewed economics as fundamental to any understanding of society. The Latin Americans view Marxist analysis as a necessity, for it provided a means of verifying the nature and extent of domination, as well as a means of clarifying ideological presuppositions and commitments. Thus, when black theologians emphasized race and did not refer to economic analysis, it provided an example of the ideological ambiguity that the Latin Americans had come to mistrust. The claim that the biblical God was on the side of the poor (blacks, women, *campesinos, obreros*) needed to be verified by some scientifically verifiable means of analysis, if ideological traps were to be uprooted.

Thus Míguez Bonino, for example, would write of the need to scientifically verify by means of analysis the prescientific notion of the poor in the Bible. In this sense Gutiérrez's discovery of the poor as a social class and as the bearers of God's word is of great significance here. Suspicion and ambivalence were a result of the Latin American perception that the black theologians' unclarity about liberation would allow them to continue to unjustly benefit from the rewards of Euro-American imperialism while advocating liberation for blacks in North America.

Concomitantly, the Latin American theologians' approach to the meaning of the Gospel, through Marxist analysis, led them to value a definition of the Gospel that was mediated through scientific analysis. The understanding of the Gospel in Black Theology had emerged out of a long-established communal reinterpretation of the Gospel and prophetic Christian activism, which appeared unscientific to Latin Americans. Understandably, ambivalence and suspicion would exist between two communities whose theological self-understanding emerged in such disparate historical circumstances.

Fourthly, the Latin Americans' primary emphasis in the early stages of the development of LALT on decolonizing Latin American theology from the colonial and neocolonial hegemony of Euro-Americanization—the process of evolving a theology grounded in the religions and cultures of Latin America—is in its early stages. This process of Latin Americanization has been done primarily under the aegis of Latin American theologians who are still ambivalent concerning their European roots and their Latin American identity. Black theologians, despite their North American base, represent the nonwhite reality in the Americas with which many Latin Americans, like Assmann, have been unable to find a common ground of communication and identity.

The Latin Americans' emphasis on the primacy of class is grounded in their own analytical understanding of Latin America, and their suspicion and ambivalence toward Black Theology is reflective of the four factors discussed above. The distinctive emphasis of LALT is therefore thoroughly grounded in its social context and gives some indication of its attitude concerning BTUSA.

The emphasis that LALT has placed on economic oppression has almost precluded the possibility of any sustained attention to race oppression. This claim is supported by the scant attention given by LALT to the matter of oppression along racial lines in Latin America. It is evident that the Latin Americans view race as secondary to class: It is class division, they believe, that is primary to the Latin American reality. Thus, the primary condition they confronted was economic domination within capitalist society. Further, they claimed that Marxist analysis afforded them an opportunity to validate scientifically and to describe comprehensively the reality of Latin America. However, did they describe the totality of the Latin American reality, or did their descriptive project fall short of its stated goal of grasping and explaining the structures and modes of domination in Latin America?

In the writings of the Latin Americans, references to race are few, yet the Latin American population is constituted by a racial mix, primarily of blacks, mestizos, and whites, but including some Asians. (There are also significant numbers of Japanese in Brazil, for example.) Lloyd Stennette, a black Costa Rican, argues that the problems of indigenous peoples and of blacks are the same in Latin America: "Having heard about the problems of indigenous peoples, I believe that the problems of blacks in Latin America are probably the same."[105] Concerning blacks specifically, he continues, "It seems as if we, as members of the Black Race, don't even exist on the continent. But there are millions of Blacks in Latin America, in Brazil especially but also in the Caribbean, the countries of Central America, Venezuela and Colombia."[106]

Apart from the problem of interpreting Latin American census reports, due to the blurring of distinctions along color lines and, in some cases, the abolition of color or race as a designation, the problem of acquiring precise figures is difficult. For example, Stennette writes, "It is hard to know how many Blacks there are in Costa Rica. The census gives no clear idea because many mulattoes do not consider themselves Blacks. But on the whole I think that about 10% of the total population of two million is Black."[107]

Concerning Brazil, Mauro Batista indicates that though blacks were the majority of Brazil's population in 1972, it is difficult to make a contemporary assessment because racial designation "does not even show up in our 1970 census."[108] He does say, however, that the black population of Brazil (including blacks and mulattoes) is around forty to fifty million. Thus, Brazil has the second-largest black population of any country in the world, coming behind Nigeria.[109] Following Batista's assessment, with further elaboration, are the footnoted comments of Anivaldo Padilha in an article by Antonio De Sant'Ana entitled, "Is Brazil Really a Racial Democracy?" Padilha writes in 1984:

> There are no conclusive statistics on the racial distribution of the Brazilian population, since questions related to race have not been included in the national census from 1930 to 1980. As a result of pressure from the Black movement, the 1980 census included questions about race. But this census produced little clarity as most people did not answer the questions properly. It is widely accepted among social scientists that about forty percent of the population is Black, and the remaining sixty percent is racially mixed with predominant African influence. By European and North American standards, whites represent a very small minority in Brazil.[110]

When Padilha's and Batista's claims are assessed alongside the official population figures for Brazil, it is possible to glimpse the complexity relative to the examination of racial distribution in Latin America. According to the 1985 edition of *The Britannica Book of the Year,* which includes extensive demographic data on nations of the world, the total population of Brazil is 132.5 million, of which 53 percent are white, 22 percent mulatto, 12 percent mestizo, 11 percent black and 0.1 percent indigenous. In comparison with Padilha's and Batista's assessments, depending on the interpretation of the statistics, the official figures appear to be quite distorted.[111] In addition, even a cursory analysis of population statistics for Latin America indicates that there is a significant presence of blacks and Indians in Latin America, which is not easily avoided.[112]

The significant presence of blacks and indigenous people in Latin America is so important that it should be impossible to do full justice to the reality of Latin America without reference to their cultures and religions. In addition, when this fact is correlated with the discernible Latin American phenomenon of the convergence of class and color/race, the earlier absence of reference to them in LALT is extraordinary.[113] While the Latin American theologians of liberation would not deny the presence of racism in Latin America, there is still the question of whether or not they have adequately accounted for this problem in their work.

The problems peculiar to blacks as victims of racial prejudice are nowhere to be found in the seminal writings of the Latin American theologians of liberation, except when they refer to Black Theology as the theology of liberation in North America. We have already documented the response of the Latin Americans when the question was raised at the Geneva meeting of 1973 (sponsored by the World Council of Churches). The "incommunication" that Hugo Assmann described as similar to the sense of incommunication he felt with non-Western persons in Brazil led to a series of dialogues in which there was interaction between blacks and Latin Americans, yet, except for some marginal references to marginalized races, there has been no sustained articulation by these theologians from the perspective of black Latin Americans.

In an interview with Assmann in 1983 at a conference in Cuba, he referred to this incommunication as something in the past and asserted that the Latin American theologians had grown beyond that point as a result of their ongoing dialogue with black theologians.[114] There are some indications of the Latin Americans' recognition of the need to give more attention to race and culture, especially in their willingness to sponsor consultations that seriously address those issues.[115]

It is worth noting that Gustavo Gutiérrez has shown an openness to struggling with the issue of racism. In the first meeting of Theology in the Americas (Detroit 1975), Gutiérrez's first point in his short speech made reference to the fact that as Christianity expanded into the New World, it was marked by a commitment to Western culture and the white race.[116] He said, "We all know that Christianity has been linked to a culture, to a race and to a mode of production."[117] He went on to suggest that there must be a rereading, and rewriting, of history in order to regain the memory of the "Beaten Christs of the Indians" in Latin America, for instance, as we reorient theology to the perspective of "those who have been beaten, the loser."[118] Thus Gutiérrez's writings have reflected an increasing sensitivity to the matter of race. In one of his books, *The Power of the Poor in History*, Gutiérrez writes about the "underdogs" and their approach to the Gospel when he says, "Indians, blacks and mestizos who had received the gospel found reasons in it for resisting the oppression to which they were subjugated."[119] He admits that recorded history has said little about blacks in Latin America and laments the paucity of historical texts about blacks.[120] James Cone attributes Gutiérrez's openness to the fact that he has learned from BTUSA in his dialogue with black theologians.[121]

Sergio Torres, the executive director of Theology in the Americas in its early years, likewise showed an openness, according to Cone:

Through his influence, Theology in the Americas was completely reorganized with an emphasis on the theology projects of Black, native, Hispanic and Asian Americans. Because minority projects did not have many resources for financial support, Torres spent some time generating help from other sources. At the second Detroit Conference of Theology in the Americas (August 1980), racial minorities, with the help of some whites, continued their reorganization of TIA for the purpose of developing a unique North American Theology of Liberation as based on the struggles of racial minorities in this country. This reorganization of TIA by racial minorities could not have happened without the support and encouragement of Sergio Torres.[122]

In addition, Cone singles out Sergio Arce Martinez from Cuba as another theologian of liberation from Latin America who exhibits an openness to black theology.[123] Concerning Arce Martinez and his role in the Encounter of Theologians in Mexico (1977), Cone writes, "The presence of Sergio Arce Martinez of Cuba at the Encounter helped our conversations. ... His public display of willingness to learn from black theology helped other Latin Americans to do the same."[124] In assessing the Mexico Conference, Cone concludes that it was "the turning point in the attitude of many Latin Americans toward black theology."[125]

In the context of CELAM—an important context for Catholic theologians of liberation in Latin America—African problems were specifically identified for the first time in 1979.[126] Enrique Dussel has written that the final document of the CELAM meeting in Pueblo, Mexico (1979), was the first document in which women, the indigenous peoples and blacks were identified as being the victims of abject poverty.[127] Dussel writes: "For the first time the indigenous peoples along with the 'Afro-Americans' were said to be suffering abject poverty."[128]

In the Ecumenical Association of Third World Theologians (EATWOT) there has been an ongoing dialogue. This context of dialogue has been supportive of learning and growth for both black and Latin American theologians of liberation. It was not until the preparatory stage for the 1980 EATWOT meeting in São Paulo, Brazil, that the specific topic of "race, class, and liberation theology" was addressed. Despite the growth of LALT's awareness of racism in Latin America, and the input that they have received from BTUSA, the earlier absence of any analysis of the problem of racism in LALT still requires explanation.

One reason for this inadequacy has been highlighted on several occasions: the Latin Americans' insistence on the form of social analysis that stressed economic rather than cultural factors. A second reason is reflected in the common Latin American belief that integration into the national identity (e.g., Cuban) is more important than the assertion of racial/cultural or ethnic particularity.[129]

The Cuban experience serves as an illustration of this reason for the earlier failure of Latin American theologians of liberation to accent the problems of blacks in Latin America: the primacy of national identity over racial or ethnic particularity. This claim gains credibility, for example, in relationship to Costa Rica. Stennette points out:

> In 1948 a law was passed stipulating that all those living in Costa Rica were to be considered Costa Ricans. The initiative did not come from Blacks. It came from José Figueres, a political leader of European descent, who would later be president of the Republic. So after a century of possessing no nationality, Blacks came to be considered Costa Rican.[130]

Prior to 1984, Stennette shows that the black West Indians brought to Costa Rica as cheap laborers were not considered Costa Ricans and suffered, as a result of this, "a profound identity crisis."[131] Stennette writes about them:

> In Costa Rica we Blacks [were] not considered to be Costa Ricans. When we go to Jamaica, we are not Jamaicans either. And those who might go to Africa are not Africans. . . . In my country we have an expression that sums it all up. We are "neither chicha (a liquor drink) nor lemonade.". . . There still exists a profound crisis of cultural and psychological identity among the Blacks of Costa Rica. For one hundred years we have been geared to feel that we cannot go on being Blacks. I don't know how we can change our color. If we want to be part of the national society of Costa Rica, the first thing we must do is learn Spanish. But our mother tongue is English, and that is what we speak to our families at home.[132]

Latin American liberation theologians, most of whom are white or in some cases mestizo, need to hear Stennette or Antonio Olimpio de Sant'Ana, a black Brazilian, both of whom question the validity of referring to national society consciousness without specifying the dominant or controlling characteristics that define it. Thus, they both question the validity of the claim that the African has been included in the national consciousness of Brazil and Costa Rica.

The Latin American liberation theologians have appropriated the notion of "national society" uncritically when, like Miguel Concha, they insist on viewing ethnic minorities as a part of the national society and seeking the resolution of their particular problems in the broader context of their national problems.[133] Accordingly, they believe that the problems of blacks in Brazil, Colombia, and other Latin American countries will have their resolution within the broader context of the demise of capitalism and imperialism and the rise of new social orders (i.e., socialist countries).

A third reason for the inadequate representation of the problems of blacks in Latin America by the Latin American theologians was suggested when we referred to their European education. Cornel West agrees when, in discussing their lack of appropriation of popular religions and cultures, he writes:

For the most part, Latin American liberation theologians belong to the dominant cultural group in their perspective. As intellectuals educated in either European schools or Europeanized Latin American universities and seminaries, they adopt cosmopolitan habits and outlooks. Like their theoretical master Karl Marx ... they tend to see popular culture and religion as provincial and parochial. It is something to be shed and ultimately discarded, replaced by something qualitatively different and better.[134]

This claim is illustrated by West when he cites Hugo Assmann, who said at a conference in Geneva:

In my opening address I was sometimes aggressive because, as a Westernized Latin American, I don't feel at ease with my color, my "Gringo" face, my German origin. I don't feel happy with the fact that my theological dissertation was written in German. I have a psychological necessity to say to you in Western language that I am not Western. We Latin Americans are still in search for a Latin American identity.[135]

This problem is exacerbated when one acknowledges the fact that, with the notable exception of Gutiérrez, who identifies himself as mestizo/Indian, there are few if any other nonwhite theologians of liberation in Latin America.

The fourth reason for the absence of black themes in the theology of liberation in Latin America is the fact that the decolonization project, which constituted the first stage of Latin Americanization, consumed the majority of the Latin American theologians' efforts. The second stage of Latin Americanization, which entails a grounding of Latin American theology in the religion and culture of the Latin American poor, is as yet in its early stages. In a sense, this accents the fact that the Latin Americans first declared their independence from Europe and North America while still valorizing European and North American sources above their own Latin American sources.

This focuses our attention on two parallel yet related problems. On the one hand the Latin American liberation theologians declared their independence from the cultural and religious centers that, through their identity, background and education, they had come to value as most significant. On the other hand, they could not bring themselves openly to utilize the sources conditioned so definitively by the nonwhite population of Latin America. Much like the early North American intellectual community, the Latin American intellectual community was saturated with what one author has called "colonial provinciality."

Cornel West writes about this in the North American context when he states that the "geographical displacement of European peoples from a European civilization whose superiority they openly acknowledged," along with "an antagonism to the indigenous American peoples and an unwillingness to mingle with unchristian African slaves" created significant tension within the North American intellectual community.[136] This is exactly what Assmann refers to when he cites his own dependence on European intellectual and cultural sources.

Thus, a thoroughgoing openness to the intellectual and cultural sources of nonwhite and non-European Latin America has been slow in coming to the Latin American liberation theologians, thereby aborting their project of Latin Americanization. Insofar as they have failed to acknowledge the presence and contribution of black Latin Americans, the Latin American theologians of liberation have manifested their failure to complete the second stage of Latin Americanization. To assert that a theology of liberation must begin with a commitment to the poor and not to acknowledge that in Latin America the poorest of the poor are most often nonwhite peoples is strange indeed.

The fifth, and perhaps the most important reason why references to blacks have been absent from LALT, is the one that is most difficult to demonstrate, and yet the aroma of the pervasive hegemony of racist ideology can be derived from the fabric that constitutes Latin American social reality. The black presence in Latin America had not been highlighted because Latin Americans did not highlight that which they did not hold in high esteem. Further, the evidence suggests that the values, sensibilities and attitudes that shape the Latin American mind are tainted with the ideology of white supremacy. In the words of Leslie Rout, the Latin American approach to the African in Spanish America has been governed by "a legacy of deceit," which suggests that racism is a profound and pervasive problem in Latin America, despite the consistent and nearly unanimous disclaimers by many Latin American governments. The record of the Latin American liberation theologians speaks by its silence at this point. What it suggests is that the Latin American liberation theologians themselves assumed the attitudes of their dominant culture, which viewed the black contribution and presence as insignificant and unimportant.

References to the distortion of census statistics and the confusing information to be derived from them has already been shown as downplaying the significant numbers of blacks present in Latin America. This is one reason why Stennette asserts that it seems as if blacks do not exist in Latin America. Correlate this fact with several other facts and a picture begins to emerge that supports my claim. First, Leslie Rout comments on the attitudes of Latin Americans when asked about racial prejudice and cites several examples to illustrate his contention that they adamantly believe that it does not exist in Latin America.

He indicated that Latin Americans tended to have racist views about blacks, often without recognizing that those views were racist.[137] Rout cites the experience of a Peace Corps volunteer, Audrey Miles, who reported that upon taking up her teaching assignment in Chiquinquira, Colombia, "she was informed by another teacher that Colombian Negroids could teach children subject matter but could not 'Give them values for living.' "[138] She further reported that, to her dismay, "she discovered that the local population generally believed Black Colombian women to be prostitutes."[139] When these experiences are linked to Anivaldo Padilha's claim that Brazilian school children are taught in school that there is no racial prejudice in Brazil, we begin to see one of the strands constituting the web of denial in Latin America.[140]

Another strand in the web has been identified by Mauro Batista as "the ideology that seeks to make Black people white."[141] It is called the process of whitenization in other parts of Latin America, but in Brazil it is "the ideology of *branquemento*."[142] Batista views this form of racial discrimination as "even more serious, insidious, and poisonous" than the racial discrimination in the United States and in South Africa.[143]

Concerning the ideology of *branquemento*/whitenization, Batista writes:

It says that white is good, Black bad, being Black means embodying everything that is worthy of discredit and hate and that should be discarded rather than given recognition. The human ideal is being white, or being human and being white are completely equated. The ideology is not just to be found in the white population. It has penetrated every level of society and struck deep roots in Blacks as well. As a result, Blacks reject their own blackness, their selfhood, and their real identity as Black human beings. ... It is easy to see the consequences—personal, social, cultural, and so forth—of this ideology which is still being upheld in our country. Black human beings are being affected at the very core of their being because this ideology suggests that being Brazilian means being white; and Brazil does not want to give up the idea that it is a white country.[144]

Batista's assertion concerning Brazil is confirmed by Antonio Olimpio de Sant'Ana:

> One part of the violence against Blacks (in Brazil) is an ideological foray which says that Blacks are at a lower cultural and racial stage of evolution and are therefore incapable of participation as subjects in the economic, social and political process. It allows Blacks certain cultural and religious manifestations which are really intended "to keep blacks in their proper place."[145]

Rout and Stennette independently confirm Batista's claim in relationship to two other countries. Rout, commenting on Colombia, writes:

> What has . . . evolved in many areas is a flexible concept called "Social Race," which allows anyone to be whatever he wishes under limited circumstances. An example is the situation in a government-built housing project in Barranquilla, Colombia. Of the people living in the development, "No one is to be seen who would not qualify as a Negro in the United States." But the machinations of the social-race concept are evident in that these same residents "Declare themselves 'white persons' and castigate slum dwellers as 'Negroes.' " Nevertheless, the inescapable fact is that this system of social categorization remains under the control of whites. Thus, the "Black white men" in the Barranquilla housing project may say that only "Negroes" live in slums, but few phenotypically white persons are going to invite either the "Negroes" or the "Black white men" home to dinner.[146]

Stennette, commenting on the Costa Rican situation, writes: "Many Blacks are ashamed to be Blacks. They would like to be white because they cannot get anywhere as Black. Since they cannot return to Jamaica or head for Africa, they try to ape white society."[147]

The process of whitenization has accompanied the dominant ideology as it has shaped Latin American attitudes toward such significant aspects of life as miscegenation and immigration. Batista, for example, claims that the ideology of whitenization "is responsible for all the distortions, prejudices, and inauthentic aspects to be found in our interracial relationships."[148]

In Brazil particularly and in Latin America generally, the integration of blacks into the national society was designed to eradicate the black presence. Thus miscegenation was encouraged in the hope that after generations of intermarriage the black-skinned would become brown and then eventually lighter. The immigration policies of most Latin American countries over the past one hundred years or more are amply documented. These policies restricted the entrance of blacks into Latin America and encouraged the immigration of Europeans. According to Rout, Juan Alberdi in Argentina wrote in 1852 that "to govern is to populate."[149] Rout elaborates on Alberdi's philosophy, outlined in his *Bases and Points of Departure for Argentine Political Organization*:

> Since he [Alberdi] also believed Europe to be "the most civilized land on the globe," the immigration of Europeans was deemed requisite for future national development. . . . The theories and arguments of Alberdi . . . and others may seem peculiar in that, even in 1852, Argentina was considered a "white" nation. Their intention was to create a people who would be physically and culturally interchangeable with the inhabitants of Spain, France and Italy. This goal achieved national acceptance, and a Europeanized Argentina became a reality. Between 1870 and 1981 the nation welcomed over 2 million immigrants, of whom only 2 percent were non-Caucasian.[150]

Integration, miscegenation, and selective immigration policies constitute dimensions of the singular strand I have called whitenization (*branquemento*).

All these factors—the ideology of whitenization, intentional distortions of census statistics, Latin American denials of the reality of racial prejudice in the face of obvious examples—show that profoundly racial value judgments are deeply rooted in the patterns of the Latin American ethos. These value judgments have misled Latin American theologians of liberation, kept them from accurately representing the presence of blacks in their homelands and made it difficult for them to interact with black North American theologians.

The Latin America liberationists' neglect of racial factors is not simply a by-product of their insistence on the primacy of economic analysis over race analysis but is profoundly rooted in the racist assumptions that permeate the fabric of Latin American civilization.[151] The lack of reference to the problem of racial oppression in the earlier work of Latin American theologians resulted from the ideological presuppositions of white supremacy imposed on them by their background and education.

The challenge to Latin American theologians of liberation is to take this criticism seriously and rescue the aborted process of Latin Americanization in order to produce a theology of liberation that applies to all the spheres of oppression in Latin America.

In summary, LALT's emphasis on the primacy of economic analysis and its inability to incorporate the race question into its discourse are direct consequences of its contextual grounding in Latin America and account for the significant differences of approaches to liberation theology that distinguish LALT from BTUSA.

What Can They Say to Each Other?

The answer to the question, "What can they say to each other?" is derived from an investigation of the methodological and contextual similarities and differences, against the backdrop of the history of their dialogue with each other. First, it is evident that BTUSA and LALT are complementary strands of a global theological tradition that is on a common pilgrimage to holistic liberation and they can affirm each other in their respective struggles to reorient the theological enterprise, so that it becomes accountable to the poor and the oppressed. A consequence of their encounter process has been the recognition of the global context of all freedom struggles. Further, their encounter with each other has been an instrument that broadens their vision of holistic liberation.

Second, at the heart of BTUSA's and LALT's contribution to each other is their mutual challenge to each other concerning the need for a comprehensive means of describing, analyzing and evaluating the diverse sensibilities, values, structures and mechanisms of domination. Indeed the final statement of the fifth EATWOT conference (India 1981) clearly affirms this when it defines one of the priorities as "developing a synthesis between the two major trends in Third World theologies: The socio-economic and the religio-cultural, both of which are essential for integral liberation."[152] In order to explicitly comprehend the nature of oppression in the modern world, it is necessary to formulate new ways of interpreting the reality of oppression. The problems of race and class domination are interrelated, but they cannot be understood simply as manifestations of an oppressive economic system. Race and class, as forms of domination, cannot be reduced simply to economics. The words of Luis Gomez de Souza of Brazil, concerning the complementarity of the various forms of oppression, must be followed up. He writes:

Mechanisms of domination exist on many different levels. There is economic domination of the land and of the means of production. There is cultural domination by the dominant classes. There is male domination of woman. There is domination over Blacks, and domination over young people. There is domination over all sorts of oppressed minorities who are subject to discrimination . . . thus Black and indigenous movements of self-assertion are historically complementary to other processes of liberation, such as those of the common people in urban and rural areas.[153]

Third, LALT and BTUSA have contributed to each other in reminding each other that insofar as they acknowledge the need for a comprehensive liberation of all those who are oppressed, there is recognition of the need for creating strategic alliances. The conditions of domination are such that none are free unless all are free. This is surely the reason why the liberation theologians in EATWOT have sought together to develop Third World theological perspectives.[154]

It is the practical struggles that necessitate what both Fidel Castro and Gayraud Wilmore, respectively and independently, have called strategic alliances.[155] A strategic alliance is an association or union entered into for the furtherance of the long-term common interests and aims of its members. A strategic alliance is one that is of greater significance within an integrated whole. A tactical alliance, by comparison, is an association or union entered into for the purpose of attaining immediate and limited, rather than long-term ends. A strategic alliance is one that will affect the outcome of the war, whereas a tactical one has significance just for one battle in the entire war. A strategic alliance has much more meaning for an integrated whole than does a tactical alliance entered into for limited and immediate ends. Castro was specifically addressing himself to the matter of Christians as allies within the revolutionary process of Latin America. Wilmore was outlining the priority for the 1980s of the liberation movement among blacks in North America, in relationship to other movements of liberation, both national and international. I wish to affirm the notion of strategic alliances as an important instrument for liberation theologies in different contexts.

Fourth, BTUSA and LALT can continue to challenge each other in the determination of the norm for and sources of their respective liberation theology traditions. If it is true, as they mutually affirm, that the norm for liberation theology is the God of the oppressed, who was and is revealed in history as the one who sides with the oppressed by suffering with them and empowering the poor to struggle against domination, then there can be no liberation theology which does not incorporate the experiences of the poor and oppressed within its theological discourses. BTUSA evolved from a long tradition of radical prophetic Christianity that viewed the black liberation struggle as its historic vocation.

However, both BTUSA and LALT can work together in a strategic alliance to better incorporate the voices and the experiences of the oppressed into the liberation discourse. The sources of theology must incorporate and be defined by those who are the victims of exploitation; the poor must speak for themselves.

Fifth, in the question of determining the sources of liberation theology, BTUSA and LALT can contribute to each other by defining a methodology for incorporating resources into their discourse. The question concerning the origin of resources to be utilized within liberation discourse (oppressed or oppressor?) need to be refined.

Can Marxist analysis be utilized as a means of social analysis in liberation theology traditions? The obvious answer is that it already has been. Nevertheless, the question of the ambiguity of ideological interests needs to be resolved, particularly if BTUSA is to view certain aspects of Marxist analysis as capable of serving the black freedom struggle. The crucial question for black theologians has been well stated by Opoku Agyeman, as he discusses the role of Marxism:

> Would a . . . Marxist government solve the problem of the black [person]? Would it hold within itself the vital therapy to cleanse the world

of racism? Or, is there something about the black [person's] history—
in its tragic dimensions of powerlessness, servitude, and persistent
subservience to others—that requires the solution of self-repair rather
than the efforts of a . . . socialist regime, however genuinely motivated?[156]

He responds to these questions by showing that the historical record of
those who espouse Marxism has not been good with regard to racism. He
writes, "It is significant that . . . like most Europeans, Marx thought of non-
whites as 'barbarians' and 'savages' whose only salvation was in the benef-
icent tutelage of European political and economic, and also of European
social and cultural, systems."[157] Marx thus found it relatively easy to dismiss
as primitive everything from the communalism of West Africa to the ancient
cultural institutions of China. This question is relevant for the future discourse of BTUSA and LALT.

Sixth, BTUSA and LALT can continue to affirm the need for dialogical
encounter, since dialogue is a context in which differences can be clarified
and similarities can be determined. In commenting on the history of the
dialogues within EATWOT, Enrique Dussel has observed that both theological traditions (BTUSA and LALT):

saw possible solutions to enable us in the first place to understand
the other's position and then to draw up methods and categories
appropriate to a future world theology, a new analogical totality,
which will be constructed in the twenty-first century after particularities have been noted and spelt out.[158]

Lastly, BTUSA and LALT can challenge each other to define the process
whereby the poor can continue to *evangelize* the church. Does LALT's
assertion that the poor evangelize the church constitute the outline of an
ecclesiological reorientation that parallels the radicalization of Black Theology by the Black Power Movement of the sixties? I would respond in the
affirmative. However, this is an insight that needs further elaboration as
BTUSA and LALT move into the future.

CHAPTER FIVE

Toward a Theology of Religio-Cultural, Socio-Economic and Political Liberation

Where Do We Go from Here?

BTUSA and LALT have manifested a capacity for growth and development as a consequence of their interaction with each other, and we have demonstrated that these two liberation theology traditions have much to contribute to each other.[1] That LALT is at least in an ongoing process of revision is admitted by Juan Luis Segundo in his book *The Liberation of Theology*. Segundo ends his book by acknowledging that neither his work nor the work of the other Latin American liberation theologians represents a final product, and suggests that their works are but partial reflections in a continuing process whereby the method and content of LALT will be developed.[2]

Segundo's statement is equally relevant to the work of black theologians in the United States, where theologians are engaged in a process of evaluating and learning from other liberation traditions. The capacity of these two traditions (BTUSA and LALT) to learn from each other is discernible from the statement which emerged from the Seventh International Assembly of the Ecumenical Association of Third World Theologians, which was held in December 1986, at Oaxtepec, Mexico.[3]

Two aspects of the statement are noteworthy. First, concerning tension over social analysis, the writers of the statement observe that the Latin Americans, on the one hand, have become less rigid in their insistence on class analysis while, on the other hand, "the U.S. minorities admit to a new realization that racism alone is not enough to understand their oppressed reality. Color and race are not the only relevant factors. The economic factor must be taken into account as is clear from the fact that an emergent black middle class refuses solidarity with the struggles of the community."[4]

Second, concerning the religio-cultural traditions of African and indigenous peoples, the statement acknowledges that the Latin Americans "have

133

ignored for a long time the native and Afro-American expression of religiosity and have been influenced by a middle-class culture, which is a minority in a vast and multi-racial continent"[5] despite the dominance of white and western culture in Latin America. However, the document continues by noting that "today Latin Americans are becoming more conscious that they come from a 'mestizo' race and are 'discovering' the existence and values of blacks and indigenous cultures in their midst."[6]

There are some key areas in which the theological enterprise among black theologians in the United States and Latin American liberation theologians must continue to grow and move forward. The specific areas of Christology, ecclesiology, eschatology and liberation will receive attention. In addition, a specific proposal for a comprehensive analytical framework that would provide an integral understanding of class and race will be elaborated.[7] Taken together, the theological and social analytical dimensions of this chapter constitute, I believe, the texture of the contours of future work which should be done and represent a mapping out of my own answer to the question: Where do we go from here?

The Thematic Universe of the Poor[8]

As a consequence of their a priori commitment to the struggles of the poor, black theologians in the United States and Latin American liberation theologians need to deepen their appreciation of the thematic universe of the poor. Despite the fact that their theological point of departure is the experience of the poor in struggle — a decisive breach that separates liberation theology from traditional bourgeois approaches to theology — neither BTUSA nor LALT has gone far enough in reorienting the theological enterprise in the light of the thematic world of the poor and their situations.[9]

Any theology of liberation that claims to represent the oppressed but does not derive its orientations, models, types, directives, principles and inspirations from their religio-cultural traditions manifests an inconsistency within itself. What does it mean to define the substance, content and method of a theology accountable to the Latin American poor without specifically referring to the experiences of exploited Africans, indigenous peoples and women in Latin America? Or, what can it mean for BTUSA to claim that it is a theology of the oppressed without referring to the oppressed classes in the United States?

Both BTUSA and LALT should be more inclusive of the perspective of the poor and oppressed in their discourse and allow them to speak for themselves by defining the contours of liberation discourse. Although the Latin Americans have discerned this problem in their work and are increasingly turning to the cultures of Africans, indigenous peoples and women in Latin America, they nevertheless ought to consistently strive to reorient themselves to this world, which has often been alien to many of them.[10]

Juan Carlos Scannone, an Argentine priest and theologian, contends that while the theologians in Latin America must inevitably bear the stamp of their European heritage and training, they must also "undergo a real cultural conversion without denying the values of the tradition and critique they got from their training."[11] If they are to be true to the people and the distinctively Latin American thematic world, then Scannone insists that LALT "must confront the various socio-cultural mediations ... through which the faith of the pueblo or of different groups read the signs of the times: the projects and utopias that articulate hope."[12]

Hence, the theological sources and norms, images and visions, projects and utopias must be conditioned by the meaning world through which the poor interpret their experiences of exploitation, suffering and hope. This point, though obvious to the theologians of both liberation traditions, is not easily implemented especially when the theologians involved are somewhat alienated from the worlds of the oppressed, for a variety of reasons. It is for this reason that a comprehensive analytic framework can be helpful, since it provides a scientific means of mediating between such prescientific notions as "the poor" and "the oppressed" and the specific nature of poverty and oppression, as well as providing a reference point for determining the priorities of the theologian.

In Latin America, for example, Gustavo Gutiérrez has maintained that it is necessary to incorporate those symbols, myths, beliefs and values which constitute the vital expressions of dynamic faith and have become subversive images as they sustain hope among the indigenous cultures of the continent. The active presence of Christ in the liberating struggles of the poor is, by means of a critical reorientation from the perspective of indigenous peoples, a representation of these hope-sustaining values and beliefs.

In the area of Christology, for example, David Batstone, a North American writer, proposes that a deepening of the indigenization process would presuppose two basic ideas: "(1) the spirit of Christ is presently active in the historical struggle of the Latin American pueblo for [religio-]cultural, socio-economic, and political freedom from colonial and neo-colonial domination and (2) a 'veiled Christ' is somehow present in the pre-Columbian religion of the native people."[13] Batstone's proposals in the area of Latin American liberation Christology are significant for two reasons. First, he intuits that the Latin Americans must account for their claim that the liberating Christ is present in the religio-cultural traditions of the poor, especially if they wish to establish liberation theology on the foundation of the worldview of the poor. Second, Batstone's positive comments concerning the need to incorporate the veiled Christ "present in the pre-Columbian religion of the native people," suggests that he, like the Latin American theologians of liberation, have downplayed the important contributions that Africans and women can make to the evolution of Latin American Christology. While Christology is not the emphasis in this section, Batstone's proposal accents the perspective that the thematic universe of the poor must be incorporated into liberation discourse.

After documenting the potential of the Inca legend of the Christ figure Inkarri, and the important contribution of José María Arguedas, one of Peru's important novelists, Batstone concludes his comments by noting that the cultural universe of the indigenous poor in Latin American "is strikingly absent from the vast majority of writings which have been produced by Latin American theologians," despite the fact that these religio-cultural traditions contain an immense, but as yet hidden, wealth of images, values and meanings that speak to the fundamental hopes of the Latin American people.[14] Hence, LALT needs to undergo a *religio-cultural* conversion to the meaning world of the poor, especially the indigenous people, Africans and women who constitute the poorest of the poor in Latin America.

An important implication for Latin American theologians of liberation should be a critical reassessment of their own cultural and intellectual self-identities in order to unmask the ideological presuppositions of their own worldviews. Insofar as the Latin Americans deny the power of racism in Latin America and the ideological hegemony of white superiority which is pervasive in the attitudes and institutions of Latin America, they continue to mask the inherently racist assumptions of an analysis based on class divisions and cultural homogeneity.

Latin American liberation theologians ought to analyze their own modes of being, as theologians, in order to identify the hegemonic culture which engenders the exclusion of degraded and oppressed cultures. In this regard, the cultivation of a group of theologians from the black and indigenous communities in Latin America would be a most significant development. The ability of Gustavo Gutiérrez, by virtue of his Peruvian indigenous heritage, to reflect sensitively on the question of racial and cultural oppression, is mute testimony to the necessity of "organic intellectuals" whose theological calling is defined by their identity as black and/or indigenous Latin Americans.[15]

A by-product of the evolution of a committed group of theologians who are sensitive to cultural and religious heterogeneity would be the application of culturally sensitized social analysis to the values and institutions of Latin American society in order to discern the positive and negative dimensions of the cultural and religious life of Latin Americans.

What does it mean that there is little indigenous or black leadership in predominantly Catholic Latin America? Are the base communities actually reflecting a different approach to leadership, or is there a predominance of white Latin American leadership in those communities also? How does the overwhelming domination of theology by white Latin Americans contribute to the perpetuation of racism? These are some of the questions which Latin American theologians of liberation should answer themselves. The Latin Americanization process is in danger of being aborted unless the theologians of liberation can begin to take seriously the blacks and indigenous, who are often the poorest of the poor on the Latin American continent. The base communities or the popular movements should be the loci of new perspectives on the contribution of these "forgotten" people.

The recognition of the ideological hegemony of whites in LALT will clarify the need to examine and explore the full potential of the popular religious and cultural expressions of nonwhite peoples in Latin America. Without denying the work that has already been done by Gutiérrez and others, there is a greater need to examine the forms of religious and cultural life in order to discern those dimensions which can contribute to revolutionary activity.

Gutiérrez has warned against the oppressor appropriating the revolutionary potentialities of the religious and cultural expressions of the oppressed.[16] While it is true that he was referring to the situation of blacks in North America, his words are equally appropriate to Latin America. Nevertheless, the Latin American liberation theologians can enhance their own project by listening to the black and indigenous poor in Latin America, rather than avoiding them.

Virgilio Elizondo, a Mexican-American theologian, for example, has indicated the significance of *La Morenita* (The Brown Lady) who is celebrated on the feast of Our Lady of Guadelupe. *La Morenita* appeared as an apparition in Guadelupe, Mexico, in 1531 and told the Indians to build a temple for her. According to Elizondo, "In the seven years that followed the apparition in Guadelupe in 1531, some eight million persons came to the church asking for Baptism."[17] In this way, Elizondo concludes "the gospel ... penetrated and permeated the Mexican-American culture."[18] The Brown Lady *(La Morenita)* "is found not only in the basilica in Mexico City but in numberless shrines throughout the Americas, in the homes of millions of persons."[19] What did it mean to the *mestizos* of Mexico? For Elizondo it meant the affirmation "of the people as *la raza* as a cultural and religious entity," which gave them a basis for their own self-identity as human beings.[20] Is it incidental that in at least three other Latin American countries—Argentina, Costa Rica and Colombia—the leading religious symbol of the struggle for freedom from oppression is a black saint? These are all phenomena that should be reassessed.

Gustavo Gutiérrez has appropriated the notion, elaborated by Bartolomé de las Casas in the sixteenth century, of the "scourged Christs of the Indies," to refer to the role of the Indian in Latin America. In las Casas, Gutiérrez has uncovered the theology of liberation of a sixteenth-century priest who once said that in the Indies he had seen, "Jesus Christ, our God, scourged and afflicted and crucified, not once, but millions of times."[21]

Gutiérrez's commitment to an evaluation of popular religion and culture is embodied in the existence of the Bartolomé de las Casas Institute in Rimac, a ghetto of Lima, Peru, where research is carried on in the following areas: popular religion and culture, workers, peasants and youth. Gutiérrez, the head of the institute, views it as the research institution of the popular liberation theology movement in Peru.[22] Gutiérrez's example needs to be followed in other parts of Latin America, where there is need for research among the poor workers and *campesinos* concerning the liberative aspects of popular religion and culture.

Key Yuasa, a Brazilian writer, has written and published an essay entitled "The Image of Christ in Latin American Indian Popular Religiosity." To my knowledge, Yuasa, a Brazilian of Japanese decent, has not been involved in the liberation theology movement in Latin America. However his work is the source of some important insights concerning popular religiosity. According to Yuasa:

> Popular religiosity can be said to include the following areas: Iberian popular Catholicism which became a member of Spanish and Portuguese Catholicism in the Americas. The Afro-American cults, Amerindian religiosity, spiritism of different levels, syncretistic religions, Pentecostalism, and modernized popular Catholicism represented by base ecclesial communities.[23]

Yuasa's interest is in examining the diverse dimensions of popular religiosity in Latin America in order to identify the specific insights which indigenous and blacks have made to Latin American Christianity. He explores, for example, the fact that "the poor and simple people may receive a revelation from God through poor people; that spiritual good be not something monopolized ... by rich, cultured, elite oriented clergy."[24] He identifies some themes which emerge consistently among the indigenous poor when he refers to the Indian emphasis on the dispossessed and land rights and refers to the ethnic symbols of popular religiosity: Guadelupe, the Indian woman in Mexico, Christo Morado, the Black Christ in Peru and Our Lady Aparecida, a black woman in Brazil.[25] These are examples of aspects of popular Latin American religiosity that can be incorporated into the liberation theology discourse and reflect the thematic universe of the poor.

Of equal importance, in this regard, is Gayraud Wilmore's admonition to black theologians in the United States that they incorporate the worldview of those who are at the bottom of the socio-economic ladder into black theological discourse.[26] Wilmore claims (and I agree) that, "the masses will not take power until there is a coherence between the world-view by which they operate and their ability to translate that position into an effective instrument against the structures which oppress them."[27] Intrinsic to Wilmore's comment is a criticism of the black theological movement's inability to root itself in the black lower class. Insofar as BTUSA is unable to develop organic ties with the black lower class and black underclass, then they will have failed to perform consistently their stated function as intellectuals who define their vocations according to their relationship to the oppressed. This problem is also intrinsic in the criticism made of BTUSA and its proponents by Randolph Outlaw.[28] After documenting his own encounter with BTUSA, Outlaw, a black writer in prison, writes:

> It has been two years since I graduated from seminary. I have continued to read literature by Black theologians, Black educators, and Black activists. They have continued to write about racism, the poor living conditions of Black urban families, the renewal and enhancement of the Black church as a community organization, the need for solidarity with the grassroots for the creation of a new Black future, and the need for Black religious leaders to deal with their credibility problem. Yet, in my community nothing has fundamentally changed from the time I was child.[29]

Outlaw continues by cautioning black theologians and clergy that

> Black theology is emerging as a tradition shaped in accord with the interests of an elite that sustains its power by excluding poor people from the decision-making that defines and shapes our struggle. If this is to change, Black theologians and ministers must ensure greater opportunity for the weak, the poor, and the uninformed to participate actively in the theological enterprise and the decision-making bodies that affect the quality of their lives.[30]

Wilmore and Outlaw have articulated a challenge to BTUSA to incorporate the thematic worldviews of the poor within their discourse. The existence of a growing class stratification in the black community in the United States constitutes an additional challenge to black theologians as they endeavor to develop a theology that is accountable to the "poorest of the poor." The black underclass represents, according to Douglas Glasgow, "a relatively new population in industrial society" who are permanently unemployed, persistently poor and perennially immobile.[31] Glasgow characterizes this development as "the single greatest danger in maintaining a healthy cohesive Black community,"[32] since it fractures an already fragmented community into even more polarized sectors. The underclass is a distinct class from the lower class in that whereas "the lower class experience is a variation of middle class adaptation and striving," the underclass experience is that of permanent poverty.[33] Glasgow emphasizes the difference in milieu, perspective and attitude between blacks of various classes when he writes:

> They remain organizationally separated, yet each group pursues survival with vigor—the underclass searches for a way, a hustle, some means to maintain itself; the middle-income group seeks to at least make secure its second-class middle classness. Thus the dialogue prevailing between Blacks of all classes in the sixties has begun to wane

in the seventies, and the underclass in its isolation threatens whatever small gains the working and middle-income population achieves, and intra-community restlessness and antagonism is ever increasing.[34]

Manning Marable supports Glasgow's intuitions when he states that in religion, blacks are categorized by class distinctions because "various social strata experience religion in diverse ways."[35] The underclass may not be a part of any institutional church and is often separated from an otherwise class-stratified black religious community. Thus, in a social environment which benefits from division in the oppressed community, increasing class stratification and its relationship to a choice of religious affiliation are directly implicated in the inability of the black North American community to be unified. Thus, the unity of discipline and commitment required for any mass movement among blacks is thwarted by the social divisions which flow from the economic order. It is, therefore, absolutely necessary that black theologians face squarely the reality and implications of class stratification in the black community, since the implications have significance for our capacity to evolve a mass movement toward liberation. The fact of class stratification in the black community in the United States is another indication of the necessity of a form of social analysis that is sensitive not only to racial oppression but also to class oppression.

The concern here, following Wilmore and Outlaw, is to demonstrate the necessity of engaging the meaning world of the black poor in BTUSA, a fact which Wilmore asserts "has not yet happened in the black theology movement, notwithstanding the fact that most of its originators and present advocates have identified with the black ghetto."[36]

Of even more significance, theologically, is Wilmore's claim that "the worldview of the masses of black [poor] people in the United States, Africa, and the Caribbean is only more or less Christian."[37] Hence, black theologians of liberation should be self-conscious about the need to incorporate the worldview of the black poor into their discourse, while acknowledging that this worldwiew entails a different view of theology than that which "has come down throughout the history of the church."[38] Hence the need for specifically theological criteria governing the incorporations of these views into the discourse of liberation theology.

BTUSA needs to incorporate into its discourse, therefore, those perspectives and images that convey the fundamental hopes of black oppressed people. Black literature, womanist writings, folk tales, slave narratives, spirituals, blues, prayers and sermons, as well as other religious-cultural expressions of the black poor, must be explored in order to discern their potential for sustaining hope and motivating action among the oppressed. Black theologians should also be converted to the meaning world of the poor, since the naming of their own reality and experiences, by the oppressed, is the beginning of a revolutionary consciousness which sustains them in their liberation struggles.

In sum, BTUSA ought to seek to make the poor not only the subjects about and for whom they theologize, but black theologians must allow the poor themselves to be co-artisans in the creation of language, images, symbols, visions and utopias that enable and empower faith in the struggle to transform their situation and awaken new hope.

Gustavo Gutiérrez acknowledged the need to be open to the thematic world of the poor when he observed that the greatest work for theologians of liberation lies ahead as they attempt to reconstruct "the memory of the poor, a memory that is . . . subversive of a social order that despoils and marginalizes," from the customs, rites, images and symbols that are manifested among the poor and represent their interpretation of faith.[39]

The recognition of the thematic universe of the poor, however, implies several problems for the theologian of liberation. First, as Wilmore indicates, there is the problem of the "more or less Christian" character of the religio-cultural traditions of the poor. This means that the specifically Christian content of these liberation theology traditions must be accounted for theologically.

This problem is highlighted in the recently published volume, edited by Dwight Hopkins and myself, entitled, *Cut Loose Your Stammering Tongue: Black Theology in the Slave Narratives*. In this volume of essays, a new generation of black theologians is engaged in reconstructing the subversive memory of poor, oppressed African-American slaves, in order to discover that which might be useful in constructing a contemporary Black Theology. In this volume, Will Coleman's article raises Wilmore's question and attempts to propose a way to advance the black theological discourse.[40]

Secondly, as David Batstone has indicated, there is the need to discern the "veiled Christs" in the religio-cultural traditions of the indigenous people of Latin America. Underlying these concerns is the need to acknowledge the impetus to liberation which manifests itself in the experiences of the poor and is a testimony to the dynamic liberating presence of God among them.

In methodological terms, the a priori commitment to the thematic world of the poor and their struggles to transform their circumstances constitutes a witness to the presence of the empowering Spirit of Christ, the Liberator, among them. This witness, in turn, is the pretext that determines the incorporation of the message of the Gospel into a coherent theology of liberation. Thus, the transforming praxis of liberation is derived from the dialectic interplay of the witness to the liberating Spirit of Christ in the meaning world of the poor, on the one hand, and the biblical witness to the liberating Christ manifested in Jesus of Nazareth, on the other hand. These two poles, through the method of correlation, constitute the basis for discerning the Christ of liberation in liberation theology.[41] The key element in this hermeneutical circle is the doctrine of the Spirit of Christ.

In sum, both BTUSA and LALT can endeavor to deepen their understanding of the thematic universe of the poor, as well as to empower the poor to be active contributors to a new theological tradition and vision of human society. Thus, the religio-cultural traditions of the poor can not only shape, but regulate, the themes and motifs, aspects and elements that are accentuated in a theology of religio-cultural, socio-economic and political liberation.

The Poor Must Evangelize the Church

The irruption of *comunidades cristianas de base* (Christian communities of the common people) constitutes the emergence of the Spirit which brings forth a new church rooted in the context of exploitation, struggle and poverty. This ecclesiogenesis, as Leonardo Boff has termed it, represents, according Gustavo Gutiérrez, a challenge which has issued from the invasion of the church by the poor. Whereas traditional ecclesiological approaches have accentuated the insight that the church is to be an instrument of evangelization to the world, the Latin Americans in particular have inverted the traditional approaches by arguing that in the light of their pastoral actions among the poor, they have come to recognize the evangelizing potential of the poor.[42] Working amid the poor, whom they were evangelizing, the Latin American liberation theologians were evangelized by them. According to Gutiérrez, this experience—the poor evangelizing the church in Latin America—is coming to

> dominate our work and our view of the church more and more. We are coming to realize that it is the poor who are doing the work of evangelization. We are coming to realize in a new way that God is revealed in history and that God is revealed through the poor. It is to them that God's love is revealed ... Viewed in this light the task of evangelization consists in involving oneself in the process of proclamation carried out by the poor. The latter are not just the privileged addressees of the gospel message. They are also its bearers by the very fact of who they are.[43]

The poor, therefore, are not the objects of the evangelizing work of the church, simply, but they become the active subjects of liberating praxis and the privileged bearers of the spirit of liberation that is Christ's presence hidden among the poor. Thus it is from the poor and by the poor that this new ecclesial experience in Latin America springs. It points in the direction of "a new spirit, a greater fidelity to the liberating wellsprings of the gospel message, and also fidelity to the transcendent destiny of the earth with all its anxieties and yearnings."[44]

The recognition, by the Latin Americans, of this reality—that God is revealed in history to and through the poor—is based on a reinterpretation of traditional christological themes and the development of a more dynamic understanding of God's presence in the world. In addition, the Latin Americans, wary that they might be guilty of romanticizing about the poor, have grounded their claim concerning the privileged status of the poor in the biblical message that identifies the Kingdom of God as belonging to the wretched of the earth (Matthew 22:1–10, Luke 14:16–21) and establishes God's presence among the despised ones of the earth as an important criterion for measuring the faithfulness of the community of faith to the Gospel (Matthew 25:31–46, the parable of the sheep and the goats). Hence, the Spirit of the liberating Christ, hidden in the experiences of the poor and marginalized of the earth, surfaces as the theological basis for establishing new priorities and principles for ecclesial practices and life.

The experience of the Latin American church, however, suggests that the *comunidades cristianas de base* are emerging as alternatives to the existing hierarchy of the established church, rather than as an invasion of traditional ecclesiastical authorities and structures. Despite the proliferation of the base communities in Latin America, the question must be posed: Will the traditional structures of the church, which are now allied to the bourgeois interests of the dominant class, be transformed? This is the challenge that the Latin Americans face as their tradition of liberation theology evolves and grows. In light of the continuing challenge to the theologians to be converted to the thematic universe of the poor, and despite the new ecclesial developments among the Latin American liberation theologians, the challenge to be evangelized by the poor is an immense one.

This challenge is especially significant for BTUSA, which, although it has evolved from a prophetic tradition of black Christianity, is currently proceeding amid a black Christian community that has largely been cut off from its roots in the prophetic tradition of the black church. The challenge, therefore, for BTUSA in this regard, is to evolve a critique of values, structures, symbols, images and practices that shape the black church. In addition, and because secular black organizations have emerged to take up the mantle of the prophetic tradition, BTUSA must develop a critique of these institutions also.

To date, no black theologian, other than James Cone, has been bold enough to set forth a critique of either the black churches or secular black Civil Rights organizations.[45] The criticisms that have often been made have come primarily from black radical organizations, such as the Black Panthers, the Student Non-Violent Coordinating Committee and the Black Muslims.

Cone is quite specific when he writes that black churches and black Civil Rights organizations reflect a lack of vision insofar as they continue the same old strategies and ministries which, in his opinion, will not be "enough for the establishment of freedom in the twenty-first century."[46] In this current period, black religious scholars are needed whose guiding principles are not limited to simple complacency within seminary professorships or privileged pulpits but whose vision is guided by the need to articulate strategies which will enhance black liberation. Also crucial are black scholars whose vocation is consistent with the words of Vincent Harding when he maintains:

> The fact still remains that for the life and work of the Black scholar in search of vocation, the primary context is not to be found in the questionable freedom and relative affluence of the American university, nor in the ponderous uncertainties of "the scholarly community," nor even in the private joys of our highly prized, individual exceptionalisms. Rather, wherever we may happen to be physically based, our essential social, political, and spiritual context is the colonized situation of the masses of the Black community in America.[47]

Cone hints at his recognition that BTUSA must allow itself to be evangelized by the poor when he comments on the future prospects of BTUSA and the black church. He writes:

> We must ask not what is best for the survival of black churches or black theology, but rather what is best for the liberation of the black poor in particular and the poor of the whole world in general. Unless we black preachers, theologians, and lay persons are prepared to measure our commitment to the gospel in terms of our participation in the liberation of the poor, then our gospel is not good news to the poor but instead an instrument of their oppression.[48]

The evangelization of the black church by the black poor in the United States will mean the development of self-critical tools whereby to evaluate the values and insights that emerge from their experiences, since it is not self-evident that these values and insights will necessarily be supportive of the liberation struggle. Regarding the development of analytic instruments, the work of Robert Franklin, a black ethicist who teaches at the Divinity School of Emory University, is noteworthy.

In an article entitled "Religious Belief and Political Activism in Black America: An Essay," Franklin analyzes the political activity of the black religious community:
1. Progressive accommodationists
2. Prophetic radicals
3. Redemptive nationalists
4. Grassroots revivalists, and
5. Prosperity positivists.[49]

These typologies function as a means of organizing the following variables:
   a. Dominant attitude and relationship of the faith community to the political establishment
   b. The central political and ethical goal of the group
   c. The intellectual heritage which informs this social orientation

d. The central theological metaphor which expresses the groups' understanding of God.

Franklin concludes that "the bulk of black middle class Christians" fall within the progressive accommodationist camp, which views their political relationship to the establishment in cooperative terms, and that the black underclass would probably be located primarily in the grassroots revivalists' camp, which views its relationship to the political establishment as one of indifference. I would conclude that the concerns of BTUSA, therefore, which Franklin locates in the prophetic radical camp and which views its relationship as confrontational, is defined by a small minority within the black Christian community and does not constitute the primary emphasis of the black poor in the United States. It becomes incumbent on the practitioners of BTUSA to continually clarify the means whereby the poor can evangelize and transform the community of faith. In the latter part of this chapter we will propose a framework within which to discern the authentic presence of the liberating Spirit of Christ among the poor.

While it was our aim in the preceding section of this chapter to highlight the need for the theologian to be converted to the thematic universe of the poor, it has been our aim in this section to encourage both BTUSA and LALT to deepen their understanding of the need to allow the church to be evangelized by the poor, who bear witness to the Spirit of the liberating Christ in their persistent struggle of faith and hope.[50]

Pneumatology as the Key Link between the Jesus of History and Christ the Liberator

The theological basis and criterion for assessing the incorporation of the thematic universe of the poor, and the liberating presence of Christ among them, is pneumatological Christology. The development of a coherent doctrine of the Spirit as a basis for establishing the historical coordinates of Jesus of Nazareth's deeds, words and destiny as the Christ, is a necessity for BTUSA and LALT.

The development of a coherent doctrine of the Spirit has received little attention in the writings of the theologians of liberation.[51] J. Deotis Roberts, a North American black theologian of liberation, acknowledges that this is true but contends that the Spirit and its presence is decisive for understanding the black religious experience, the context of BTUSA.[52]

A fully developed doctrine of the Spirit can contribute to the resolution of some of the more complex issues facing the liberation theological enterprise, and to the development of a theology of religio-cultural, socio-economic and political liberation. The christological interpretations of BTUSA and LALT are based on the experiences of those who are struggling in the present to make God's liberation a concrete reality, and are dependent on a dynamic understanding of the Spirit of Christ (*pneumatos*) as the theological link between Jesus of Nazareth and the liberating presence of Christ among the poor.[53]

The development of an internally coherent linkage between the christological insights of BTUSA and LALT via pneumatology is an area of theological work that reflects both the continuity and discontinuity that characterizes liberation theology's relationship to the Christian tradition. In continuity with the Christian tradition, LALT and BTUSA view the ongoing task of the theologian as the explication of the meaning of the Gospel of Jesus Christ in each new age and situation. In contrast to the traditional theological approaches, BTUSA and LALT insist that the dynamic presence of God the Messiah is uniquely accessed in the experience of the wretched of the earth: the poor.

Pneumatology is an important key to linking Jesus of Nazareth and his message concerning the reign of God, with the manifestation of God as the liberator in black history and black culture. This is the methodological ground whereby the black theologian in the United States is able to assert that the Christ is black. The answer to Lessing's classical "ugly ditch" question is the theological appropriation of a doctrine of the Spirit as the creative, empowering, hope-inducing power in the black experience.[54]

The importance of this insight lies in the assertion that the Spirit of Christ provides a hermeneutical key by which to establish continuity between Jesus of Nazareth and the liberating presence of Christ as the black Messiah. A similar perspective might be articulated by LALT, wherein the Spirit of Christ manifested in Jesus of Nazareth is the key to linkage with the liberating presence of Christ in the history and experiences of the Latin American poor.[55]

There are five aspects of the biblical tradition and the church's belief in the Holy Spirit that are relevant for this thesis:
1. The Spirit of God as the gracious gift of God
2. The Spirit as a means of preventing us from objectifying God
3. The Spirit as the Spirit of Christ
4. The Spirit as stressing the eschatological character of God
5. The Spirit as the Spirit of mission.

First, the Holy Spirit is understood in the biblical tradition as a gracious gift from God (Ephesians 2:8) that liberates us from all that restricts and restrains human potentiality. The testimony and experiences of the poor witness to the miraculous and gracious gift of God's Spirit in their midst.

Second, the doctrine of the Spirit in the biblical tradition helps to prevent the objectification of God (John 3:8). Paul's testimony at the Areopagus, to the Athenians, is that faith in Christ entails the belief in a God that cannot be reduced to temples or objects of human worship (Acts 17:16–31). Paul's stress is upon the God of life as a creative presence within the same reality shared by humanity (v. 24). This refers to the trust entailed by Christian faith in a living God "in whom we live and move and have our being" (v. 28), and the fact that finding God is a matter of reaching out and discerning God's presence, for God "is not far from each one of us" (v. 27). The story of Cornelius and Peter, the God-Fearer (Acts 10), reminds us that the Spirit of God cannot be limited to the community of faith (*ekklesia*), nor to its ritual acts and places, since God's Spirit is accessible even to outsiders. This concept of the Holy Spirit can assist us in resisting the temptation to objectify God as a means of control and manipulation.

Third, the Christian tradition stresses that the Spirit is the Spirit of Christ (Luke 1:35; Romans 1:4; John 16:13–15). Thus Cone's insistence on the distinctively Christian character of BTUSA. The black Messiah is the dynamic presence of the Spirit of Christ empowering the poor to struggle for liberation. The Christian perspective is grounded distinctively in our memory of Jesus of Nazareth, who was called the Messiah and whose presence must continually be discerned in the struggles of the poor.

Fourth, the biblical concept of the Spirit stresses the eschatological character of the reality of God as a presence that points to a new and transformed future (2 Corinthians 5:1–5; Ephesians 1:11–15). We will return to eschatology later, but presently I wish to note the promissory nature of the presence of the Spirit as a means of discovering new horizons of faith and hope.

Fifth, the Spirit in the Bible points to a commitment in mission to the poor (Luke 4:16–19). The pneumatological obligation to which I have referred is a consequence of the impingement of the Spirit in calling forth and motivating faith and hope in struggle. In sum, the Spirit of Christ is God's gift to the poor; it empowers and motivates them in the struggle; it resists the temptation of reducing God's Spirit to the historical struggle; it encourages them to look for God in all creation; and motivates the mission of religio-cultural, socio-economic and political liberation among them.

So defined, the Spirit of Christ, understood as the embodiment of the values and commitments manifested in the life, ministry and message of Jesus of Nazareth, and as the gift of the liberating presence of the Messiah among the poor, can provide the liberation theology enterprise with five important intuitions.

First, a historical interpretation of the meaning of the Spirit of Christ provides BTUSA's and LALT's belief in the presence of Christ the Liberator among the poor with historical coordinates in Jesus' life.[56] The danger of religious belief without historical coordinates is that it is subject to manipulation. Further, the historical tendency in the Christian tradition, which has been termed "docetic," is inconsistent with a biblical understanding of faith in Jesus Christ. The historical creeds of the church have affirmed that the confession "Jesus is the Christ" entails the acknowledgment not only of "Very God," but also of very (hu)man, thus ensuring against docetism in the creed. Any religious message that is void of historical grounding is likely to be perceived as transcending the conflictive social situations that characterize human history.

Secondly, the importance of pneumatology as the basis for connecting Jesus of Nazareth to the liberating presence of Christ in the poor is that it allows us to explore the meaning world of Jesus of Nazareth in order to discover the images and models which transmitted the utopic message of the reign of God as a message with peculiar significance for the poor. Juan Luis Segundo has observed that the parables, for example, represent Jesus' unique method of communicating the apocalyptic message of the reign of God to the people of his day.[57] Thus, according to Segundo, the parables constitute the subversive denunciation of the existing structures of domination and "are attacks on the oppressive religious ideology of the Israelite majority and, for that reason, a revelation and defence of the God who has chosen the poor as the preferred recipients of the kingdom."[58]

The apocalyptic imagery appropriated by Jesus in the parable of the sheep and goats (Matthew 25:31–46) functions as a subversive element within the thematic universe of the hearers of the parable and challenges the existing religious ideology of the Pharisees, who had previously utilized that imagery as a means of supporting the oppressive social structures and divisions in Palestine. Jesus, in his word and deeds, highlighted the place of the hungry, thirsty, imprisoned, poor, sick and needy as the privileged location of Christ's hidden presence in the world.

It should be noted that although BTUSA and LALT both view the reign of God as significant for understanding the significance of Jesus' life and message, few of them have incorporated this insight into their investigation of the historical Jesus. Segundo, one of the few to do so, views the challenge of establishing Jesus of Nazareth as the historical ground of belief in the liberating Spirit of Christ, as a means of (1) highlighting the values which Jesus lived by and promulgated, (2) revealing the God in whom he believed and (3) discovering the practical and theoretical means whereby Jesus set forth those values in his own context, Palestine.

Third, the use of the pneumatological schema provides BTUSA and LALT with a historically grounded hermeneutical basis for discerning the authentic liberating presence of Christ that is hidden in the history and experiences of the oppressed. In contrast to the often prevailing demonic spirits of this world (i.e., oppressive ideologies that operate in the world of the poor and function to sustain their oppression), and within the conflictive history that characterizes human existence, this pneumatological schema allows liberation theologians to discern and to acknowledge the liberating presence of Christ among the poor. This presence is a historical correlate of those values and commitments which were revealed in the words and deeds of Jesus of Nazareth.

Hence, the liberation theologians can refrain from the danger of romanticizing deeds and actions within the struggle and begin utilizing the dynamic presence of Christ the Liberator as a means of establishing a self-critical dimension to the words and deeds of the poor, who are also sinners. The self-critical principle that should be used in a theological evaluation of the words and practices of the black church or black nationalism, and in the base communities and historical projects, is dynamic presence of Jesus the Christ who was revealed in the person of Jesus of Nazareth.

James Cone, for example, highlights the problem of finding a theological self-critical principle for adjudicating the distinctive Christian character of Black Theology within the context of his discussions with Gayraud Wilmore and others in the BTUSA movement.[59] This pneumatological schema provides BTUSA and LALT with a historically grounded self-critical means and methodology for assessing the authentic liberational content of the themes, images, principles, practices and values that define and determine the universe of the poor. Further, it provides a means to not only acknowledge the presence of the liberating Spirit of God hidden in the experiences of the poor, but also for discerning the Spirit of Christ among the competing spirits of the world. This is the meaning of the biblical writer's injunction that we "do not believe every spirit, but [must] test the spirits to see whether they are from God, because many false [spirits] have gone out into the world" (1 John 4:1–3). Thus, liberation theologians are prevented from confusing the Spirit of Christ with various competing and conflicting spirits that are present in each social context.

Fourth, the development of this pneumatological framework provides BTUSA and LALT with the means of evaluating the liberational content in the words and deeds of the Christian community as a means of challenging the people of God to incarnate the Gospel in a manner that is consistent with the Spirit of Christ. Within the context of the North American theological scene, the church is indebted to James Cone, whose writings erupted with the challenge to the churches to embrace the Spirit of the Christ of freedom in the battle for the Gospel.

The contemporary presence of the reign of the Spirit of Christ (God) in the church meant that the primordial elements, themes, motifs and values which had been incarnated in Jesus of Nazareth were to be fleshed out in the concrete reality of the contemporary situation. Hence, Cone's challenge to the church to embrace the black Messiah, while at the same time acknowledging that the Spirit of Christ cannot be reduced to the black experience.

The dialectic is thereby established whereby the church, as the people of God gathered around the memory of Jesus Christ, is compelled to a historical engagement in service to the poor while simultaneously acknowledging that God is already with the poor and that the church ought to open itself to being evangelized by them. This is an aspect of the self-critical process. Gustavo Gutiérrez contributes to Cone's insights by highlighting the need for radical discipleship, in this sense, when he posits:

> The practice of the following of Jesus will show what lies behind the acknowledgement of the Messiah. It will show whether our thoughts are those of God or only our own—the ideas we have of Jesus and

our discipleship. . . . To the question "Who do you say that I am?" we cannot give a merely theoretical or theological answer. What answers it, in the final analysis, is our life, our personal history, our manner of living the gospel.[60]

The people of God are to be the historical manifestation of the values and insights, themes and motifs which reflect the presence of Christ the Liberator, and must define their mission in a manner consistent with such a commitment. In the absence of such a commitment, the church is guilty of apostasy, as in the case of racist white ecclesial structures or the oppressive Latin American church of the hierarchy, and must be challenged to return to the Christ of freedom.

Finally, pneumatological Christology enables liberation theologians to recognize the eschatological presence of God's Spirit, which points beyond each historic project to a more universal message of liberation that encompasses within it the struggle for religio-cultural, socio-economic and political liberation, but is not reduced to it. The hope and faith sustained by the Spirit of Christ among the poor empowers them to believe in a transformed future and draws them beyond themselves.

My use of the term "the Spirit of Christ" places stress upon the multidimensional character of the message of the Gospel, both as it was promulgated by Jesus of Nazareth in its seminal form, and as it was articulated to the post-Easter community for whom Jesus was the primordial revelation of God's action in their world. Jesus' central message concerning the Kingdom of God is acknowledged by the theologians of liberation as an important key to discovering the values, insights, themes and motifs that shaped his faith and practice. Hence, the proclamation of the Kingdom, as the content of the message of the pre-Easter Jesus, and the thrust of the message of the post-Easter resurrection community stands at the heart of Christian expectation about the future.

For the early Christian community, God's Kingdom was Christ's Kingdom manifested in the presence of the Spirit as they [the community of Jesus] incarnated the values that Jesus promulgated. They struggled to create the Kingdom, at the same time recognizing that the coming Kingdom stands *extra nos* (beyond us). Hence my view of pneumatology is one that views the Spirit of Christ as extending beyond Jesus of Nazareth, the church and the poor to a God whose resurrection is the concrete basis of the hope of the poor for a new and different future. The Spirit of Christ is a living presence that points beyond the limitations of each historical situation and is the ongoing basis for the community's will and struggle for brokenness and exploitation toward wholeness and *shalom*. This is true even for Jesus of Nazareth, who came to understand his message as one of universal significance.

Closely linked to Christology, and confirming the eschatological perspective articulated by BTUSA and LALT, is the view that historical projects of liberation are comprehended by the Kingdom of God, but that the Kingdom of God cannot be reduced to historical projects. The final document of the 1980 São Paulo, Brazil, Congress document of EATWOT, for example, explicates the eschatological perspective of Third World liberation theologians by stating:

> The coming of the Kingdom of God's final design for his creation is experienced in the historical processes of human liberation.
>
> On the one hand the Kingdom has a utopian character, for it can never be completely achieved in history; on the other hand, it is foreshadowed and given concrete expression in historical liberation. The Kingdom pervades human liberations; it manifests itself in them, but it is not identical with them. Historical liberations, by the very fact that they are historical, are limited, but open to something greater.[61]

The comments in this document reflect the common perspective of the liberation theologians that historical projects of liberation point beyond themselves "and can never be achieved in history." But what does it mean to affirm this view, as do the theologians in both liberation camps, while at the same time claiming that the resolution of conflictive theological claims must be resolved within the dialect of human history? The appropriation of the concept of the Kingdom of God, based on a pneumatological Christology as the ground of establishing the historical coordinates of Christian faith and practice, can provide us with a key wherein to explicate the relationship between historical liberation struggles and God's final and ultimate design for creation.

From the viewpoint of BTUSA and LALT, the heart of Christian expectation and hope is that the Resurrected One, whose presence *(parousia)* is celebrated in the community of faith, and who invades the church through the poor as the liberating presence of God, is present in a manner that points beyond the limitations of each historical project. Cornel West provides us with an important clarification when he attempts to distinguish between historical projects of liberation, which he deems to be penultimate, and ultimate salvation, which comprehends God's final design. He writes:

> Penultimate liberation is the developmental betterment of humankind, the furtherance of the uncertain quest for human freedom in history. Ultimate salvation hopes for the transcendence of history, the deliverance of humankind from the treacherous dialectic of human nature and human history. The process of penultimate liberation can culminate within history, whereas the process of ultimate salvation is grounded in history but promises to proceed beyond it.[62]

West's point in making this distinction is to highlight the necessity of acknowledging the tragic nature of human existence (caught inextricably between our ideals and hopes and the inexplicable vicissitudes of human existence), while affirming the hope, spirit and commitment to struggle which has emerged in BTUSA and LALT, as well as in other liberation traditions.

The distinctive contribution of the Christian message within the historical struggles for liberation is that the expectation of the parousia lives. It is based on the resurrection (which Karl Barth has called the first form of the parousia-event),[63] the gift of the Spirit of Christ present in the church (which Barth calls the second form of the parousia), and the presence of the Spirit among the poor (highlighted by LALT and BTUSA). It is also based on the expectations of the community that the one who was already present in their midst is coming at some time in the near future to consummate the establishment of the Kingdom of God, where "God will be all in all." The God who revealed her/himself to Moses in the Hebrew Bible as "I will be who I will be" will be in the end "all in all." For this reason the use of the metaphor "the Kingdom of God" as a utopic symbol by Jesus of Nazareth is to be understood as a key to comprehending the values for which he died, the strategies which he employed, and the God in whom he believed.

In sum, pneumatological Christology establishes theological criteria for pushing forward the work of BTUSA and LALT and provides a partial answer to the question: Where do we go from here?

Toward a Comprehensive Framework for Understanding the Dynamics of Domination

The concept of hegemony can be utilized to enhance the theologians' capacity to discern the liberating presence of the Spirit of Christ in the world. While a pneumatological Christology is a means of testing the spirits that inhabit the universe of the poor, it is also evident that a coherent concept of analysis could enhance the work of liberation theology in this regard. As noted by Jose Míguez Bonino, particularly, social analysis can mediate between important prescientific liberation themes, such as "poor" and "oppressed," and the scientific facts about the poor in each historical situation.

The tension between BTUSA and LALT over the primacy of class or race has led both traditions to acknowledge their respective shortcomings. The formation of a specific framework that would facilitate the inclusion of both race and class as equally significant was originally proposed by Cornel West. In *Prophesy Deliverance: An Afro-American Revolutionary Christianity,* West suggests that both black theologians and Latin American theologians of liberation "can learn from the most penetrating Marxist theorist of culture in this century, Antonio Gramsci," who, West continues, "provides a valuable framework in which to understand culture, its autonomous activity and status, while preserving its indirect yet crucial link with power in society."[64] West's proposal explicitly identifies a progressive Marxist concept that facilitates the integration of class and race oppression into a more comprehensive analysis of domination, thus satisfying the need to promote an analysis of both race and class oppression.

The difficulty of integrating race and class within traditional Marxist analysis is fundamentally grounded in a Marxist social analysis that focuses on the economic factor as the most determinative factor in understanding the structures of society. Therefore, an investigation of the problem necessarily entails the unraveling of Marxist social theory in order to establish its theoretical basis.

The foundation of Marx's theory of society was historical materialism, a materialistic conception of history that viewed the structures of society and its historical development as being determined by the material conditions of life or the mode of production of the material means of existence. The guiding thread of Marx's work was that the sum total of the relationships of productions—the way humans organized their social production as well as the instruments they used—constituted the real basis of society on which an ideological superstructure arose and to which definite forms of consciousness corresponded. Thus, the way humans produced their means of subsistence conditioned their whole social, political and intellectual life. The materialist conception was intended to be a naturalistic, empirical, and scientific explanation of historic events that interpreted industrial and economic factors as basic. Concerning his conception of history, Marx writes:

> This conception of history depends on our ability to expound the real process of production, starting from the material production of life itself, and to comprehend the form of intercourse connected with this and created by this mode of production as the basis of all history.[65]

According to Marx, then, social analysis assumes a distinction between the economic basis of the material conditions of human society and the ideological superstructure, which serves as the legitimizing and sustaining force of any particular economic order. The economic base is essentially constituted by the productive forces (producers) and the means of production (economic structure). For Marx, everything—from habits of thought to political and legal institutions, religion and morality, theology and philosophy, ethics, art and culture—is a part of the ideological structure that serves to justify the self-interest of those who control the means of production and thereby dominate society. Marx's definition of the ideological superstructure is encompassed in his famous words:

> The ideas of the ruling class are in every epoch the ruling ideas: i.e., the class which is the ruling material force of society, is at the same time its ruling intellectual force. The class which has the means of material production at its disposal, has control at the same time over

the means of mental production, so that thereby, generally speaking, the ideas of those who lack the means of mental production are subject to it. The ruling ideas are nothing more than the ideal expression of the dominant material relationships, grasped as ideas; hence of the relationships which make the ruling class the ruling one, therefore, the ideas of its dominance.[66]

Marx's system, then, views the ideological superstructure as reflecting the productive relationships (economic base). Whether or not Karl Marx himself viewed the economic base as absolutely determinative of the ideological superstructure is still being debated. It is important to note that the orthodox Marxist perspective interprets Marx's view as economic determinism: the view that the economic base determines the superstructure. A major problem in interpreting Marx, of course, lies in the fact that his writings did not explicitly elaborate on many of these questions. Engels, in responding to early Marxists who had simplistically interpreted Marx's works as economic determinism, denied a simplistic interpretation for Marx. In a letter, Engels wrote:

According to the materialist conception of history, the ultimately determining element in history is the production and the reproduction of real life. More than this neither Marx nor I have ever asserted. Hence if somebody twists this into saying that the economic element is the only determining one, he transforms that proposition into a meaningless, abstract, senseless phrase. The economic situation is the basis, but the various elements of the superstructure: political forms of the class struggle and its results, to wit: constitutions established by the victorious class after a successful battle, etc., juridical forms, and then even the reflexes of all these actual struggles in the brains of the participants, political, juristic, philosophical theories, religious views and their further development into systems of dogmas, also exercise their influence upon the course of the historical struggles and in many cases preponderate in determining their form.[67]

From Engels's letters one can glean the following insights. The superstructure evolves out of, and occasionally alongside, the economic base. The superstructure could have a relative autonomy, and structure and laws peculiar to itself. There is reciprocal interaction between superstructure and base, and even, in some circumstances and for a limited period, the superstructure could determine the evolution of the base, but nevertheless, in the long term, the superstructure is determined by the base.[68]

Despite Engels' clarification, there has been a persistent debate among Marxists concerning the relationship of the economic base to the superstructure. Insofar as Marxists have viewed culture and religion as aspects of the ideological superstructure, they have interpreted them as being ulti-mately determined by the economic base.

Michael Omi and Howard Winant have suggested that there are two difficulties that confront any attempt to comprehend racism within the context of traditional Marxist analysis: (1) the traditional Marxist definition of class-formation is inadequate, and (2) the traditional Marxist analysis of race is problematic. According to Winant and Omi, the traditional Marxist definitions of class and race are inadequate because:

> It defines classes solely in terms of economic relationships, thus reduc-ing them to mere locations or positions in the production process. Such an approach says nothing about the actual occupants of these locations, their capacity for organization, or their ideology.[69]

Winant and Omi also observe that the traditional Marxist analysis of race and racism is problematic, primarily because it views race "as an epi-phenomenon or manifestation of class. Race is explained by reference to class and thus reduced to an aspect of class struggle."[70] Continuing their criticism of the orthodox Marxist analysis of race, they reject an economi-cally determinist understanding of class.[71] They also reject various neo-Marxian revisions of the traditional Marxist explanation of class formation, because they judge those revisions to be dependent on economic deter-mination.

Progressive Marxists have developed their own understanding of Marxist social theory and have criticized orthodox Marxism for its narrow emphasis on the primacy of the economic base. Cornel West, for example, writes:

> The orthodox Marxist analysis of culture and religion that simply relates racist practices to misconceived material interests is only par-tially true, hence deceptive and misleading. These practices are fully comprehensible only if one conceives of culture, not as a mere hoax played by the ruling class on workers, but as the tradition that informs one's conception of tradition, as social practices that shape one's idea of social practice.[72]

For the Marxist tradition, issues such as race and ethnicity are a part of the ideological superstructure under the control of the ruling class, and as such are the ideological instruments the ruling class uses to perpetuate its dominance by dividing the working class. Thus, the orthodox Marxist would argue, race and ethnicity are secondary matters, which will be resolved within the framework of a united working-class movement.

Lucius Outlaw, Maulana Karenga, and Amilcar Cabral are three think-ers who have enhanced Marx's social theory by critiquing it. Lucius Outlaw suggests that Marx's anthropology is basic to the inability of Marxist social theory to deal with race and ethnicity:

It is to Marx's philosophical anthropology that we must turn to locate a principal source for the difficulty the Marxian tradition has had in coming to terms with race/ethnicity, racism, and nationalism. For it is his view of human "being" in its essence, in its species being, that grounds the critique of capitalist social formations and subsequently grounds the revolutionary project on behalf of a society free of (class) oppression. And it is this view of humanity that implicitly and explicitly conditions the thinking of many Marxists such that they give primacy to class oppression as the condition to be overcome.[73]

Outlaw's conclusion is that Marx's anthropological definition of the human species as producer of its own existence is abstracted from the real particulars of human life, such as ethnic background, religious perspective, and so on.

In reaction to this flaw, Outlaw proposes a reworking of Marxist philosophical anthropology in such a manner that race and ethnicity (culture) are viewed as relatively autonomous and sometimes positive determinants of human existence. Outlaw, committed both to black nationalism and to Marxism, encourages the development of an analysis that takes account of both racism, in its structural/relational, dynamic manifestations, and class and subclass stratifications, their sources and their consequences.

Maulana Karenga essentially concurs with Outlaw in his assessment of why Marxist social analysis has had difficulty in viewing race and ethnicity other than as secondary to class. For Karenga, a human being is essentially a cultural being:

This contention challenges Marx's philosophical anthropology, which posits the human being as essentially a Gattugswesen or species being. For though the image of humans may transcend a given socio-historical or cultural context, the concrete human being as species being is an abstraction from his/her socio-historical particularity; i.e. his/her cultural particularity.[74]

Karenga asserts that the tendency to reduce racial oppression to class oppression is therefore incorrect and analytically unproductive.

For Karenga, race and ethnicity must necessarily be a fundamental part of any theory of society and culture designed for freeing a racially oppressed people from the impositions of a racist society.

Amilcar Cabral and José Carlos Mariátegui are also progressive Marxists from the Third World who acknowledge the inadequacy of defining human beings in a purely economic manner. Cabral argues for a more central role in culture when he writes:

There is a strong dependent and reciprocal relationship existing between the cultural situation and the economic situation in the behavior of human societies. In fact, culture is always in the life of a society.[75]

Mariátegui, in Peru, also asserts the necessity of developing the idea of culture alongside the economic factor as important determinants of social identity and status.[76]

The problem of economic determinism in Marx and in classical (orthodox) Marxism may in the end be irrelevant; there are many progressive Marxists who acknowledge the deficiencies of an analysis based exclusively on the economic factors and who argue persuasively for both a more real definition of human beings and for a more dynamic understanding of the economic base and the superstructure. Culture is an additional fundamental factor that is decisive in relationship to the problem of racial oppression.

Culture, then, defined as a historically grounded total mode of existence, is proposed as a more comprehensive description of the real human being. Inasmuch as culture, in the Marxist framework, is viewed as superstructure, then there must be an acknowledgment of the dynamic interplay between the economic base and the superstructure in order to define a social theory that would integrate race and ethnicity. Culture, according to various African and African-American theorists, is inclusive of the historically grounded experiences of a particular people and, as such, reflects the peculiar habits, traditions, values, sensibilities, ways of interpreting life and death, and ways of struggle of the particular group and is linked reciprocally with social and economic reality while having, at the same time, a measure of autonomy from the economic base. Noneconomic factors such as racial, ethnic or sexual identity are relatively autonomous in the defining of social relations. It is at this point that the work of Antonio Gramsci becomes very important.

Marx viewed the ideological superstructure as the apparatus of legitimation for the ruling class and, as such, relegated the superstructure to being an epiphenomenon of the economic order of society. Orthodox Marxist social theory understood economic relations as basic and the ideological superstructure as derivative, even though Engels appeared to argue for a more dynamic view of the relationship between the base and the superstructure. Within this framework, culture was seen as a part of the ideological superstructure that served to legitimize the domination of the working class by the ruling class. This view on culture restricts it to its negative and repressive aspects. Culture, however, can be seen in a positive light as supporting and fostering liberation struggles. Cornel West proposed Antonio Gramsci as providing "a valuable framework in which to understand culture, its autonomous activity and status, while preserving its indirect yet crucial link with the power in society."[77]

According to West's assessment of Gramsci:

Unlike the Latin American liberation theologians, he does not downplay the importance of popular culture; unlike the black theologians, he does not minimize the significance of class. Instead, he views the system of production and culture in a symbiotic relationship, each containing internal tension, struggle, and even warfare.[78]

Marx set forth his notion of ideology in his famous dictum "the ruling ideas of any particular epoch are the ideas of the ruling class," in which he viewed ideology as the structural legitimization of the rule of the oppressor class.

According to West:

Gramsci deepens Marx's understanding of the legitimation process by replacing the notions of ideology with his central concept of hegemony. For Marx, ideology is the set of formal ideas and beliefs promoted by the ruling class for the purpose of preserving its privileged position in society; for Gramsci, hegemony is the set of formal ideas and beliefs and informal modes of behavior, habits, manners, sensibilities, and outlooks that support and sanction the existing order.[79]

Gramsci used the term *hegemony* in the sense of the process by which the proletariat gained leadership over all the forces opposed to capitalism and welded them into a new homogenous politico-economic historical bloc. Concerning hegemony, he writes, "The realization of hegemonic apparatus, in so far as it creates a new ideological terrain, determines a reform of consciousness and of methods of knowledge."[80] Michael Omi and Howard Winant, Marxist writers who concur with West that Gramsci's concept of hegemony is valuable in rating race and class, give us a good definition of the concept when they write:

Hegemony is the thoroughgoing organization of society on behalf of a class which has gained the adherence of subordinate as well as dominate sectors and groups. Often summarized as rule by means of a combination of coercion and consent, hegemony is better understood as the creation of a collective popular will by what Gramsci calls "intellectual and moral leadership." The exercise of hegemony extends beyond the mere dissemination of "ruling class" ideas and values. It includes the capacity to define, through a vast array of channels (including the basic structures of economic, political, and cultural life) the terms and meanings by which people understand themselves and their world.[81]

Within this framework, then, Omi and Winant conclude it is possible to reinterpret the process of class formation as not simply economically determined.[82] Classes can then be viewed "as (1) multiply determined, (2) historical actors (which) themselves are (3) effects of the social struggles in which they were formed."[83]

Hegemonic culture, then, is comprised of the traditions and current practices that "subtly and effectively" encourage people to identify themselves with the habits, sensibilities, and worldviews supportive of the status quo and the class interests that dominate it. It is a culture successful in persuading people to "consent" to their oppression and exploitation.[84] For Gramsci, hegemonic culture could be manifested in support of whatever class was in the dominant position. The critical link for Gramsci was the role that intellectuals played in obtaining the consent of the subordinate group to their own domination. Gramsci writes:

The intellectuals of the historically progressive class, in the given conditions, exercise such a power of attraction that, in the last analysis, they end up by subjugating the intellectuals of the other social groups; they thereby create a system of solidarity between all the intellectuals, with bonds of a psychological nature and often of a caste character.[85]

In this way the worldview of the ruling class was so diffused by its intellectuals as to become the "common sense" of the whole society. As long as capitalist hegemony continued, the proletariat remained unaware of the contradictory nature of capitalist society and of the possibility of transforming it. A necessary part of the ideological hegemony of capitalists was their ability to represent their own interests as those of society as a whole. Gramsci became the first Marxist theorist to analyze seriously the way in which the bourgeoisie perpetuate their domination through consent rather than coercion based on the manipulation of the "so-called organs of public opinion — newspapers and associations."[86]

In order to establish its own hegemony, the working class has to be able to present itself as the guarantor of the interests of society as a whole. Here again the intellectuals of the working class become the critical link, because in Gramsci's framework their contribution is to establish the contours of a counterhegemonic culture, grounded in the oppositional forces that could be disseminated throughout the society. According to Gramsci:

Every social class . . . creates together with itself, organically, one or more strata of intellectuals which give homogeneity and an awareness of its own function not only in economic but also in the social and political fields.[87]

Organic intellectuals articulate the collective consciousness of their class in the political, social and economic sphere, and are mediating links between the "world of production" (economic base) and "the complex of superstructures." They secure the consent of the masses for the policies of society. Thus, the development of a group of intellectuals organically connected to the oppressed class becomes a necessary precondition for revolutionary transformation, because they are able to articulate a counterhegemonic culture, that "represents genuine opposition to hegemonic culture of habits, sensibilities, and world views that cannot be realized within the perimeters of the established order."[88]

West elaborates on Gramsci's notion of hegemonic culture by defining four categories for understanding cultural processes: hegemonic, prehegemonic, neohegemonic, and counterhegemonic.[89]

> Hegemonic culture is to be viewed as the effectively operative dominate worldviews, sensibilities, and habits that sanction the established order. Pre-hegemonic culture consists of those residual elements of the past which continue to shape and mold thought and behavior in the present ... Neo-hegemonic culture constitutes a new phase of hegemonic culture; it postures as an oppositional force, but, in substance, is a new manifestation of peoples' allegiance and loyalty to the status quo. Counter-hegemonic culture represents genuine opposition to hegemonic culture.[90]

The acknowledgment of the relative autonomy of the cultural dimensions (and others) of the superstructure allows us to have a more dynamic understanding of the relationship between an economic-based and a culture-based definition of the ideological superstructure of society.

Secondly, the appropriation of Gramsci's notion of hegemony restrains the tendency to view culture as simply a negative influence or simply the creation of the ruling class for purposes of self-legitimation. Counterhegemonic culture presumes the significance of culture from the "underside of history" as expressing the oppositional aspirations and hopes of the oppressed class. Within this framework it is possible to perceive the value of popular culture, insofar as it is counterhegemonic. This is the reason for the black theologians' insistence on the value of the contribution of black culture.

Black culture and black religion have often been counterhegemonic cultural expressions against the hegemonic culture of white racists, and herein lies its importance as a struggle-sustaining worldview for blacks. West is correct in asserting that the "present challenge confronting black theologians is to discover and discern that aspect of Afro-American culture and religion that can contribute to a counterhegemonic culture in American society" and to connect these discoveries with a special analysis of the economic conditions that also define black lives.[91]

This is also true of the Latin American liberation theologians who have in the past tended to downplay the importance of popular religion and culture for the liberation struggle. The acknowledgment of the power of racism, in their context, would enhance the possibility of an intentioned quest for the counterhegemonic culture that exists in Latin America among the indigenous and black oppressed.

Thirdly, the notion of hegemony allows for the dialectical interplay of the economic base and the superstructure. This understanding of the relationship between the economic base and the superstructure makes it possible to refrain from narrow interpretations whereby economic factors have absolute determining influence on the evolution of human society.

Thus, the claim that racism is derived from the economic needs of capitalism to exploit the labor and resources of the nonwhite world can be seen as only a partial truth. As the work of Frank Snowden, Thomas Gossett, and others has shown, color prejudice in the form of racism against the darker peoples of the world is a phenomenon that goes back to antiquity.[92] Racism against blacks, Gayraud Wilmore asserts, has existed for thousands of years, in all kinds of societies:

Some people evidently assigned a pejorative meaning to Blackness long before the beginning of African slavery—for whatever reason—and if the Bible itself seems relatively free of this prejudice it is only because the Jews, after many years of residence and inter-marriage in Africa, were themselves a dark-skinned people by the time the Old Testament was written.[93]

This acknowledgment enhances the possibility of analyzing class (the economic factor) and race (the cultural superstructure) as two relatively autonomous factors in any comprehensive overview of the structures of domination in both the United States of America and in Latin America. Both factors (class and race) function dialectically within the course of a society that is multiracial and multiethnic. Gramsci's contribution, therefore, enables both black theologians and Latin American theologians to accept the significance of both factors—race and class—for their respective analyses.

On the basis of the commitment to the Gramscian notion of hegemonic and counterhegemonic culture, it is possible for black theologians and Latin American theologians of liberation to acknowledge the relative significance of both race and class for their respective situations. BTUSA can acknowledge the fact that their social analysis must contain both the religio-cultural and the socio-economic dimension. Although Julius Wilson has argued that race has declining significance and Cornel West has asserted that "class position contributes more than racial status to the basic form of powerlessness in America," black thinkers such as Cone, Wilmore and Karenga continue to affirm that "Afro-Americans . . . cannot simply have a general theory, they must have an afro-centric theory, i.e., one that rises from, is focused on and is on behalf of them."[94]

This is not to suggest that the debate should terminate; rather it is a recognition that the concepts of class and race are different concepts that are grounded on different bases and have some relative degree of autonomy from each other, though influencing each other.

West can affirm on the basis of his scientific analysis of American economic structures that class is more basic to the definition of one's social status. But he would also have to acknowledge that racism within the United States has an unscientific and irrational character and power that cannot simply be deduced from economic analysis.

Marx's interest was the identification of the principal divisions of human society based on the means of production. His criteria were, primarily, economic criteria. Because race, as a category, is never simply an economic category, Marx's economic base should be enhanced by a more comprehensive understanding of the diverse factors that condition social relationships.

In the final analysis, black theologians—if their decisions were based solely on economic data—would have to agree with West that with respect to "the basic form of powerlessness" in the United States, "class position contributes more than racial status."[95] However, this need not mean that they view race as any less important than class. It only means that black theologians have come to understand that Marx's definition of social class is based on economic criteria and that with respect to the issue of "powerlessness" in the United States, the economic factor is paramount, at least in a scientific sense.

Black theologians can then insert their contribution on the emergence of counterhegemonic culture into the discussion among progressive Marxists and black nationalists. Black theologians would, therefore, be reflecting their important contribution that the cultural basis is important as a factor in defining the social status of African-Americans and that at times it is a relatively autonomous factor in this process.

On their part, the Latin Americans should acknowledge that insofar as they have defined oppression within a narrow economy-based social analysis, they have failed to comprehensively appreciate the dynamic reality and influence of racism in determining social status in Latin America. Their emphasis on the primacy of class is correct insofar as they, like orthodox Marxists, tend to view the productive relationships of a society as being grounded in the economic base. However, the voices of African and Indian intellectuals in Latin America, as well as those of African-American, Asian and African theologians, can serve as a corrective intended to enhance the class analysis that has been utilized by the Latin Americans.

In Latin America there ought to be intentional inquiry into the specific nature of the dynamic between race and class that will take seriously the relative autonomy and influence of racism there. Although some scholars have noted the convergence of class distinctions along color lines, not many in Latin America have been willing to take seriously the cultural factor in defining social relations.[96]

For Latin American theologians, the acknowledgment of the appropriateness of these insights need not be viewed as a negation of their claim that class is primary in Latin America; such an acknowledgment can be a way to correct the narrowness of economic-base social analysis.

Appropriation of the insights of Gramsci and Mariátegui, with respect to hegemonic and nonhegemonic culture, can be an enhancement of the Latin Americans' analytic framework. Until there is conscientious and committed action to broaden their analysis in this way, their emphasis on the primacy of class and their inability, so far, to value and appropriate popular culture and religion will continue to be viewed as debilitating by indigenous and blacks in Latin America. By appropriating the notion of hegemonic and counterhegemonic culture, Latin American liberation theologians would be highlighting the significant insights that have resulted from their analysis based simply on the economic conditions of oppression in Latin America and the world, because such an appropriation would stress the connection between the socio-economic and the religio-cultural dimensions of the struggle for liberation.

The use of the concepts of hegemonic and counterhegemonic culture provide BTUSA and LALT with (1) a framework for incorporating race and class analysis in an integral framework, (2) a conceptual instrument of analysis which, alongside theological criteria, can be a means of assessing the words, practices and institutions which shape human society, and (3) a means of mediating between basic prescientific conceptions within liberation theology and the scientific basis for their use by liberation theologies.

An additional consequence of the use of Gramsci's explanatory framework is that it enhances BTUSA and LALT's capacity to address the important issue of gender oppression. The development of feminist, womanist and *mujerista* theologies in the context of the Americas has issued a challenge to all liberation theologies of the need to analyze the structures of domination in order to discern the patriarchal values, attitudes, sensibilities and institutions which define women's lives. White feminist theologians emerged, in the late sixties, alongside BTUSA and LALT, in order to affirm the existence of sexism within the values, structures and language of broader community, and to specifically critique the inherent patriarchy of the religions and theologies of Euro-American culture. Womanist theologians emerged from the African-American community about a decade later, in order to articulate a critique of both BTUSA and white feminist theology for the lack of inclusivity.

On the one hand, the womanist critique of BTUSA noted that black women's experiences were conspicuously absent from early Black Theology; that exclusive language with reference to God was lacking for some black women; and that the black Christian community was characterized by black male dominance. On the other hand, the womanist critique of white feminist theology pointed to the lack of nonbourgeois black women's perspective in early feminist theology; that white women's definition of women's struggle was inadequate, and that white women had manifested their own racism with regard to the struggles of their sisters.[97] Yolanda Tarango and Ada Isasi-Diaz, two Hispanic women theologians, have in recent years begun to establish a theological tradition derived from the experiences of

Hispanic/Latina women. Their critique of feminist theologies parallels the womanist critique from the perspective of Hispanic women. In one of the first published works that drew Latin American liberation theologians into the dialogue about women's oppression in Latin America, Elsa Tamez notes that liberation theology in Latin America has increasingly seen women joining in the discourse of liberation theology.[98] Of noteworthy mention, again, is the role of EATWOT, which recently entered into its second five-year period of focusing on women's oppression in Latin America. Tamez's challenge is clearly stated:

> If Latin American men do not recognize the reality of women's oppression, if they do not admit that they are promoters or accomplices of the ideology of machismo that permeates our culture, if they do not realize how great the riches that are lost to society due to the marginalization of women, if they do not move from theoretical conviction to liberating practice, if they do not join in solidarity with women in their struggle, the path of the feminist movement in Latin America will be longer, the progress slower and often more bitter, with more frustrations than joys.[99]

In the same manner that the differences between BTUSA and LALT can be viewed as an opportunity for mutual enrichment, so also can the varieties of theologies based on women's oppression contribute to the evolution of a more comprehensive theology of socio-economic, religio-cultural and political liberation. Gramsci's notion of hegemony, with some revision, allows for the possibility of viewing race, class and gender as specific threads within the structures of domination in the United States and in Latin America. Thus, both BTUSA and LALT can be more comprehensive in relation to the human experience.

Conclusion

The evolution of theologies of religio-cultural, socio-economic and political theologies of liberation in Latin America and the United States will be enhanced by the appropriation of a commitment to the concept of pneumatological Christology and the usage of the hegemonic and counterhegemonic framework. In light of an a priori commitment to the struggles of the poor, the incorporation of these themes by BTUSA and LALT will provide both theological traditions with another reason for affirming their mutual dedication to be co-artisans of liberating praxis and a transformed future.

In this context, the interpretive guide to the Gospel of Jesus Christ becomes the historical event of Jesus of Nazareth as the liberating presence of Christ, calling the oppressed and endowing them with the self-consciousness (faith) that they are the true subjects of God's redemptive project. On this basis, this common vision, then, both BTUSA and LALT can join in affirming that:

We can be for ourselves . . . if we are for others; these others can be for themselves only if they are for others—as long as we all share the understanding of the need for a vision of a shared world of the highest levels of progressive existence that are humanly possible.[100]

Notes

Introduction

1. Black Theology in the United States (BTUSA) and Latin American Liberation Theology (LALT) can be more accurately referred to as "Black Theologies" and "Latin American Liberation Theologies." In this publication, however, the emphasis will be on the nuances of emphasis that may characterize particular manifestations in each tradition. For this reason I will use "Black Theology" and "Latin American Liberation Theology" as two broad rubrics that contain the diverse manifestations of each tradition.

2. See James Cone's comment in the preface of the 1986 edition of his *A Black Theology of Liberation* (Maryknoll, N.Y.: Orbis Books, 1987, Second Edition), xiii, and also see Gustavo Gutiérrez's discussion of this issue in his *The Power of the Poor in History* (Maryknoll, N.Y.: Orbis Books, 1983), 193.

3. See Cone, xi. While this comment only reflects the thoughts of a black theologian, it is not difficult to find this idea articulated by Gutiérrez, Chapter 7, or by Juan Luis Segundo in *The Liberation of Theology* (Maryknoll, N.Y.; Orbis Books, 1979), Chapter 1.

4. For a discussion of this interpretation of the development of liberation theology, see Cone, xv, or his *God of the Oppressed* (New York: Seabury Press, 1975), 54–56. Also see Gustavo Gutiérrez's distinction between progressive theology and liberation theology, 196–201, and Theo Witvliet's discussion of the same in *A Place in the Sun: An Introduction to Liberation Theology in the Third World* (Maryknoll, N.Y.: Orbis Books, 1985), Chapters 1, 2, 3.

5. For an understanding of paradigms in theology, see Sallie McFague, *Metaphorical Theology: Models of God in Religious Language* (Philadelphia, Pa.: Fortress Press, 1982). Here *paradigm* is used to refer to a framework of interpretation which involves certain basic assumptions and issues. Both McFague and Rebecca Chopp have argued that the development of liberation theology represents a paradigm shift in contemporary theology. See Rebecca Chopp, *The Praxis of Suffering* (Maryknoll, N.Y.: Orbis Books, 1986), 4.

6. The commitment of both black theologians (USA) and LALT is evident in the documents emerging from their joint venture in EATWOT. See Virginia Fabella and Sergio Torres, eds., *Irruption of the Third World* (Maryknoll, N.Y.: Orbis Books, 1983), 205, or James Cone, *For My People* (Maryknoll, N.Y.: Orbis Books, 1984), Chapters 9 and 10, and Gutiérrez, Chapters 7 and 8.

7. In this discussion the terms *integral* and *holistic* will be used interchangeably to refer to a comprehensive liberation which integrates politics, economics, culture, religion and theology into one whole vision.

8. EATWOT is the Ecumenical Association of Third World Theologians. This

organization is constituted of theologians from the oppressed Third World communities who began a commitment in 1976 to work together in developing the liberation theology enterprise. The first meeting organized for EATWOT was in 1976 in Tanzania, and since that time they have been meeting at regular intervals.

9. Fabella and Torres, eds., 205.

10. James H. Cone is currently Charles Briggs Professor of Systematic Theology at Union Theological Seminary and has been the most prolific and consistent black theologian writing. Gayraud S. Wilmore is Professor of Church History and Afro-American Religious Studies at the Interdenominational Theological Center in Atlanta, Georgia, a theologian and an outstanding historian of the black religious experience. J. Deotis Roberts is currently Professor of Philosophical Theology at Eastern Baptist Theological Seminary and has also written a great deal on Black Theology.

11. Gustavo Gutiérrez, often referred to as the "Father of Latin American Liberation Theology," is a Peruvian priest and theologian whose importance to LALT is evidenced by his published work. Jose Míguez Bonino, a Protestant minister, is an Argentinean theologian whose contribution to the Protestant movement's development of LALT is important. Hugo Assmann, a regular participant in the early encounters of BTUSA and LALT, is a theologian living and working in Brazil.

12. James H. Cone, "Christianity and Black Power," in *Is Anybody Listening to Black America?*, ed. C. Eric Lincoln (New York: Seabury Press, 1968).

13. The Chimbote meeting was a conference sponsored by a group of radical priests that Gutiérrez had helped organize. They gathered in preparation for the Medellín Conference of Latin American Bishops, and Gutiérrez presented the basic outlines of what he called, for the first time, "a theology of liberation." See Robert McAfee Brown, *Makers of Contemporary Theology: Gustavo Gutiérrez* (Atlanta, Ga.: John Knox Press, 1980), 25, or see Edward L. Cleary, *Crisis and Change: The Church in Latin America Today* (Maryknoll, N.Y.: Orbis Books, 1985), 78.

14. This preliminary assessment is based on my own evaluation of the statement issued following its meeting in Oaxtepec, Mexico. Selected passages were published in *Ecumenical Review*. See "Commonalities, Differences and Cross-Fertilization Among Third-World Theologians," [Ecumenical Association of Third World Theologians document, Mexico, Dec. 1986], *Ecumenical Review* 40 (April 1988): 287–91.

15. Key Yuasa, "The Image of Christ in Latin American Popular Religiosity," in *Sharing Jesus in the Two-Thirds World*, ed. Vinay Samuel and Chris Sugen (Grand Rapids, Mich.: Eerdmans Pub. Co., 1983), 42–43.

16. For a representative reading of black theologians, see the following: James Cone, *Black Theology and Black Power* (New York: Seabury Press, 1969); *A Black Theology of Liberation* (Maryknoll, N.Y.: Orbis Books, 1987, Second Edition); *God of the Oppressed* (Maryknoll, N.Y.: Orbis Books, 1984); J. Deotis Roberts, *Liberation and Reconciliation: A Black Theology* (Philadelphia: Westminster Press, 1974); *Black Theology Today: Liberation and Contextualization* (New York: Edwin Hellen Press, 1983); *Black Theology in Dialogue* (Philadelphia: Westminster Press, 1987); Major Jones, *Black Awareness: A Theology of Hope* (New York: Abingdon Press, 1971); *The Color of God* (Macon, Ga.: Mercer University Press, 1987); Cecil Cone, *The Identity Crisis in Black Theology* (Nashville, Tenn.: The African Methodist Episcopal Church, 1975); William R. Jones, *Is God a White Racist?* (New York: Doubleday/Anchor Books, 1973): Albert Cleage, *The Black Messiah* (New York: Sheed and

Ward, 1969); and *Black Christian Nationalism* (Detroit, Mich.: Luxor Pub. PAOCC, 1987); Gayraud Wilmore, *Black Religion and Black Radicalism* (Maryknoll, N.Y.: Orbis Books, Second Edition, 1983); and *Last Things First* (Philadelphia: Westminster Press, 1982).

17. For a representative reading of Latin American theology of liberation, see the following: Gustavo Gutiérrez, *A Theology of Liberation* (Maryknoll, N.Y.: Orbis Books, 1973); *The Power of the Poor in History* (Maryknoll, N.Y.: Orbis Books, 1983); and *We Drink from Our Own Wells* (Maryknoll, N.Y.: Orbis Books, 1984); Juan Luis Segundo, *The Liberation of Theology* (Maryknoll, N.Y.: Orbis Books, 1976); José Míguez Bonino, *Doing Theology in a Revolutionary Situation* (Philadelphia, Pa.: Fortress Press, 1975); Hugo Assmann, *Theology of a Nomad Church* (Maryknoll, N.Y.: Orbis Books, 1976); Rubem Alves, *What Is Religion?* (Maryknoll, N.Y.: Orbis Books, 1981); Enrique Dussel, *A History of the Church in Latin America* (Grand Rapids, Mich.: Wm. B. Eerdmans Publishing Company, 1981).

Chapter 1

1. For the most thorough study of the relationship between black radicalism and black religion, see Gayraud Wilmore's outstanding work, *Black Religion and Black Radicalism* (Maryknoll, N.Y.: Orbis Books, 1983, Second Edition), in which he documents the development of the historical struggle for black freedom and its relationship to black religion.

2. Herbert O. Edwards, "Black Theology and Retrospect and Prospect," *Journal of Religious Thought* 17, No. 2 (Fall–Winter 1975): 46–47.

3. For a thorough discussion of black religion and culture as resources for black struggle against racism, see Gayraud Wilmore, *Black Religion and Black Radicalism* (Maryknoll, N.Y.: Orbis Books, 1983, Second Edition) and Cedric Robinson, *Black Marxism: The Making of the Black Radical Tradition* (London, England: Zed Press, 1983).

4. The word *theology* is being used here as referring to the technical discipline of a "systematic, rational reflection on the meaning of God." James Cone, in "Black Religious Thought in American History, Part I: Origins," has indicated, correctly so, that black slaves had neither the time, tools nor disposition to do "theology as 'rational reflection' about God."

5. Ibid., 83.

6. For the best treatment of this subject, see Albert J. Raboteau, *Slave Religion* (New York: Oxford University Press, 1978).

7. Herbert Aptheker, *A Documentary History of the Negro People in the U.S.* (New York: Citadel Press, 1951), 11.

8. Raboteau's work in *Slave Religion* is still one of the best texts for documenting this claim.

9. Wilmore, 11–28.

10. Robert Bruce Simpson, "A Black Church Ecstasy in a World of Trouble," (Ph.D. Dissertation, Washington University, 1970), 175–211.

11. Wilmore, 37.

12. For a complete discussion of this claim, see any of the following: George P. Rawick, *From Sundown to Sunup: The Making of the Black Community* (Westport, Conn.: Greenwood Publishing Company, 1972), especially chaps. 1–3; Raboteau; Wilmore; Cornel West, *Prophesy Deliverance: An Afro-American Revolutionary Chris-*

tianity (Philadelphia, Pa.: Westminster Press, 1982), especially chaps. 1, 4, 5.

13. Raboteau, 147.

14. Ibid., 163.

15. Cited in Wilmore, 52.

16. Ibid., 54–55.

17. For Walker's appeal, see Herbert Aptheker, *"One Continual Cry," David Walker's Appeal* (New York: Humanities Press, 1965).

18. Wilmore, 108.

19. Raboteau, 319.

20. Carter G. Woodson, ed., *Negro Orators and Their Orations* (Washington, D.C.: Associated Publishers, 1925), 150ff.

21. Wilmore, 319.

22. For Delaney's comments, see Martin Delaney, *The Condition, Elevation, Emigration and Destiny of the Colored People of the United States, Politically Considered* (Philadelphia, Pa., 1852), 38ff. This interpretation of Delaney's comments is found in Wilmore, 111.

23. Wilmore, 157.

24. Ibid., 197.

25. Gayraud S. Wilmore and James H. Cone, *Black Theology: A Documentary History, 1966–1979* (Maryknoll, N.Y.: Orbis Books, 1978), 245.

26. For Cone's interpretation, see James H. Cone, *Speaking the Truth: Ecumenism, Liberation and Black Theology* (Grand Rapids, Mich.: William B. Eerdmans Publishing Company, 1986), 95–96. Cone's perspective is supported by Wilmore in *Black Religion and Black Radicalism*, chapter 6.

27. Cone, *Speaking the Truth*, 97.

28. While acknowledging the debate on African retention which transpired between Melville Herskovits, E. Franklin Frazier and other scholars during the past several decades, it is the conviction of this writer that the work of Albert J. Raboteau, George Eaton Simpson, Gayraud Wilmore, George Rawick, and Eugene Genovese has amply demonstrated the African-American's continuity with Africa. See Raboteau, *Slave Religion*; Gayraud S. Wilmore, *Black Religion and Black Radicalism*; George P. Rawick, *From Sundown to Sunup*; Eugene Genovese's *Roll, Jordan, Roll* (New York: Pantheon Books, Random House, 1972); and George Eaton Simpson, *Black Religions in the New World* (New York: Columbia University Press, 1978). For Herskovitz and Frazier's views, see Melville J. Herskovits, *The Myth of the Negro Past* (Boston: Beacon Press, 1958), or *The New World Negro: Selected Papers in African Studies*, ed. Frances S. Herskovits (Indiana: Indiana University Press, 1966); and E. Franklin Frazier, *The Negro Church in America* (New York: Schocken Books, 1964) or *The Negro in the United States* (New York: Macmillan Co., 1949).

29. For an excellent example of this, see Martin Luther King, Jr., "Letter From a Birmingham Jail," in *Why We Can't Wait* (New York: Signet Books, New American Library, 1963), 76–95.

30. For an excellent discussion of King's academic preparation, see Ira Zepp and Kenneth L. Smith, *The Search for the Beloved Community* (Valley Forge, Pa.: Judson Press, 1974), or David Garrow, *Bearing the Cross* (New York: Vintage Books, Random House, 1988).

31. Martin Luther King, Jr., *Stride toward Freedom* (New York: Harper and Row, 1958), 33.

32. Ibid., 36.

33. Ibid., 106.

34. King's perspective is echoed in the work of Jürgen Moltmann, the European theologian, Kitamori, the Japanese theologian, and Takatso Mofekeng, the South African theologian. See Jürgen Moltmann, *The Crucified God: The Cross of Christ as the Foundation and Criticism of Christian Theology* (New York: Harper and Row, 1974); Kazo Kitamori, *The Theology of the Pain of God* (Richmond, Va.: John Knox Press, 1965); and Takatso Mofekeng, *The Crucified Among the Cross Bearers* (Kampton: J. H. Kok, 1983).

35. This pneumatological point is also made in Theo Witvliet's discussion of the Spirit in his text, *The Way of the Black Messiah* (Oak Park, Ill.: Meyer, Stone Books, 1987), 218–30.

36. For reference to these clergy, see Robert H. Brisbane, *Black Activism: Racial Revolution in the United States 1954–1970* (Valley Forge, Pa.: Judson Press, 1974), 65; or Jim Bishop, *The Days of Martin Luther King, Jr.* (New York: G. P. Putnam's Sons, 1971), 239.

37. King, *Why We Can't Wait*, 77.

38. Ibid., 90.

39. Ibid., 91.

40. This statement is taken from a speech which Albert Cleage delivered in Detroit on February 24, 1967, entitled "Myth About Malcolm X." The speech was published in a compendium of articles on Malcolm X edited by John Henrick Clarke, *Malcolm X and His Times* (New York: Macmillan Company, 1969), 24.

41. Insofar as I affirm Black Power as the immediate antecedent to Black Theology, it then becomes important to view Malcolm X and the Black Power Movement and Martin Luther King, Jr., and the Civil Rights Movement as a part of the ebb and flow of the same black freedom impulse which gave rise to Black Theology. Therefore Malcolm X's significance must be evaluated in the context of the frustration that was being felt by some of those in the Civil Rights Movement.

42. James H. Cone, "America: A Dream or a Nightmare?" *Journal of the Inter-denominational Theological Center,* Spring, 1986, vol. 12, no. 2, 271–272.

43. See Cone's complete discussion of this issue in his book *Martin and Malcolm and America: A Dream or a Nightmare* (Maryknoll, N.Y.: Orbis Books, 1991).

44. Malcolm X, *The Autobiography of Malcolm X*, with the assistance of Alex Haley (New York: Ballantine Books, 1964), 241.

45. See Cone, *Martin and Malcolm and America*, 1–16.

46. West, *Prophesy Deliverance*, 69–91.

47. Wilmore, *Black Religion and Black Radicalism*, 267.

48. Brisbane, *Black Activism*, 139.

49. Ibid.

50. See Floyd B. Barbour, ed., *The Black Power Revolt: A Collection of Essays* (Boston, Mass.: Horizon Books, Imprint).

51. Brisbane, *Black Activism*, 139.

52. On June 6, 1966, at a meeting in Memphis, Tennessee, Floyd McKissick, Stokely Carmichael and Martin Luther King, Jr., agreed that their organizations, the Congress of Racial Equality (CORE), the Student Non-Violent Coordinating Committee (SNCC), and the Southern Christian Leadership Conference (SCLC) would jointly sponsor the Meredith March, and invite other civil rights organizations to join them. See Brisbane, *Black Activism*, 140.

53. Martin Luther King, Jr., *Where Do We Go from Here: Chaos or Community?*

(Boston, Mass.: Beacon Press, 1967), 29. King documents his perspective on the development of the Black Power cry at a mass meeting in the south.

54. Robert Brisbane expressed this judgment in his book, *Black Activism*. I concur from my own review of some of the documents which discuss the issue of Black Power in 1966. See Brisbane, *Black Activism*, 148.

55. *New York Times*, August 5, 1966, 10. For an elaboration of Carmichael's views on Black Power, see Stokely Carmichael and Charles Hamilton, *Black Power: The Politics of Liberation in America* (New York: Random House, Inc., 1967) and Stokely Carmichael, *Stokely Speaks: Black Power Back to Pan-Africanism* (New York: Vintage Books, Random House, Inc., 1971).

56. Nathan Wright, Jr., "Black Power: A Religious Opportunity," in Wilmore and Cone, *Black Theology: A Documentary History*, 59.

57. Wilmore and Cone, *Black Theology: A Documentary History*, 23.

58. Ibid., 100–101.

59. James H. Cone, *For My People* (Maryknoll, N.Y.: Orbis Books, 1983), 19–24.

60. Wilmore and Cone, *Black Theology: A Documentary History*, 67.

61. For a good evaluation of the origin of the term "Black Theology," see Cone, *For My People*, 19–20.

62. See, for example, these documents: The Black Declaration of Independence, July 4, 1970 (NCB); The President's Message to the Progressive National Baptist Convention, Inc., September, 1968; the statement by black Methodists for church renewal, 1968; the Episcopal address to the 27th General Conference of the Christian Methodist Episcopal Church, 1976; statement from the Black Christian National Church, Inc., 1976. These documents are all to be found in Gayraud S. Wilmore and James H. Cone, *Black Theology: A Documentary History*, 108–331.

63. Wilmore and Cone, *Black Theology: a Documentary History*, 68.

64. Ibid., 111.

65. See Brisbane, *Black Activism*, Chapter 7, for a good description of the violent riots which wreaked havoc on America from 1964–1970.

66. James Cone has argued that Washington's publication is an important part of the framework of the development of Black Theology. While I agree, I would designate its importance as being secondary to Civil Rights, Black Power and the riots. For Cone's discussion, see James Cone, *For My People*, 6.

67. Joseph Washington, Jr., *Black Religion* (Boston: Beacon Press, 1964), 155.

68. Wilmore, *Black Religion and Black Radicalism* (First Edition), 286.

69. Wilmore's claim is made in "Black Theology: Its Significance for Christian Mission Today," *International Review of Mission* 63, No. 250 (April 1974).

70. This view is supported by both James Cone in his *For My People*, 8–9, and by Gayraud Wilmore in his article, "Black Theology: Its Significance for Christian Mission Today," 211.

71. Cone, *For My People*, 9.

72. Ibid.

73. Wilmore and Cone, *Black Theology: A Documentary History*, 610.

74. Quotation from a public statement made by Camilo Torres in 1966 and cited by Walter J. Broderick in *Camilo Torres: A Biography of the Priest-Guerillero* (Garden City, N.Y.: Doubleday and Company, Inc., 1975), 254.

75. An excellent source of historical data on the struggle of Latin Americans

for independence is Eduard Galeano's *Open Veins in Latin America* (New York: Monthly Review Press, 1973).

76. These periodizations were appropriated from Enrique Dussel in *History and the Theology of Liberation* (Maryknoll, N.Y.: Orbis Books, 1976), 80–81 and by Pablo Richard in an unpublished paper entitled "The Theology of Liberation in the Current Situation of Latin America."

77. For a comprehensive description of these factors, see Enrique Dussel, *A History of the Church in Latin America: Colonialism to Liberation* (Grand Rapids, Mich.: Wm. B. Eerdmans Publishing Co., 1981), especially Chaps. 10, 11, 12.

78. José Míguez Bonino, *Doing Theology in a Revolutionary Situation* (Philadelphia, Pa.: Fortress Press, 1970), 17.

79. Ibid.

80. The specific figures cited here are taken from Penny Lernoux's "The Long Path to Puebla," which was printed in *Puebla and Beyond,* John Eagleson and Philip Scharper, eds. (Maryknoll, N.Y.: Orbis Books, 1979), 4.

81. Míguez Bonino, *Doing Theology in a Revolutionary Situation,* 12.

82. Ibid., 12–13.

83. For a complete description of these characteristics, see the data cited by Míguez Bonino in *Doing Theology in a Revolutionary Situation,* 22–23, and taken from a United Nations report entitled *Inform Preliminar Sobre la situation del Mundo* (New York: United Nations Publications, 1952).

84. Míguez Bonino, *Doing Theology in a Revolutionary Situation,* 21.

85. Ibid., 26.

86. Ibid., 14.

87. Gustavo Gutiérrez, *A Theology of Liberation* (Maryknoll, N.Y.: Orbis Books, 1975), 25.

88. Edward Cleary, *Crisis and Change: The Church in Latin America Today* (Maryknoll, N.Y.: Orbis Books, 1985), 30.

89. Ibid., 30–31.

90. Míguez Bonino, *Doing Theology in a Revolutionary Situation,* 25.

91. Ibid.

92. Ibid., 26.

93. Walter Rodney, *How Europe Underdeveloped Africa* (Washington, D.C.: Howard University Press, 1974), 14.

94. For a full discussion of *dependencia,* see Míguez Bonino, *Doing Theology in a Revolutionary Situation,* 27.

95. Penny Lernoux, "The Long Path to Puebla," 5.

96. Broderick, *Camilo Torres,* 300.

97. Gustavo Gutiérrez, *The Power of the Poor in History* (Maryknoll, N.Y.: Orbis Books, 1983), 190–91.

98. Ibid., 191.

99. Ibid.

100. Phillip Berryman, *The Religious Roots of Rebellion* (Maryknoll, N.Y.: Orbis Books, 1983), 28.

101. See the published address of Archbishop Ricketts in *The Church in the Present-Day Transformation of Latin America in the Light of the Council: I,* published by the General Secretarial of CELAM (Bogotá, Colombia: Apartado Aereo 5278, 1970), 21–26.

102. Cleary, *Crisis and Change,* 22.

103. Ibid.

104. Enrique Dussel, *History and the Theology of Liberation*, 111–12. For a more extensive discussion of the church in Latin America, see Enrique Dussel, *A History of the Church in Latin America*.

105. Cleary, *Crisis and Change*, 19.

106. Ibid., 18.

107. Ibid., 20.

108. Ibid.

109. Ibid.

110. Ibid., 19. See also Appendix II of Enrique Dussel, *A History of the Church in Latin America*, 326.

111. Cleary, *Crisis and Change*, 19.

112. Gutiérrez, *The Power of the Poor in History*, 26.

113. Cleary, *Crisis and Change*, 22. For another account of the intervening years, see Alfonso Lopez Trujillo, *Medellín: Reflexiones en el CELAM* (Madrid, Spain: Biblioteca de Autores Christianos, 1972), 11–12, where Trujillo indicates that the turn to Latin America had been set in process from the time of Vatican II.

114. Cleary, *Crisis and Change*, 23.

115. Noel Erskine has set forth the claim that the theology of the Caribbean must be decolonized and has attempted to demonstrate this process in his book *Decolonizing Theology. A Caribbean Perspective* (Maryknoll: N.Y.: Orbis Books, 1981). I am applying this term to Latin America.

116. For documentation on this process, see Cleary, *Crisis and Change*, 27–29.

117. Ibid., 30.

118. Gutiérrez, *The Power of the Poor in History*, 28.

119. Cleary, *Crisis and Change*, 34–35.

120. Dussel, *History and the Theology of Liberation*, 114–15.

121. The final documents of the Medellín Conference were published in English under the auspices of the Latin American Episcopal council and entitled *The Church in the Present Day Transformation of Latin America in the Light of the Council* (Bogota: General Secretariat of CELAM, 1970), vol. 2, hereafter cited as *Medellín Conclusions*, 58.

122. *Medellín Conclusions*, 72–75, 78.

123. Ibid., 60.

124. Gutiérrez, *The Power of the Poor in History*, 26.

125. Cleary, *Crisis and Change*, 43.

126. Ibid., 35.

127. Ibid.

128. For this evolution in thinking, see "Chronology of Theology of Liberation," which appeared in the mimeographed bulletin "CIDALA Forum," published in Bogotá, Colombia, by the Committee for Intercultural Dialogue and Action in Latin America (CIDALA). It was the outline of a lecture given by the Catholic Way theologian Rafael Avila at CIDALA headquarters in 1973.

129. Míguez Bonino, *Doing Theology in a Revolutionary Situation*, 54–55.

130. For a description of their views on the development of ISAL, see Hugo Assmann, *Oppresion-Liberacion: Desafio a los Cristianos* (Montevideo, Uruguay: Tierra Nueva, 1971), 79; and Julio de Santa Ana, "Protestantismo Cultura y Sociedad" (Buenos Aires, Argentina: La Aurora, 1970), 29, 114; or "ISAL, un Movimiento en March," *Cuadernos en Marcha*, No. 29 (September, 1969).

131. Cleary, *Crisis and Change,* 39.

132. Cone expresses this perspective in the prefaces of his *God of the Oppressed* and in *Black Theology of Liberation.*

133. Gayraud S. Wilmore, "Afro-American and Third World Theology," in *African Theology En Route,* Kofi Appiah-Kubi and Sergio Torres, eds. (Maryknoll, N.Y.: Orbis Books, 1979), 206.

134. For an exposition of the reason Latin American liberation theologians view class analysis as basic to their enterprise, see Míquez Bonino, *Doing Theology in a Revolutionary Situation.*

135. Gustavo Gutiérrez, "Liberation Theology and Progressivist Theology," in *The Emergent Gospel,* Sergio Torres and Virginia Fabella, eds. (Maryknoll, N.Y.: Orbis Books, 1978), 240.

136. For a discussion of black Christologies of liberation, see Albert B. Cleage, Jr., *The Black Messiah* (New York: Sheed and Ward, 1968); James H. Cone, *God of the Oppressed,* (New York: Seabury Press, 1975), especially Chap. 6; and J. Deotis Roberts, *Liberation and Reconciliation: A Black Theology* (Philadelphia: The Westminster Press, 1971), Chap. 6.

137. Vincent Harding, "Black Power and the American Christ," published in *Black Theology: A Documentary History, 1966-1979,* ed. Gayraud S. Wilmore and James H. Cone (Maryknoll, N.Y.: Orbis Books, 1979), 35–42.

138. Gustavo Gutiérrez, *The Power of the Poor in History,* 92–93.

139. For a thorough explication of Latin American Christologies of liberation see Jon Sobrino, *Christology at the Crossroads* (Maryknoll, N.Y.: Orbis Books, 1976); *Jesus in Latin America* (Maryknoll, N.Y.: Orbis Books, 1987); José Miranda, *Being and the Messiah* (Maryknoll, N.Y.: Orbis Books, 1973); José Cardenas Pallares, *A Poor Man Called Jesus* (Maryknoll, N.Y.: Orbis Books, 1982); Orlando Costas, *Christ Outside the Gate* (Maryknoll, N.Y.: Orbis Books, 1982); and Ignacio Ellacuría, *Freedom Made Flesh* (Maryknoll, N.Y.: Orbis Books, 1976).

140. Sergio Torres and John Eagleson, *The Challenge of Basic Christian Communities* (Maryknoll, N.Y.: Orbis Books, 1981), 263.

Chapter 2

1. The black radical tradition of the 60s, as it is represented in the statements of the era, suggests a critical attitude toward American economic structures and a commitment to their radical transformation. See "The Black Manifesto," for example, published and adopted on April 26, 1969, by the National Black Economic Development Conference in Detroit, Michigan, and affirmed by the National Conference of Black Churchmen on May 7, 1969. Both documents suggest a clear recognition of the need for economic liberation and were republished in Gayraud S. Wilmore and James H. Cone, *Black Theology: A Documentary History 1966-1979* (Maryknoll, N.Y.: Orbis Books, 1979), 80–92.

2. "Message to the Churches from Oakland, California," a statement by the National Committee of Black Churchmen (sic) published in Wilmore and Cone, *Black Theology: A Documentary History,* 103–104.

3. The National Committee of Black Churchmen's (sic) Statement, "The Black Declaration of Independence," July 4, 1970, in Wilmore and Cone, *Black Theology: A Documentary History,* 111.

4. Gayraud S. Wilmore is a church historian in discipline. I acknowledge here

that I am referring to him as a black theologian, in an extraordinary fashion. Although trained in Ethics and teaching primarily Church History, Wilmore is an important pioneer in the Black Theology Commission of the National Conference of Black Churchmen and provided an important contribution to Black Theology in publishing his text *Black Religion and Black Radicalism*. This book is the basis for much of BTUSA's later development.

5. See Cone's first published essay, "Christianity and Black Power," in *Is Anybody Listening to Black America?*, ed. C. Eric Lincoln (New York: Seabury Press, 1968).

6. James H. Cone, *Black Theology and Black Power* (New York: Seabury Press, 1969), 2.

7. The notion of praxis used throughout this publication refers to the technical philosophical term which signifies the inseparably connected human actions of historical reflection and practical activity. Although there is disagreement among Marxist scholars concerning the meaning of the term *praxis* in Marx's written work, this concept is explicated by him in his well-known "Theses on Feuerbach" (especially the third and the eighth thesis). The word *praxis*, of course, has deep roots in the Aristotelian school of Greek antiquity, where the word referred to practical knowledge, or the application of theory in a practical way so as to determine its validity as true knowledge. For this writer, praxis is the integral relationship of theoretical reflection and practical activity in a dynamic and ongoing process which creates and transforms.

8. Gayraud S. Wilmore, "Black Theology: Review and Assessment," *Voices From the Third World* 5, no. 2 (December 1982).

9. Cone, *Black Theology and Black Power*, 5–12.

10. James H. Cone, *My Soul Looks Back* (Nashville, Tenn.: Abingdon Books, 1982), 44.

11. For an account of the struggle of other black Christians with this question, see Gayraud S. Wilmore's references to himself and other prominent black Christian leaders in this period, in his article, "Black Theology Review and Assessment."

12. Cone, *My Soul Looks Back*, 44.

13. See Cone's discussion of sources and norms of BTUSA in his *The God of the Oppressed* (New York: The Seabury Press, 1975), chaps. 1–4, or *A Black Theology of Liberation* (second edition), (Maryknoll, N.Y.: Orbis Books, 1986), chaps. 1 and 2.

14. Cone, *God of the Oppressed*, 3.

15. Ibid.

16. Ibid., 17.

17. Ibid., chaps. 3, 4, 5.

18. Ibid., 31.

19. Ibid.

20. Ibid., 39.

21. Ibid., 81.

22. Wilmore and Cone, *Black Theology: A Documentary History*, 603.

23. Cone's more recent work on Martin Luther King, Jr., and Malcolm X promises to provide BTUSA with a rich source for further theological work. See James Cone, "America: A Dream or a Nightmare," in *The Journal of the Interdenominational Theological Center*, 13, No. 2 (Spring 1986): 263–78, or *Martin and Malcolm and America* (Marynoll, N.Y.: Orbis Books, 1991).

24. For a discussion of the interpretation of the dialogue between black theologians, see James Cone, "An Interpretation of the Debate Among Black Theologians," in Wilmore and Cone, *Black Theology: A Documentary History*, 609–22. See also Cecil W. Cone, *The Identity Crisis in Black Theology* (Nashville, Tenn.: AMEC, 1975).

25. Gayraud S. Wilmore, "Black Theology: Review and Assessment," 14.

26. Ibid., 15.

27. Gayraud S. Wilmore, *Black Religion and Black Radicalism* (first edition) (Garden City, New York: Doubleday, 1972), 296.

28. J. Deotis Roberts, *Black Theology Today: Liberation and Contextualization* (New York: The Edwin Mellen Press, 1983), 55.

29. Gayraud S. Wilmore, *Black Religion and Black Radicalism* (second edition) (Maryknoll, N.Y.: Orbis Books, 1983), 235.

30. Ibid.

31. Cone, *God of the Oppressed*, 130.

32. Ibid., 134.

33. Ibid., 135.

34. Wilmore, *Black Religion and Black Radicalism* (second edition), 216.

35. Albert Cleage had argued that Jesus Christ was the black Messiah based on a historical analysis of the literal significance of Jesus. Cone's position is distinctly different from Cleage's, since Cone tends to reject Cleage's stress on the literal blackness of the historical Jesus of Nazareth as unbiblical, and to place emphasis on the symbolic identification of Jesus the Jew with those who are oppressed by virtue of their blackness.

36. James H. Cone, *A Black Theology of Liberation* (Philadelphia: Lippincott, 1970), 27–28.

37. Cone, *God of the Oppressed*, 136.

38. See Roderick M. McLean, *The Theology of Marcus Garvey* (Washington, D.C.: University Press of America, 1982), especially chapters 3 & 4.

39. Cone, *God of the Oppressed*, 129.

40. Gayraud S. Wilmore, "The Black Messiah: Revising the Color Symbolism of Western Christology," *Journal of the Interdenominational Theological Center*, 2 (Fall 1974): 14, especially chaps. 3 and 4.

41. Ibid., 17–18.

42. Ibid.

43. J. Deotis Roberts, *Liberation and Reconciliation: A Black Theology* (Philadelphia: Westminster Press, 1974), 136.

44. Ibid.

45. Ibid., 137.

46. Ibid., 124.

47. Ibid., 137.

48. J. Deotis Roberts, *Black Theology Today: Liberation and Contextualization*, 55.

49. J. Deotis Roberts, *A Black Political Theology* (Philadelphia: Westminster, 1974), 138.

50. Ibid.

51. See, for example, Malcolm X's critique of Christian religion in *The Autobiography of Malcolm X* (New York: Ballantine Books, 1964), 241, 368–71. The black Messiah as a christological image developed in response to the call for black-

ness in all things. Albert Cleage published his book, *The Black Messiah,* in 1968 (New York: Sheed and Ward, 1968).

52. See the comments by Malcolm X in *The Autobiography of Malcolm X,* 241–42, and C. Eric Lincoln's *The Black Muslims in America* (Boston: Beacon Press, 1961), 76–80.

53. James H. Cone, *Speaking the Truth: Ecumenism, Liberation and Black Theology* (Grand Rapids, Mich.: William B. Eerdmans Pub. Co., 1986), 47.

54. See John S. Mbiti, *African Religions and Philosophy* (Garden City, N.Y.: Doubleday and Company, Inc., 1969), Chaps. 6 and 7.

55. Wilmore, "Black Theology: Review and Assessment," 15.

56. Wilmore's text, *Black Religion and Black Radicalism,* published in 1975, is a testimony to the historically grounded black political struggle in the radical prophetic tradition of the black church.

57. Wilmore, *Black Religion and Black Radicalism* (second edition), chap. 9.

58. Gayraud S. Wilmore, "Black Christians, Church Unity and One Church Expression of Apostolic Faith," in *Black Witness to the Apostolic Faith,* ed. David T. Shannon and Gayraud S. Wilmore (Grand Rapids, Mich.: William B. Eerdmans Pub. Co., 1985), 14.

59. Ibid.

60. James Deotis Roberts, *Black Theology Today,* 131.

61. Ibid., 135.

62. Ibid., 137.

63. Ibid., 54–55.

64. Ibid., 55–56.

65. Cone, *Black Theology and Black Power,* 6.

66. Wilmore, *Black Religion and Black Radicalism* (second edition), 27.

67. Ibid.

68. Roberts, *A Black Political Theology,* 221.

69. Ibid., 219.

70. James H. Cone, *The Spirituals and the Blues* (New York: Seabury Press, 1972; Maryknoll, N.Y.: Orbis Books, 1991), 97.

71. Cone, *A Black Theology of Liberation* (second edition), 141.

72. Cone, *The Spirituals and the Blues,* 100.

73. Gayraud S. Wilmore, *Last Things First* (Philadelphia, Pa.: Westminster Press, 1982), 83.

74. Ibid., 88–89.

75. Albert Raboteau, *Slave Religion* (New York: Oxford University Press, 1978), 291.

76. Cone, *The Spirituals and the Blues,* 98.

77. Joseph R. Washington, Jr., *Black Religion* (Boston: Beacon Press, 1964), 217.

78. Raboteau, *Slave Religion,* 291.

79. Ibid.

80. Cone, *The Spirituals and the Blues,* 94.

81. Ibid., 92.

82. Ibid., 89.

83. Clifton H. Johnson, ed., *God Struck Me Dead* (Philadelphia: Pilgrim Press, 1969), 165–66.

84. Ibid., 59–60.

85. Ibid., 122.

86. Dr. Martin Luther King, Jr., "A Christmas Sermon on Peace," in *A Testament of Hope*, ed. James Melvin Washington (San Francisco: Harper & Row, Publishers, 1986), 258.

87. Dr. Martin Luther King, Jr., "I Have Dream," in Washington, ed., *A Testament of Hope*, 218-20.

88. Dr. Martin Luther King, Jr., "The Most Durable Power," in Washington, ed., *A Testament of Hope*, 10.

89. The two best examples of how the future is experienced in the present come from the beginning and end of King's leadership in the Civil Rights Movement: the January 27, 1956, experience in his kitchen, and his final sermon the night before he was murdered. See David J. Garrow, *Bearing the Cross* (New York: Vintage Books, 1988), 58; and Martin Luther King, Jr., "I See the Promised Land," in Washington, ed., *A Testament of Hope*, 286.

90. Roberts, *Black Theology Today: Liberation and Contextualization*, 43.

91. Cone, *Black Theology and Black Power*, 17.

92. Nathan Wright, Jr., "Black Power and Urban Unrest: Creative Possibilities," in Wilmore and Cone, *Black Theology: A Documentary History*, 49.

93. See James H. Cone, *For My People: Black Theology and the Black Church* (Maryknoll, N.Y.: Orbis Books, 1984), Cha4; and *My Soul Looks Back*, chaps. 4 and 5. Martin Luther King, Jr., "I See the Promised Land," in Washington, ed., *A Testament of Hope*, 286.

94. See Roberts, *Black Theology Today*, Part II, and *Black Theology in Dialogue* (Philadelphia: The Westminster Press, 1987), Chap. 11.

Chapter 3

1. Gustavo Gutiérrez, *The Power of the Poor in History* (Maryknoll, N.Y.: Orbis Books, 1983), 200.

2. See, for example, Lloyd Stennette, Mauro Batista, and Barry Chavangs, "The Situation of the Black Race in Latin America and the Caribbean," in *The Challenge of Basic Christian Communities*, ed. Sergio Torres and John Eagleson (Maryknoll, N.Y.: Orbis Books, 1981), 46–69.

3. Gutiérrez, *The Power of the Poor in History*, 46–69.

4. Ibid., 92. See also "Praxis de Liberacion, Teologia y Anuncio," in *Liberacion: Dialogos en el CELAM* (Bogota: CELAM, 1974).

5. Ibid., 92–93.

6. José Míguez Bonino, *Doing Theology in a Revolutionary Situation* (Philadelphia: Fortress Press, 1975), 90.

7. Ibid.

8. Ibid., 88.

9. Gutiérrez, *The Power of the Poor in History*, 201.

10. Míguez Bonino, *Doing Theology in a Revolutionary Situation*, 61.

11. Gustavo Gutiérrez, *A Theology of Liberation* (Maryknoll, N.Y.: Orbis Books, 1976), 11.

12. Ibid.

13. Juan Luis Segundo, *The Liberation of Theology* (Maryknoll, N.Y.: Orbis Books, 1976), 13.

14. Ibid.

15. Ibid.
16. Míguez Bonino, *Doing Theology in a Revolutionary Situation,* 95.
17. Ibid., 96.
18. Arthur F. McGovern, *Liberation Theology and Its Critics: Toward an Assessment* (Maryknoll, N.Y.: Orbis Books, 1989), 145.
19. Juan Luis Segundo, "Two Theologies of Liberation," *Etudes* (September 1984) (my trans.), 323.
20. Hugo Assmann, *Theology of a Nomad Church* (Maryknoll, N.Y.: Orbis Books, 1976), 103. This book was first published in 1973 in Spanish under the title, *Teología desde la praxis de la liberación: Ensayo teológico desde la América dependiente.*
21. Ibid., 103.
22. Hugo Assmann, "The Actuation of the Power of Christ in History: Notes on the Discernment of Christological Contradiction," in *Faces of Jesus: Latin America Christologies,* ed. José Míguez Bonino (Maryknoll, N.Y.: Orbis Books, 1985), 125–26.
23. Ibid., 127.
24. Ibid., 129.
25. During the last 18 years a variety of Latin American Christologies have emerged. See Leonardo Boff, *Jesus Christ Liberator: A Critical Christology for Our Time,* trans. Patrick Hughes (Maryknoll, N.Y.: Orbis Books, 1978), Portuguese ed., *Jesus Cristo Libertador. Ensaio de Cristologia Crítica para O nosso Tempo* (Petrópolis, Brazil: Editora Vozes Ltda., 1972); *Passion of Christ, Passion of the World: The Facts, Their Interpretation, and Their Meaning Yesterday and Today,* trans. Robert R. Barr (Maryknoll, N.Y.: Orbis Books, 1987), Portuguese ed. *Paixão de Cristo — Paixão do Mundo* (Petrópolis: Editora Vozes, 1977); Jon Sobrino, *Christology at the Crossroads: A Latin American Approach,* trans. J. Drury (Maryknoll, N.Y.: Orbis Books, 1978), Spanish ed. *Cristología desde américa latina* (Mexico City: CRT, 1976), and his *Jesus in Latin America* (Maryknoll, N.Y.: Orbis Books, 1987), Spanish ed. *Jesus en America Latina: Su Significado Para La Fe Cristologica* (San Salvador, El Salvador: UCA Editoriales, 1982); José Porfirio Miranda, *Being and the Messiah: The Message of St. John,* trans. John Eagleson (Maryknoll, N.Y.: Orbis Books, 1977), Spanish ed., *El Ser y el Mesías* (Salamanca, Spain, Ediciones Sigueme, 1973); Ignacio Ellacuría, *Freedom Made Flesh: The Mission of Christ and His Church,* trans. John Drury (Maryknoll, N.Y.: Orbis Books, 1985), Spanish ed., *Teología Politica* (San Salvador, El Salvador, Ediciónes del Secretariado Social Interdiocesano, 1973). The basic hermeneutical methodology of LALT is explicated by Juan Luis Segundo, *The Liberation of Theology* (Maryknoll, N.Y.: Orbis Books, 1976), 6–34.
26. José Míguez Bonino, "Who Is Jesus Christ in Latin America Today?" in *Faces of Jesus,* ed. José Míguez Bonino (Maryknoll, N.Y.: Orbis Books, 1987), 5. Míguez Bonino is a Protestant theologian and Professor Emeritus of Systematic Theology and Ethics at the Instituto Superior Evangélico de Estudios Teológicos in Argentina.
27. Ibid., 6.
28. Gutiérrez, *The Power of the Poor in History,* 60–61. The historical Jesus of the Latin Americas is to be distinguished from the historical Jesus of the European theologians engaged in the quest for the historical Jesus. For the European quest, Christology was to be based on that which could be verified according to the canons of modern historiography. For the Latin Americans, the term simply refers to the

person, teaching, attitudes and deeds of Jesus of Nazareth insofar as they are accessible to historical and exegetical investigation.

29. Gutiérrez, *A Theology of Liberation* (1988 Edition), 116.

30. Jon Sobrino, *Christology at the Crossroads* (Maryknoll, N.Y.: Orbis Books, 1978), 9.

31. Míguez Bonino, "Who Is Jesus?" in *Faces of Jesus*, 3-4.

32. Gutiérrez, *A Theology of Liberation*, 226-32.

33. Ibid., 227.

34. Ibid., 227–28.

35. Ibid., 228.

36. Ibid., 247, note 94.

37. Pedro Negre Rigol, "Popular Christology—Alienation or Irony?" in *Faces of Jesus*, 67.

38. Míguez Bonino, *Faces of Jesus*, 9-76. Here in this text are several articles by different authors discussing these various Christologies.

39. Assmann, "The Actuation of the Power of Christ in History," 135.

40. Gutiérrez, *The Power of the Poor in History*, 21.

41. Saul Trinidad, "Christology, Conquista, Colonization," in *Faces of Jesus*, ed. José Míguez Bonino, 60.

42. Hugo Assmann, *Teología desde la praxis de la liberacion* (Salamanca: Ediciones Sigueme, 1973, Spanish edition), 149. This is my own translation of the passage.

43. The term *ecclesiogenesis* is used here in the same manner in which it is used by Leonardo Boff in his text *Ecclesiogenesis: The Base Communities Reinvent the Church,* trans. Robert R. Barr (Maryknoll, N.Y.: Orbis Books, 1986).

44. Gutiérrez, *Power of the Poor in History,* 38.

45. Gutiérrez, *A Theology of Liberation,* 255.

46. Míguez Bonino, *Doing Theology in a Revolutionary Situation,* 159.

47. Ibid., 156.

48. Ibid., 158.

49. Gutiérrez, *A Theology of Liberation,* 276–77.

50. Ibid., 277.

51. Ibid., 276.

52. Míguez Bonino, *Doing Theology in a Revolutionary Situation,* 57.

53. Gutiérrez, *A Theology of Liberation,* 260–61.

54. Míguez Bonino, *Doing Theology in a Revolutionary Situation,* 161.

55. Ibid.

56. Ibid.

57. Ibid., 166.

58. Ibid., 164.

59. Ibid., 170.

60. For a complete exposition of this idea, see Gustavo Gutiérrez, *A Theology of Liberation,* 258–65, or José Míguez Bonino, *Doing Theology in a Revolutionary Situation,* 160-61.

61. Míguez Bonino, *Doing Theology in a Revolutionary Situation,* 167.

62. For a discussion of the basic Christian communities, see the following texts: *The Challenge of Basic Christian Communities,* ed. Sergio Torres and John Eagleson (Maryknoll, N.Y.: Orbis Books, 1981), and Leonard Boff, *Ecclesiogenesis*.

63. Boff, *Ecclesiogenesis,* 42.

64. Míguez Bonino, *Doing Theology in a Revolutionary Situation,* 170.

65. Ibid., 132.

66. Ibid., 138.

67. Ibid., 133.

68. The final document from the International Ecumenical Congress of Theology, February 20–March 2, 1980, São Paulo, Brazil, published in *The Challenge of Basic Christian Communities,* ed. Sergio Torres and John Eagleson, 236.

69. Ibid.

70. Ibid., 236–37.

71. See Jürgen Moltmann, *A Theology of Hope* (New York: Harper and Row, 1967), for an example of a European political theology.

72. Míguez Bonino, *Doing Theology in a Revolutionary Situation,* 134–35.

73. Ibid.

74. Ibid., 134.

75. Assmann, *Theology for a Nomad Church,* 144.

76. Míguez Bonino, *Doing Theology in a Revolutionary Situation,* 152.

77. See Gutiérrez, *A Theology of Liberation,* 149–78.

78. Ibid., 153, 177, 237. This discussion of the relationship between salvation and history is a contemporary variation on the classical issue of the relationship between nature and grace. *Salvation* in this context has often been used in classical theology to refer to the convent of redemption, or God's redemptive project, while the term *liberation* is used to refer to the human project of historical liberation. While Gutiérrez, Míguez Bonino and Assmann would affirm a dynamic connection between the two in history, they also want to be wary of reducing the salvific intentions of God to historical projects, since the intention of God's salvific work involves more than historical projects of liberation. In the author's view, the term *liberation,* as an all-encompassing term, is entirely appropriate as a description of the central focus of the Gospel. Nevertheless, it is important to distinguish the two interrelated moments of the one history.

79. Gutiérrez, *The Power of the Poor in History,* 69.

80. Gutiérrez, *A Theology of Liberation,* 153.

81. Ibid., 37.

82. Assmann, *Theology for a Nomad Church,* 55. Gutiérrez outlines a similar threefold definition in *A Theology of Liberation,* 36-37.

83. Gutiérrez, *A Theology of Liberation,* 37.

84. Assmann, *Theology for a Nomad Church,* 47.

85. Míguez Bonino, *Doing Theology in a Revolutionary Situation,* 70.

86. Ibid.

87. For a more comprehensive description of Gutiérrez's concept of liberation, see Gustavo Gutiérrez, *A Theology of Liberation,* 36-37.

88. The philosophical works of Kant, Hegel, Marx and Marcuse, as well as others, are vitally important for an understanding of the Latin Americans' conception of liberation. See Gustavo Gutiérrez, *A Theology of Liberation,* 28-37 or Jon Sobrino, *Christology at the Crossroads,* 19.

89. It cannot be denied that the major theological themes of liberation theology have been worked out primarily within the philosophical and conceptual framework of post-Enlightenment European theology, and that LALT depends on the research of that heritage for its support. While Gutiérrez, Míguez Bonino and Assmann have independently acknowledged this fact, they also agree with Enrique Dussel, who

contends that LALT, while utilizing the European theological categories, has reorganized these theological categories in the militant struggles of the oppressed class. Hence LALT's use of the philosophical and theological categories of Europe is different. See Enrique Dussel, "Sobre La Historia De La Theologia En America Latina," in *Liberacion y Cautivero: Debates en Torno al Metoso De La Teologia En America Latina*, ed. Enrique Ruiz Maldanado (Mexico City: Venecia, 1976), 55-70.

90. Jon Sobrino, *Jesus in Latin America* (Maryknoll, N.Y.: Orbis Books, 1987), 19-29.

91. Ibid., 81.

92. Gutiérrez, *A Theology of Liberation*, 36.

93. Note here that the emphasis on culture liberation is directed toward breaking away from the cultural formations of post-Enlightment Europe, not toward an emphasis on the cultures of the poor in Latin America. The Latin Americanization of LALT, which I understand to be in the second stage, and in process, is a different emphasis which I have been highlighting throughout this thesis. While the Latin Americans acknowledged very early in the development of LALT the need to reject the dominant culture of Europe, they were not equally acknowledging their need to utilize the religio-cultural sources and traditions of the Latin American poor. See Gustavo Gutiérrez's admission that "it is obvious ... that the native peoples and cultures of Latin America are not taken into account in our present efforts at theological reflection," in *Frontiers* 33, No. 13, 25.

94. Gutiérrez, *The Power of the Poor in History,* 65. In footnote 30, Chap. 3, 73 of this text, Gutierrez comments that "It is clear ... that the native peoples and cultures of Latin America are not adequately represented in our efforts of theological reflection."

95. See Juan Luis Segundo, "Two Theologies of Liberation," in Alfred Hennelly, ed., *Liberation Theology: A Documentary History* (Maryknoll, N.Y.: Orbis Books, 1990), 353-66. See also "Commonalities, Differences and Cross-Fertilization Among Third World Theologies," *Ecumenical Review* 40 (April 1988), especially 289, 290.

96. Ibid., 356.

Chapter 4

1. See, for example, Theo Witvliet's assessment of LALT and Black Theology in *A Place in the Sun* (Maryknoll, N.Y.: Orbis Books, 1985), chaps. 3 and 6.

2. An account of this meeting is found in *Risk* 9, No. 2 (1973). The major figures in this encounter were Paulo Freire, Hugo Assmann, Eduardo Bodipolmalumba, and James H. Cone. See page 1.

3. See the panel discussion comments of Hugo Assmann, ibid., 59.

4. Ibid.

5. Ibid., 62.

6. Ibid.

7. Ibid.

8. James Cone, "From Geneva to São Paulo: A Dialogue Between Black Theology and Latin American Liberation Theology," in *The Challenge of Basic Christian Communities*, ed. Sergio Torres and John Eagleson (Maryknoll, N.Y.: Orbis Books, 1981), 267.

9. At the Geneva meeting, Paulo Freire of Brazil indicated that the represen-

tatives of black America were clearly Third World persons, for they lived in a world of dependence and exploitation in the First World. His comments closely paralleled Assmann's comments cited above. See *Risk,* 58.

10. The full documentation of this conference has been published in Sergio Torres and John Eagleson, eds., *Theology in the Americas* (Maryknoll, N.Y.: Orbis Books, 1976).

11. The major participants in this encounter included Hugo Assmann, José Míguez Bonino, Enrique Dussel on the LALT side and James H. Cone, Preston Williams, J. Deotis Roberts and Herbert Edwards on the BTUSA side. See ibid., 263–356.

12. For a record of this essay, see Herbert O. Edwards, "Black Theology and Liberation Theology," in Gayraud S. Wilmore and James H. Cone, eds., *Black Theology: A Documentary History, 1966–1979,* (Maryknoll, N.Y.: Orbis Books, 1985).

13. See "The Black Theology Panel Report," in Torres and Eagleson, *Theology in the Americas,* 351.

14. Cone, "From Geneva to São Paulo," 268.

15. Ibid., 269.

16. The proceedings of the conference were published in Cornel West, Caridad Guidote, and Margaret Corkley, eds., *Theology in the Americas: Detroit II Conference Papers,* (Maryknoll, N.Y.: Orbis Books, 1982).

17. The term "Third World" is used here to denote those oppressed groups who represent dependent and exploited segments within the context of the United States.

18. West, Guidote, and Coakley, *Theology in the Americas: Detroit II,* 83–84.

19. Enrique Dussel, "Theologies of the 'Periphery' and the 'Center': Encounter of Confrontation?" *Concilium* 171 (February 1984): 87.

20. For an account of the beginning of EATWOT, see James H. Cone, "Ecumenical Association of Third World Theologians," in *Ecumenical Trends* (September, 1985), 119; Enrique Dussel, "Theologies of the Periphery and the Center," 87; Sergio Torres, "Opening Address to the Ecumenical Dialogue of Third World Theologians" (Dar-es-Salaam, August 5-12, 1976), published in *The Emergent Gospel,* edited by Sergio Torres and Virginia Fabella (Maryknoll, N.Y.: Orbis Books, 1978), 1–2. For an additional account from another perspective, see O. K. Bimwenyi, "The Origins of EATWOT," *Bulletin of African Theology,* 2, no. 3 (January-June, 1980), 19.

21. Cone, "From Geneva to São Paulo," 265.

22. Ibid., 272.

23. This citation is taken from the final communique of the 1976 Dar-es-Salaam, Tanzania, Ecumenical Dialogue of Third World Theologians which was published in *The Emergent Gospel,* 273.

24. For a record of the list of black participants from the U.S., see Kofi Appiah-Kubi and Sergio Torres, eds., *African Theology En Route* (Maryknoll, N.Y.: Orbis Books, 1979), 212.

25. Cone, "From Geneva to São Paulo," 274. For an account and record of the EATWOT meeting in Sri Lanka, see Virginia Fabella, ed., *Asia's Struggle for Full Humanity* (Maryknoll, N.Y.: Orbis Books, 1980).

26. Cone, "From Geneva to São Paulo," 279.

27. Ibid., 276–77.

28. See the comments of Cornel West (African-American-USA), Ruvimbo Tek-

ere (African-Zimbabwe), and Alfred Reid (Afro-Caribbean-Jamaica), in Torres and Eagleson, *The Challenge of Basic Christian Communities*, 255-64.

29. Ibid., 257.

30. Cone, "From Geneva to São Paulo," 277.

31. Ibid.

32. See the final statements in Virginia Fabella and Sergio Torres, eds., *Irruption of the Third World: Challenge to Theology* and *Doing Theology in a Divided World* (Maryknoll, N.Y.: Orbis Books, 1983 and 1985 respectively).

33. See the "Final Statement of the Sixth EATWOT Conference," in Fabella and Torres, *Doing Theology in a Divided World*, 183.

34. The Latin Americans have subsequently sponsored conferences on black and indigenous culture and religion and liberation theology. See the report on the second consultation of black pastoral agents held in São Paulo, Brazil (September 6–7, 1983), in *Voices From the Third World* 8, No. 1 (June 1984): 25-26. The report refers to a first consultation on "Indigenous Struggle, Theological Reflection and Pastoral Action," held in Brasilia, Brazil (May 10–14, 1984), in the same volume. See also the reference to a preparatory meeting (December 6–8, 1984) in São Paulo and a conference (July 8–12, 1985) on Black Culture and Theology, in *Voices From the Third World* 8, No. 2 (June 1985). These are suggestive of the Latin Americans' recognition of the need to incorporate the concerns of black and indigenous Latin Americans into their theologies.

35. Cone, "From Geneva to São Paulo," 277. See also his comments in *Black Theology: A Documentary History, 1966-1979*, 451-53.

36. Ibid., 452.

37. Ibid., 453. See also Cone's record of having encountered Cuban theologians at a conference in Mexico City (1977) where he was favorably impressed by their willingness to learn from BTUSA. This record is noted in his essay, "From Geneva to São Paulo," 275.

38. Cone, *Black Theology: A Documentary History, 1966-1979*, 453.

39. Cone, "From Geneva to São Paulo," 275.

40. The theological homage to Martin Luther King, Jr., was held in June 1984, in Havana, Cuba. Representatives of the Black Theology Project included James Cone, Gayraud Wilmore, Dwight Hopkins, Carolyn Knight, Jualynne Dodson, Calvin Butts and George Cummings.

41. For this affirmation see James H. Cone, "Black Theology: Its Origin, Methodology and Relationship to Third World Theologies," in Fabella and Torres, *Doing Theology in a Divided World*, 99-101. Also see J. Russell Chandran, "A Methodological Approach to Third World Theology," in Fabella and Torres, *The Irruption of the Third World*, 79-86; or Gustavo Gutiérrez, *The Power of the Poor in History* (Maryknoll, N.Y.: Orbis Books, 1983), 169-214.

42. Anselm Kyongsuk Min develops this argument in his *Dialectic of Salvation: Issues in Theology of Liberation* (Albany, N.Y.: State University of New York Press, 1989), 91-97.

43. This acknowledgment is implicit in the affirmation of racism as an evil present in the societies of the world and in the call for a comprehensive analysis encompassing all major forms of domination. See the final statement of Fabella and Torres, *Doing Theology in a Divided World*, 182.

44. The images of liberator, co-sufferer and co-creator are derived from BTUSA and LALT. The notion of co-creator, while I believe it is implicit in the theological

ideas of BTUSA and LALT, receives its fullest elaborations in the works of feminist and womanist theologians of liberation. See Carter Heyward (*The Redemption of God*), Katie Geneva Cannon (*Black Womanist Ethics*) and Rita Nakashima Brock (*Journeys By Heart*).

45. These comments were made by Alfred Reid, a Jamaican, in "The Challenge of Non-Latin Americans," in Torres and Eagleson, *The Challenge of the Basic Christian Communities*, 263.

46. See, for example, James H. Cone's discussion of this issue in *Black Theology and Black Power* (New York: Seabury Press, 1969), 5-61.

47. Gustavo Gutiérrez, *The Power of the Poor in History*. 201.

48. See Gustavo Gutiérrez, "The Irruption of the Poor in Latin American and the Christian Communities of the Common People," or Miguel D'Escoto, "The Church Born of the People in Nicaragua," in Torres and Eagleson, *The Challenge of Basic Christian Communities*, 107-23 and 189-96.

49. Cone, "From Geneva to São Paulo," 279.

50. James H. Cone, "Reflections from the Perspective of U.S. Blacks: Black Theology and Third World Theology," in *Irruption of the Third World*, 242-43.

51. James H. Cone, *For My People* (Maryknoll, N.Y.: Orbis Books, 1983), 151.

52. The term "social analysis" is often used interchangeably with the term "economic analysis." I use the term "social analysis," however, in the precise sense that it indicates a coherent analysis of the factors that constitute a particular social situation. Thus, there are many factors which are constitutive of social analysis. The distinctive characteristic of Marxist social analysis is its view that the economic factor is primary.

53. For an elaboration of the ideas of Albert Cleage, see his *Black Christian Nationalism* and *The Black Messiah*.

54. "Statement by the National Committee on Negro Church Men" (June 31, 1966). Recorded in Wilmore and Cone, *Black Theology: A Documentary History, 1966-1979*, 25-26.

55. My view that both the integrationist and the nationalist perspectives had limitations is derived from my study of these movements and my agreement with James H. Cone, who states this view in his book, *For My People*, 193, and Cornel West, who does extensive typological studies of both traditions in his *Prophesy Deliverance* (Philadelphia: Westminster Press, 1982), Chap. 3.

56. Cone, *For My People*, 193.

57. Wilmore and Cone, *Black Theology: A Documentary History, 1966-1979*, 344.

58. Ibid., 348.

59. James H. Cone, "Black Theology and the Black Church: Where Do We Go From Here?" in Wilmore and Cone, *Black Theology: A Documentary History, 1966-1979*, 353.

60. See Martin Luther King, Jr., *Stride Toward Freedom* (New York: Harper and Row Publishers, 1958), 95.

61. Cone, *For My People*, 175-76.

62. Wilmore and Cone, *Black Theology: A Documentary History, 1966-1979*, 80.

63. Ibid., 107.

64. See the statement of Cone, footnote 50 above.

65. James Theodore Holly, "Socialism from the Biblical Point of View," *A.M.E. Church Review* 9 (1892–1893): 252.

66. Phillip Foner, *American Socialism and Black Americans* (Westport, Conn.: Greenwood Press, 1977), 44.

67. Ibid., 59.

68. Ibid., 247.

69. Ibid., 357.

70. Harold Cruse, *Rebellion or Revolution?* (New York: William Morrow and Company, Inc., 1968), 77.

71. Ibid., 93.

72. See Robert Allen, *Reluctant Reformers: The Impact of Racism on American Social Reform Movements* (Washington, D.C.: Howard University Press, 1974), especially Chapter 7. In addition, Phillip Foner's historical review and analysis of these issues is to be found in *American Socialism and Black Americans: From the Age of Jackson to World War II* (Westport, Conn.: Greenwood Press, 1977), and *American Communism and Black Americans: A Documentary History, 1919-1929* (Philadelphia, Pa.: Temple University Press, 1987).

73. Cone, *For My People*, 176.

74. See James H. Cone's acknowledgment of this fact in *For My People*, 88-89.

75. Manning Marable, *How Capitalism Underdeveloped Black America* (Boston, Mass.: South End Press), 206-7.

76. Wilmore and Cone, *Black Theology: A Documentary History, 1966-1979,* 358.

77. Arthur McGovern, "Dependency Theory, Marxist Analysis, and Liberation Theology," in *Expanding the View*, ed. Marc Ellis and Otto Maduro (Maryknoll, N.Y.: Orbis Books, 1988), 82.

78. Ibid., 89.

79. See Giulio Girardi, *Faith and Revolution in Nicaragua: Convergence and Contradictions* (Maryknoll, N.Y.: Orbis Books, 1987), especially Chap. 14.

80. Ibid., 175.

81. Edward L. Cleary, *Crisis and Change: The Church in Latin America Today* (Maryknoll, N.Y.: Orbis Books, 1985), 200.

82. Juan Luis Segundo, *The Liberation of Theology* (Maryknoll N.Y.: Orbis Books, 1976), 47-66.

83. José Míguez Bonino, *Doing Theology in a Revolutionary Situation* (Philadelphia: Fortress Press, 1975), 95.

84. Gregory Baum, "The Christian Left at Detroit," in Torres and Eagleson, *Theology in the Americas*, 422.

85. Ibid., 423.

86. Ibid.

87. Ibid.

88. Míguez Bonino, *Doing Theology in a Revolutionary Situation*, 95-96.

89. Ibid., 107.

90. See, for example, Paul Baran and Paul Sweezy, *Monopoly Capital* (New York: Monthly Review, 1966), Chaps. 5-8.

91. Cleary, *Crisis and Change*, 71.

92. Victor Westhelle, "Dependency Theory: Some Implications for Liberation Theology," *Dialogue: A Journal of Theology* 20 (Fall 1981): 294.

93. Míguez Bonino, *Doing Theology in a Revolutionary Situation*, 108.

94. Ibid., 109.

95. Ibid., 111.

96. Ibid., 113.

97. Ibid.

98. Ibid., 96.

99. Cited in Gustavo Gutiérrez, *A Theology of Liberation* (Maryknoll, N.Y.: Orbis Books, 1970), 90.

100. Ibid., 123.

101. Segundo, *The Liberation of Theology*, 58-60.

102. Ibid., 58.

103. Ibid., 60.

104. This is the force of Juan Carlos Scannone's point that "Since Latin American theologians usually have been formed in the culture of the Enlightenment . . . they must undergo a real cultural conversion." See "Theology, Popular Culture and Discernment," in Rosino Gibellini, *Frontiers of Theology in Latin America* (Maryknoll, N.Y.: Orbis Books, 1979), 225.

105. Lloyd Stennette, "The Situation of Blacks in Costa Rica," in Torres and Eagleson, *The Challenge of Basic Christian Communities*, 47.

106. Ibid.

107. Ibid., 48.

108. Mauro Batista, "Black and Christian in Brazil," ibid., 51.

109. Ibid.

110. Unpublished essay by Antonio Olimpio de Sant'Ana, "Is Brazil Really a Racial Democracy?," 27. Rev. De Sant'Ana is a Methodist minister who serves as one of the leaders of the civil rights movement in Brazil.

111. These statistics are taken from *The Britannica Book of the Year*, 1985 edition, under the heading, "Britannica World Data."

112. For a comparison of the situation in Brazil with that of Costa Rica, compare Stennette's estimate of blacks in Costa Rica being 10 percent of the population with the official statistics. According to the official 1980 census of Costa Rica there are no blacks, creoles, or mulattoes living in Costa Rica. Even if one assumes that the category of "other" (4.5 percent) might include blacks, the difference between 10 percent (Stennette's figures) and 4.3 percent (census statistics) is quite significant. See the "Britannica World Data," in *The Britannica Book of the Year* (1985) for the statistics on Costa Rica.

113. This thesis is supported by Charles W. Anderson in his essay, "The Concepts of Race and Class and the Explanation of Latin American Politics," in *Race and Class in Latin America,* ed. Magnus Morner (New York: Columbia University Press, 1970), 231-54, as well as by Leslie B. Rout, Jr., in his book, *The African Experience in Spanish America: 1502 to the Present Day* (New York: Cambridge University Press, 1976).

114. Hugo Assmann made this comment during an interview I held with him during the Second International Meeting of Social Scientists and Theologians held at the Protestant Seminary in Matanzas, Cuba, in November 1983.

115. James Cone refers to these consolations in an article on the Ecumenical Association of Third World Theologians found in the column, "Spotlight On" in *Ecumenical Trends* 14, No. 8 (September 1985): 119-22.

116. Gustavo Gutiérrez. This statement is recorded in Torres and Eagleson, *Theology in the Americas*, 309-10.

117. Ibid., 309.

118. Ibid., 310.

119. Gutiérrez, *The Power of the Poor in History*, 189.

120. Ibid., 216, footnote 43.
121. Cone, "From Geneva to São Paulo," 270.
122. Ibid.
123. Ibid., 272.
124. Ibid.
125. Ibid.
126. Enrique Dussel, *A History of the Church in Latin America: Colonialism to Liberation* (Grand Rapids, Mich.: Wm. B. Eerdman's Publishing Co., Inc., 1981), 234.
127. Ibid.
128. Ibid.
129. Pedro Santiago presented this perspective in a paper entitled, "Racial Integration in Cuban Society." This paper was presented at the Jornada Teológica, en Memoria de Martin Luther King, Jr., April 3, 1984. I attended this conference and recorded notes on the presentation. Santiago's point of view is consistent with those espoused in the writings of the Latin Americans. In this point of view the essential unity of Latin American culture is affirmed via a process called transculturation, and racial or ethnic identity is subordinated to the national identity or culture.
130. Stennette, "The Situation of Blacks in Costa Rica," 48.
131. Ibid.
132. Ibid.
133. See Miguel Concha, "Interpreting Situations of Domination: The Poor, Ethnic Groups, and Classes Made up of the Common People," in Torres and Eagleson, *The Challenge of Basic Christian Communities*, 57-61.
134. West, *Prophesy Deliverance,* 118.
135. Cited in ibid., Chap. 4, footnote 26, 171.
136. Ibid., 29.
137. Rout, *The African Experience,* 316.
138. Ibid., 317.
139. Ibid.
140. Olimpio de Sant'Ana, "Is Brazil Really a Racial Democracy?," 27.
141. Batista, "Black and Christian in Brazil," 52.
142. Ibid.
143. Ibid.
144. Ibid.
145. Olimpio de Sant'Ana, "Is Brazil Really a Racial Democracy?"
146. Rout, *The African Experience*, 319.
147. Stennette, "The Situation of Blacks in Costa Rica," 49.
148. Batista, "Black and Christian in Brazil," 49.
149. Rout, *The African Experience*, 191-93.
150. Ibid., 193.
151. My use of the term *civilization* is informed by Cornel West's definition of it as "self-images, self-identity, values and sensibilities, institutions and associations, ways of life and ways of struggle," *Prophesy Deliverance*, 123.
152. Fabella and Torres, *Irruption of the Third World*, 205.
153. Luis H. Gomez de Souza, "Structures and Mechanisms of Domination in Capitalism," in Torres and Eagleson, *The Challenge of Basic Christian Communities*, 21.

154. Chandran, "A Methodological Approach," in Fabella and Torres, eds., *Irruption of the Third World,* 83.

155. Castro's remarks concerning strategic alliances are cited in Torres and Eagleson, *The Challenge of Basic Christian Communities,* 69. Wilmore's comments were made during an address at a symposium on the black church at Union Theological Seminary, New York City (February 1980), in which he outlined the priorities of the black church movement for liberation in the eighties.

156. Opoku Agyeman, "The Super-Marxists and Pan-Africanism," *Journal of Black Studies* 8, No. 4 (June 1978): 499.

157. Ibid., 500.

158. Dussel, "Theologies of the 'Periphery' and the 'Center'," 94.

Chapter 5

1. The evidence for BTUSA's and LALT's capacity to learn and grow from each other is clearly represented in a statement that was issued subsequent to the December 1986 International Assembly of EATWOT in Oaxtepec, Mexico, in which both BTUSA and LALT are noted as having shifted in their perspectives on class and race, as well as in their perspectives on the religio-cultural traditions of blacks, indigenous peoples and women, who often constitute the poorest of the poor in Latin America and the U.S. See "Commonalities, Differences and Cross-Fertilization Among Third World Theologies," *Ecumenical Review* 40 (April 1988): especially 289, 290.

2. Juan Luis Segundo, *The Liberation of Theology* (Maryknoll, N.Y.: Orbis Books, 1976), 241.

3. "Commonalities," 287-91.

4. Ibid., 289.

5. Ibid., 288, 290. Gustavo Gutiérrez confirms his agreement with this assessment, in *A Theology of Liberation* (Maryknoll, N.Y.: Orbis Books, 1973), 307 and I believe that Hugo Assmann and José Míguez Bonino would concur.

6. "Commonalities," 290.

7. My reference here to the need for a comprehensive analytical framework integrating the socio-economic and the religio-cultural dimensions of oppression is a common enterprise supported by Third World theologians of liberation in EATWOT. See for example the final statement of the Sixth EATWOT Conference (Geneva, Switzerland, January 1983), where the writers of the document observe that "A comprehensive analysis should encompass all the major forms of oppression including religious and cultural domination. Although these oppressions cannot be subordinated one to another or merely listed serially, they are not separate, isolated issues but are linked in the working of a single world system of domination which involves a way of life," Virginia Fabella and Sergio Torres, eds., *Doing Theology in a Divided World* (Maryknoll, N.Y.: Orbis Books, 1985), 182.

8. The term *thematic universe* is being used here to refer to the religio-cultural universe which characterizes any historical experience and which becomes the basis upon which people interpret their experience and struggles. Within this religio-cultural universe one receives clues to the values and sensibilities that determine the pretextual awareness which any community brings to its appropriation of the Christian texts. The notion of thematic universe is defined by Paulo Freire as constituting the "generative themes" within the world of the poor and refers to those

symbols, images, concepts and values which make up the pretextual framework and grid through which the message of the Gospel is filtered. See Paulo Freire, *Pedagogy of the Oppressed* (New York: Seabury Press, 1970), 86-118.

9. This claim is implicit in Gayraud S. Wilmore's comments when he states, "I do not believe that a theological movement can have significant impact ... without being taken over by the segment of the church that is at the bottom of the socio-economic ladder. It is not a question of doing something for the poor; it is a matter of their taking control. That has not yet happened in the black theology movement, notwithstanding the fact that most of its originators and present advocates have identified with the black ghetto." "Black Theology: Review and Assessment," *Voices From the Third World* 5, No. 2 (1982). In addition, I have already referred to Gutiérrez's affirmation of this point of view that LALT has much to do in regard to orienting itself to the world of the poor. See also Juan Carlos Scannone, "Theology, Popular Culture and Discernment," in *Frontiers of Theology in Latin America*, ed. Rosino Gibellini, trans. John Drury (Maryknoll, N.Y.: Orbis Books, 1979), 213-39.

10. The Latin Americans' recognition of this deficiency is reflected in the fact that the Latin Americans in EATWOT have sponsored a series of regional meetings on blacks, indigenous peoples and women in LALT. See references to these meetings in *Voices From the Third World,* the semi-annual bulletin of EATWOT: "The Report on the Second Consultation of Black Pastoral Agents" (São Paulo, Brazil, September 6–7, 1983); "Report on the Women's Theology Encounter" (Santiago, Chile, November 21–22, 1983), and the report on the Ecumenical Consultation on "Indigenous Struggle, Theological Reflection and Pastoral Action" (Brasilia, Brazil, May 10–14, 1984), in *Voices From the Third World* 7, No. 1 (June 1984): 25-28. In addition, see the preliminary report on the preparatory meeting for a conference on black culture and theology, which was held December 6–8, 1984, in São Paulo, Brazil, in *Voices From the Third World* 8, No. 2 (June 1985). This meeting was held in preparation for a meeting on black culture and theology, scheduled for July 8–12, 1985, in Nova Iguaca, state of Rio de Janeiro, Brazil. Moises Sandoval also notes the weakness of LALT in relation to the indigenous peoples of Latin America. See Moises Sandoval, "Report from the Conference" (Puebla 1979), *Puebla and Beyond*, ed. John Eagleson and Philip Scharper (Maryknoll, N.Y.: Orbis Books, 1979), 141.

11. Juan Carlos Scannone, "Theology, Popular Culture and Discernment," in Gibellini, *Frontiers of Theology in Latin America*, 225.

12. Ibid., 231.

13. David Batstone, "From Conquest to Struggle: Jesus of Nazareth in the Liberation Christology of Latin America" (Ph.D. Dissertation, Graduate Theological Union, 1989), 276. Published under the same title (Albany: SUNY Press, 1991).

14. Ibid., 282. Batstone indicated that his research shows that "the Inkarra legend is an alternative vision of life which incorporates elements of the Inca tradition together with those of the Christian faith to create an indigenous Christology which speaks to the ... hopes of the Latin American pueblo," 282. Key Yuasa, a Brazilian theologian of Japanese descent, has noted the importance of the religio-cultural traditions of Indians and Africans when he writes of the Christ incognito (veiled Christ) encountered in the Indian and the ethnic figures of Latin American religiosity. See "The Image of Christ in Latin American Indian Popular Religiosity," in *Sharing Jesus in the Two Thirds World*, ed. Vinay Samuel and Chris Sugdon (Grand

Rapids, Mich.: Wm. B. Eerdmans Publishing Company, 1983), 55-57.

15. See, for example, Gustavo Gutiérrez, *Entre Las Calandrias* (Lima: Centro de Estudios y Publicaciones del Desarrollo, 1982), 243, where Gutiérrez acknowledges the importance of the Quechua contribution to the development of alternative visions of hope.

16. Gustavo Gutiérrez, "Address to Theology in the Americas" (1980), Cornel West, Caridad Guidote, and Mavi Coakley eds., *Theology in the Americas: Detroit II Conference Papers* (Maryknoll, N.Y.: Orbis Books, 1982), 82.

17. Virgilio Elizondo, *Galilean Journey: The Mexican-American Promise* (Maryknoll, N.Y.: Orbis Books, 1983), 45.

18. Ibid., 46.

19. Ibid., 45.

20. Ibid., 43.

21. Quotation of Bartolomé de las Casas was cited by Gustavo Gutiérrez in his book, *The Power of the Poor in History* (Maryknoll, N.Y.: Orbis Books, 1983), 197.

22. My knowledge of Bartolomé de las Casas Institute was fostered when in the summer of 1982 I spent two weeks in Lima, Peru, examining the work of Gustavo Gutiérrez and the institute.

23. Key Yuasa, "The Image of Christ in Latin American Indian Popular Religiosity," 45.

24. Ibid., 57.

25. Ibid.

26. Gayraud S. Wilmore, "Black Theology: Review and Assessment," 14.

27. Ibid.

28. Randolph Outlaw, "Prison and Liberation: Elites, Outcasts, Community," *Christianity and Crisis* (September 30, 1985): 367-69.

29. Ibid., 369.

30. Ibid.

31. Douglas G. Glasgow, *The Black Underclass: Poverty, Unemployment and Entrapment of Ghetto Youth* (New York: Vintage Books, Random House, 1980), 9.

32. Ibid., 15.

33. Ibid., 8.

34. Ibid., 15.

35. Manning Marable, *How Capitalism Underdeveloped Black America* (Boston, Mass.: Southend Press, 1983), 212.

36. Wilmore, "Black Theology: Review and Assessment," 14.

37. Ibid.

38. Ibid.

39. Gutiérrez, *The Power of the Poor in History*, 94-95.

40. Dwight N. Hopkins and George C. L. Cummings, eds., *Cut Loose Your Stammering Tongue: Black Theology in the Slave Narratives* (Maryknoll, N.Y.: Orbis Books, 1992). See Will Coleman's essay.

41. The method of correlation outlined by Paul Tillich as an analytical framework for a theological system, in his text, *Systematic Theology*, vol. 1 (Chicago: University of Chicago Press, 1951), 60, buttresses the view of BTUSA and LALT that the dialectical interplay between Jesus of Nazareth as God's historical act of liberation and the Spirit of Christ the Liberator, present among the oppressed, provides a methodological context for discerning the contemporary meaning of the gospel.

42. For a clear statement on the inversion of the traditional approach to "preaching the good news to the poor," see Gustavo Gutiérrez in Sergio Torres and John Eagleson, eds., *The Challenge of Basic Christian Communities*, (Maryknoll, N.Y.: Orbis Books, 1981), 120-21. See also Gutiérrez, *The Power of the Poor in History*, 105-7.

43. Ibid., 120.

44. Leonardo Boff, "Theological Characteristics of a Grassroots Church," in Torres and Eagleson, *The Challenge of Basic Christian Communities*, 143.

45. James H. Cone, *For My People: Black Theology and the Black Church* (Maryknoll, N.Y.: Orbis Books, 1983), 99-121. See also *Black Theology and Black Power*, (New York: Seabury Press, 1969; San Francisco: HarperCollins, 1989), 103-5, and *My Soul Looks Back* (Nashville, Tenn.: Abingdon Books, 1982; Maryknoll, N.Y.: Orbis Books, 1986), Chap. 4.

46. Cone, *For My People*, 197.

47. Vincent Harding, "The Vocation of the Black Scholar and the Struggles of the Black Community," *Harvard Educational Review* (1974), Monograph No. 2 (3–29), 6.

48. Cone, *For My People*, 116-17.

49. Robert Michael Franklin, "Religious Belief and Political Activism in Black America: An Essay," *The Journal of Religious Thought* 43, No. 2 (Fall-Winter, 1986-1987): 63–67.

50. The inversion of the traditional approach of the church evangelizing the poor to a perspective of the poor evangelizing the church is not a rejection of the notion that the Christian church, in all situations, exists to bear witness to Jesus Christ. Churches exist in all classes and sectors of society, but this methodological shift establishes the priority of liberation theology which places the witness to Jesus Christ among the poor in a position of providing prophetic and self-critical means of assessing the faithfulness or faithlessness of the churches to Jesus Christ.

51. Deotis Roberts supports my claim in his book, *Black Theology in Dialogue* (Philadelphia, Pa.: Westminster Press, 1987). See Chapter 5, "The Holy Spirit and Liberation," where he writes "the Holy Spirit had been neglected in recent black theology [in the U.S.]." Roberts concludes that the subject of the Holy Spirit has received "little direct attention" in the literature of liberation theology. For additional direct references to the doctrine of the Holy Spirit in liberation theology, see James H. Cone, *Black Theology and Black Power*, esp. Chap. 2; and Major Jones, *The Color of God: The Concept of God in Afro-American Thought* (Macon, Ga.: Mercer University Press, 1987), esp. Chap. 7, where Jones explicates a doctrine of the Spirit but also acknowledges that black theologians have neglected a discussion of the Holy Spirit. These comments are equally true for LALT, except for Leonardo Boff, *Church, Charism and Power* (New York: Crossroad, 1988), esp. 144-64, and José Comblin, *The Holy Spirit and Liberation* (Maryknoll, N.Y.: Orbis Books, 1989), published in Brazil in 1987 under the title *O Espiritu e a Libertacão* (São Paulo, Brazil: Editora Vozes). Since the scope of this publication is 1969–1986, these recently published texts (1987–1989) confirm my position that little or no attention had been given to a specific doctrine of the Spirit prior to 1986, and indicate the recognition in both camps of the need to develop one. Prior to that, Leonardo Boff's dissertation on the Holy Spirit and the church is noteworthy.

52. It is my intention to build upon the doctrine of the Spirit elaborated in the work of Roberts and other black theologians. Roberts's explication of the doctrine

of the Holy Spirit is basically limited to the elaboration of the biblical meaning of the Spirit and its meaning for the church, although he links pneumatology and Christology. See also James H. Cone's explicit acknowledgment of the importance of the Spirit in "Sanctification and Liberation in the Black Religious Tradition," in *Sanctification and Liberation*, ed. Theodore Runyan (Nashvile, Tenn.: Abingdon Press, 1981), 176-80.

53. This claim, though largely undeveloped in liberation theology, is implicitly present in the writings of the liberation theologians. See, for example, James Cone's *God of the Oppressed*, and his discussion of God's presence as the Black Messiah who is in the experiences of the black oppressed, or Gustavo Gutiérrez's discussion of the presence of God in the poor in Latin America in his book, the *Power of the Poor in History*. This insight is explicitly identified in J. Deotis Roberts, *Black Theology in Dialogue*, 55-64, and Theo Witvliet's important text, *The Way of the Black Messiah* (Oak Park, Ill.: Meyer Stone Books, 1987), 219-30.

54. Theo Witvliet articulates this point of view by writing of a "pneumatological obligation." See *The Way of the Black Messiah*, 218.

55. Batstone, *From Conquest to Struggle*, 228-84.

56. Underlying my interpretation of the Spirit is a philosophical commitment to historical dialectical materialism which views the adequate understanding and assessment of any image or idea as inextricably linked to its development in a particular historical setting.

57. Juan Luis Segundo, *The Historical Jesus of the Synoptics,* vol. 2, *Jesus of Nazareth Yesterday and Today*, trans. by John Drury (Maryknoll, N.Y.: Orbis Books, 1985), 120-49.

58. Ibid., 120.

59. Gayraud S. Wilmore and James H. Cone, *Black Theology, A Documentary History, 1966-1979* (Maryknoll, N.Y.: Orbis Books, 1978), 629.

60. Gustavo Gutiérrez, *We Drink from Our Own Wells: The Spiritual Journey of a People* (Maryknoll, N.Y.: Orbis Books, 1984), 50-51.

61. The final document, International Ecumenical Congress of Theology, February 20–March 2, 1980, São Paulo, Brazil, Torres and Eagleson, *The Challenge of Basic Christian Communities*, 237.

62. Cornel West, *Prophesy Deliverance* (Philadelphia: Westminster Press, 1982), 18.

63. Karl Barth, *Church Dogmatics*, vol. 4, 3 (Edinburgh: T & T Clark, 1961), 274-367.

64. West, *Prophesy Deliverance*, 118. West has been a member of EATWOT and has participated in several of their conferences.

65. Karl Marx, "The German Ideology: Part I," in *The Marx-Engels Reader*, ed. Robert C. Tucker (New York: W. W. Norton and Company, Inc.), 164.

66. Ibid., 172.

67. Friedrich Engels, "Letters on Historical Materialism," in Tucker, *The Marx-Engels Reader*, 760.

68. Ibid., 760-68.

69. Michael Omi and Howard Winant, "By the Rivers of Babylon: Race in the United States," *Socialist Review* 13, No. 5 (September–October 1983): 41.

70. Ibid.

71. Ibid., 35.

72. West, *Prophesy Deliverance*, 117-18.

73. Lucius Outlaw, "Race and Class in the Theory and Practice of Emancipatory Social Transformation," in *Philosophy Born of Struggle: Anthology of Afro-American Philosophy from 1917*, ed. Leonard Harris (Dubuque, Iowa: Kendall/Hunt Publishing Company, 1983), 121.

74. Maulana Karenga, "Society, Culture, and the Problem of Self-Consciousness: A Kawaida," in Harris, *Philosophy Born of Struggle*, 213.

75. Amilcar Cabral, "National Liberation and Culture," in *Return to the Source: Selected Speeches by Amilcar Cabral* (New York: Monthly Review Press, 1973), 41.

76. José Carlos Mariátegui, *Seven Interpretive Essays on Peruvian Reality* (Austin, Tex.: University of Texas Press, 1971), 22-30, 124-52.

77. West, *Prophesy Deliverance*, 118.

78. Ibid.

79. Ibid., 119.

80. Antonio Gramsci, *Selections from the Prison Notebooks* (New York: International Publishers, 1971), 365.

81. Michael Omi and Howard Winant, "By the Rivers of Babylon," 43.

82. Ibid.

83. Ibid.

84. West, *Prophesy Deliverance*, 119.

85. Gramsci, *Selections from the Prison Notebooks*, 60.

86. Ibid., 80

87. Ibid., 5.

88. West, *Prophesy Deliverance*, 120.

89. Ibid., 20.

90. Ibid., 120.

91. Ibid., 121.

92. See Frank M. Snowden, Jr., *Blacks in Antiquity* (Cambridge, Mass.: The Belknap Press of Harvard University Press, 1970).

93. Gayraud S. Wilmore, "The Black Messiah: Revising the Color Symbolism of Western Christology," *The Journal of the Interdenominational Theological Center* 2 (Fall 1984): 9.

94. The idea that class position has contributed more than race to the basic powerlessness of black Americans has been articulated by Cornel West in *Prophesy Deliverance*, 115. Also see Karenga, "A Kawaida," in Harris, *Philosophy Born of Struggle*, 223.

95. West, *Prophesy Deliverance*, 115.

96. For a comprehensive discussion of race and class in Latin America, see *Race and Class in Latin America*, ed. Magnus Morner (New York: Columbia University Press, 1970), or Carl N. Degler, *Neither Black Nor White* (New York: Macmillan Publishing Co., Inc., 1971).

97. For a discussion of the content of womanist theology, see Jacquelyn Grant, *White Women's Christ, Black Women's Jesus* (Alpharetta, Ga.: Scholar's Press, 1989), Katie Geneva Cannon, *Black Womanist Ethics* (Alpharetta, Ga.: Scholar's Press, 1978), or Delores S. Williams, *Sisters in the Wilderness: The Challenge of Womanist God-Talk* (Maryknoll, N.Y.: Orbis Books, 1993).

98. *Against Machismo*, interviews by Elsa Tamez (Oak Park, Ill.: Meyer-Stone Books, 1987, English translation). See the Preface, viii.

99. Ibid., vii.

100. Lucius Outlaw, "Philosophy, Hermeneutics, Socio-Political Theory: Critical Thoughts in the Interests of African-Americans," in *Philosophy Born of Struggle*, 85.

Index